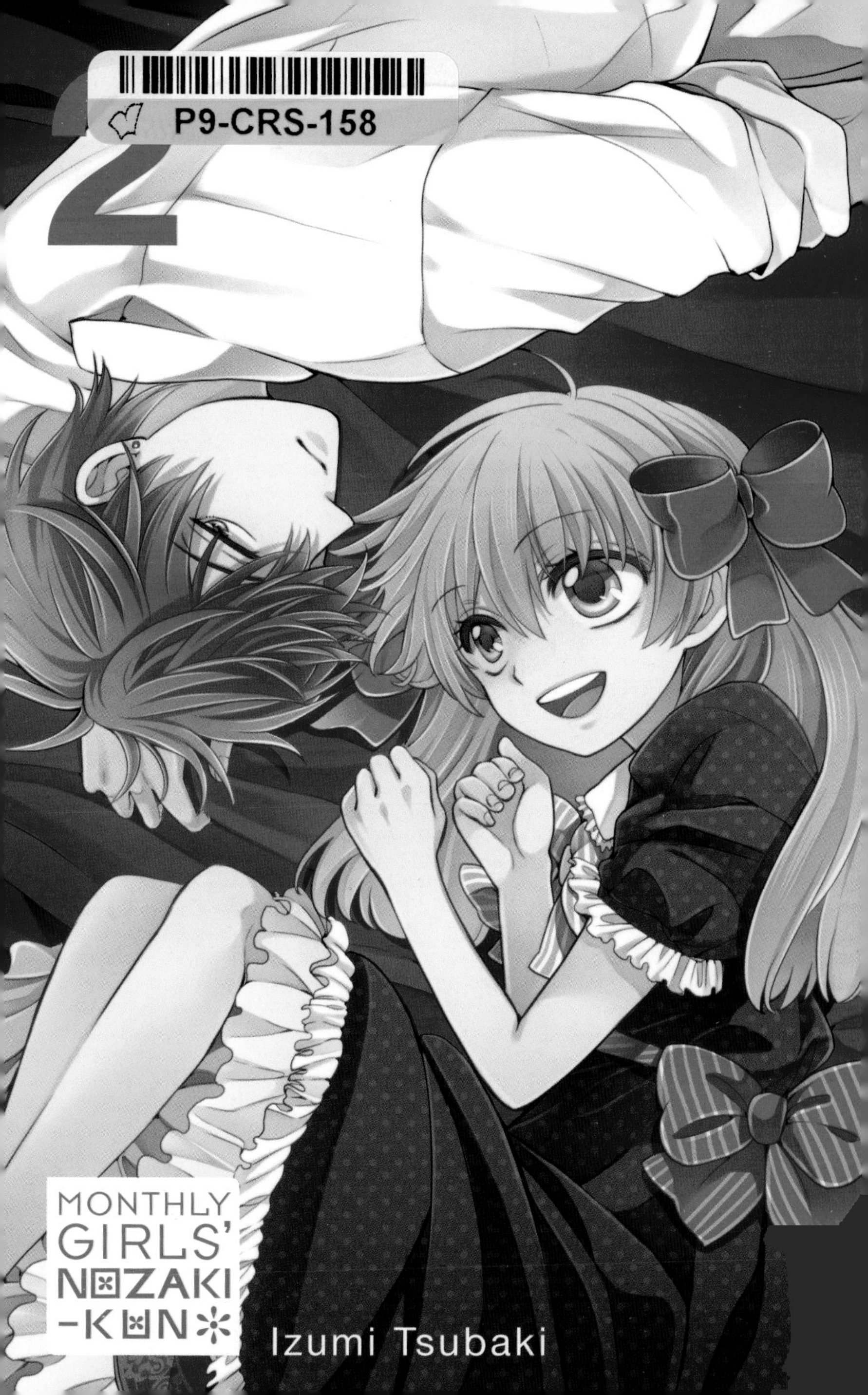

2

MONTHLY GIRLS' NOZAKI-KUN

Izumi Tsubaki

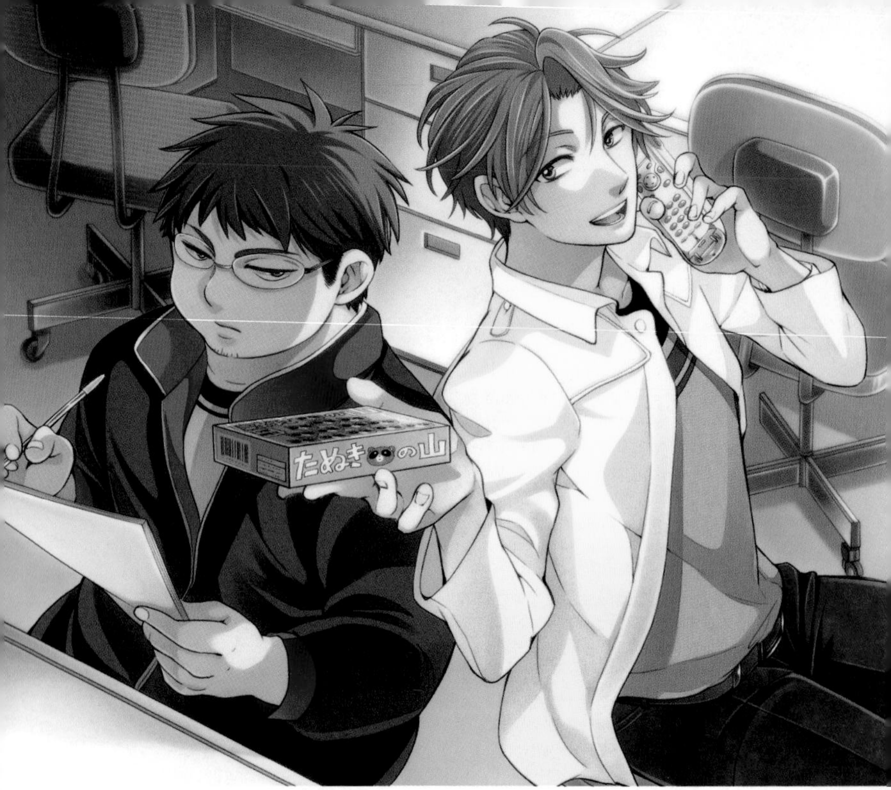
たぬきの山

MONTHLY GIRLS' NOZAKI-KUN 2

contents

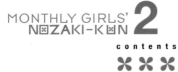

[ISSUE 11]

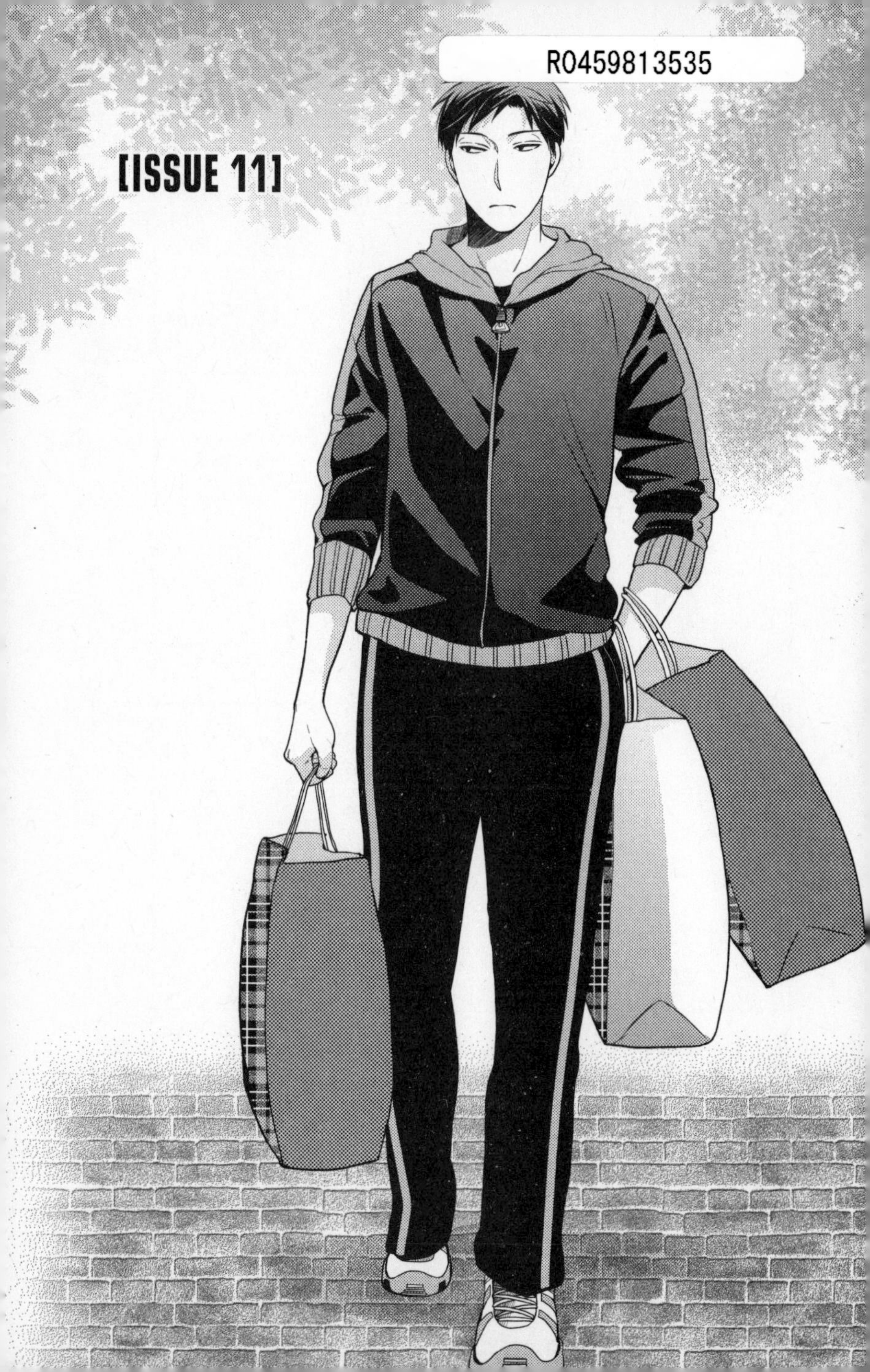

VACATIONING

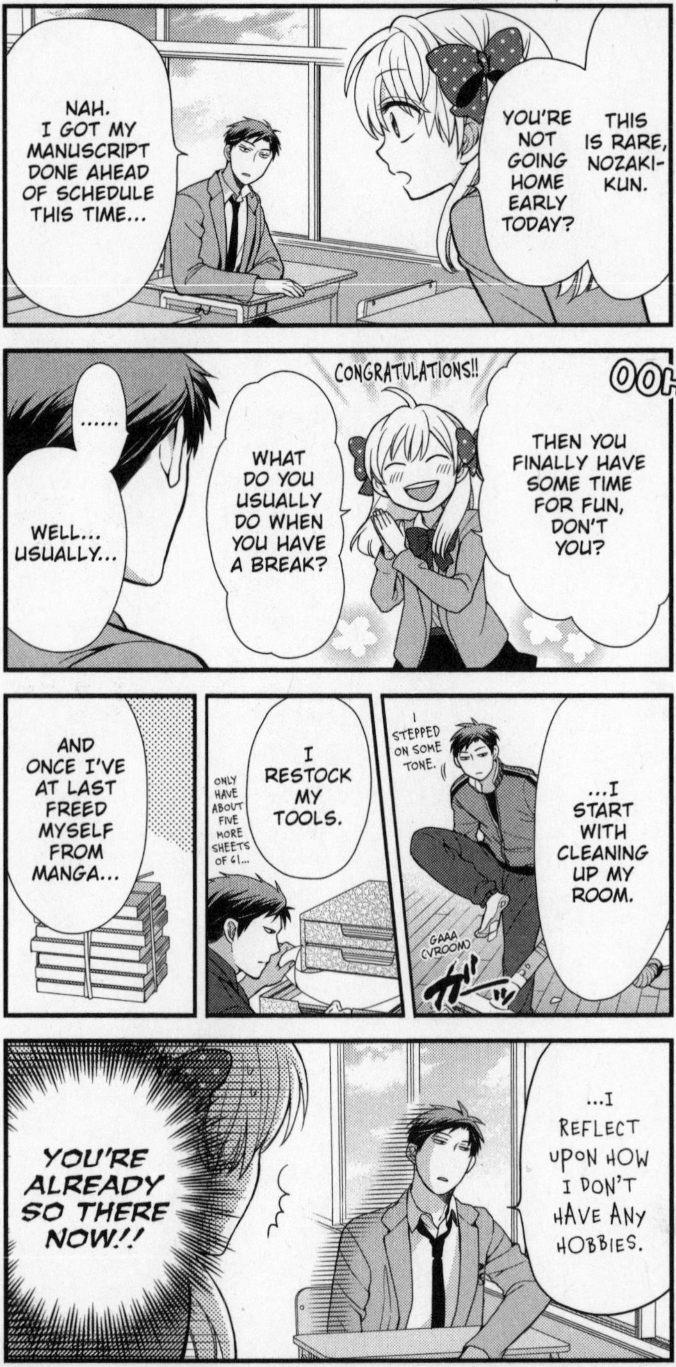
THIS IS RARE, NOZAKI-KUN.
YOU'RE NOT GOING HOME EARLY TODAY?
NAH. I GOT MY MANUSCRIPT DONE AHEAD OF SCHEDULE THIS TIME...
OOH!
THEN YOU FINALLY HAVE SOME TIME FOR FUN, DON'T YOU?
CONGRATULATIONS!!
WHAT DO YOU USUALLY DO WHEN YOU HAVE A BREAK?
......
WELL... USUALLY...
...I START WITH CLEANING UP MY ROOM.
I STEPPED ON SOME TONE.
GAAA (VROOM)
I RESTOCK MY TOOLS.
ONLY HAVE ABOUT FIVE MORE SHEETS OF 61...
AND ONCE I'VE AT LAST FREED MYSELF FROM MANGA...
...I REFLECT UPON HOW I DON'T HAVE ANY HOBBIES.
YOU'RE ALREADY SO THERE NOW!!

AT THE DATE SPOT

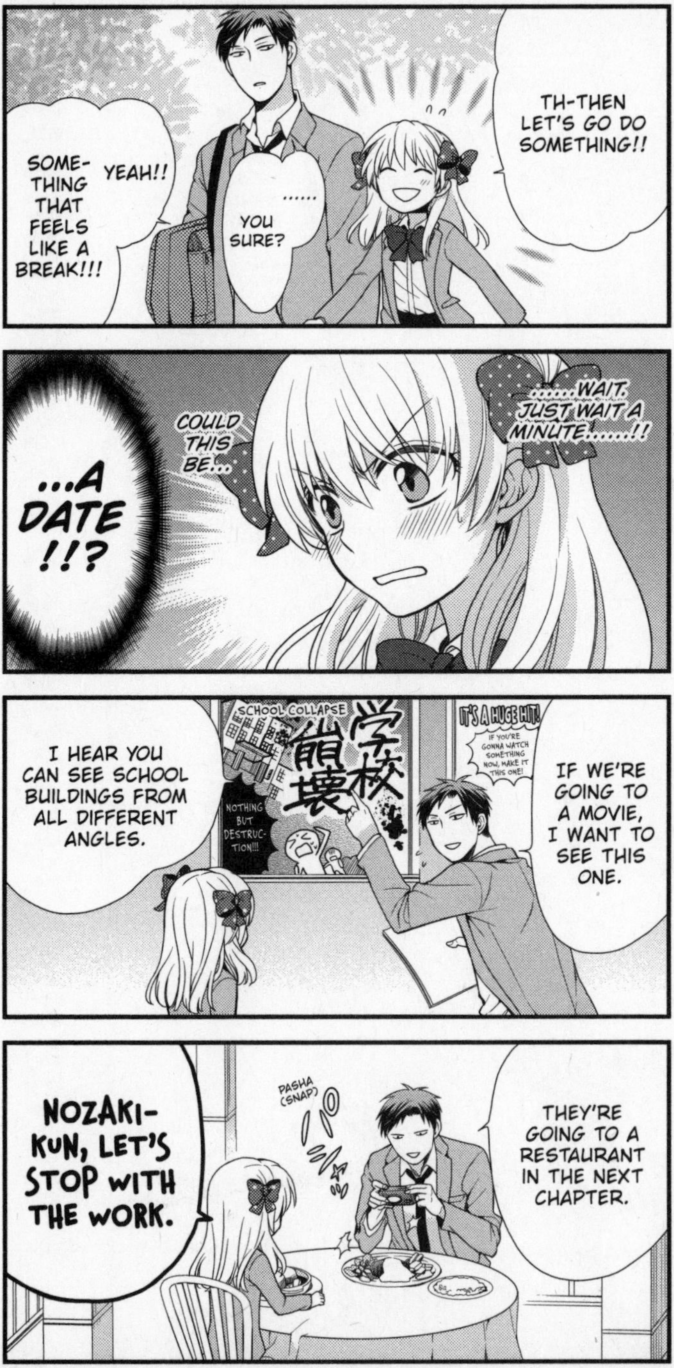
TH-THEN LET'S GO DO SOMETHING!!
......
YOU SURE?
YEAH!!
SOME-THING THAT FEELS LIKE A BREAK!!!
......WAIT. JUST WAIT A MINUTE......!!
COULD THIS BE...
...A DATE!!?
IF WE'RE GOING TO A MOVIE, I WANT TO SEE THIS ONE.
IT'S A HUGE HIT!
IF YOU'RE GONNA WATCH SOMETHING NOW, MAKE IT THIS ONE!
学校崩壊
SCHOOL COLLAPSE
NOTHING BUT DESTRUC-TION!!!
I HEAR YOU CAN SEE SCHOOL BUILDINGS FROM ALL DIFFERENT ANGLES.
THEY'RE GOING TO A RESTAURANT IN THE NEXT CHAPTER.
PASHA (SNAP)
NOZAKI-KUN, LET'S STOP WITH THE WORK.

A REFRESHING HIGH SCHOOL CONVERSATION

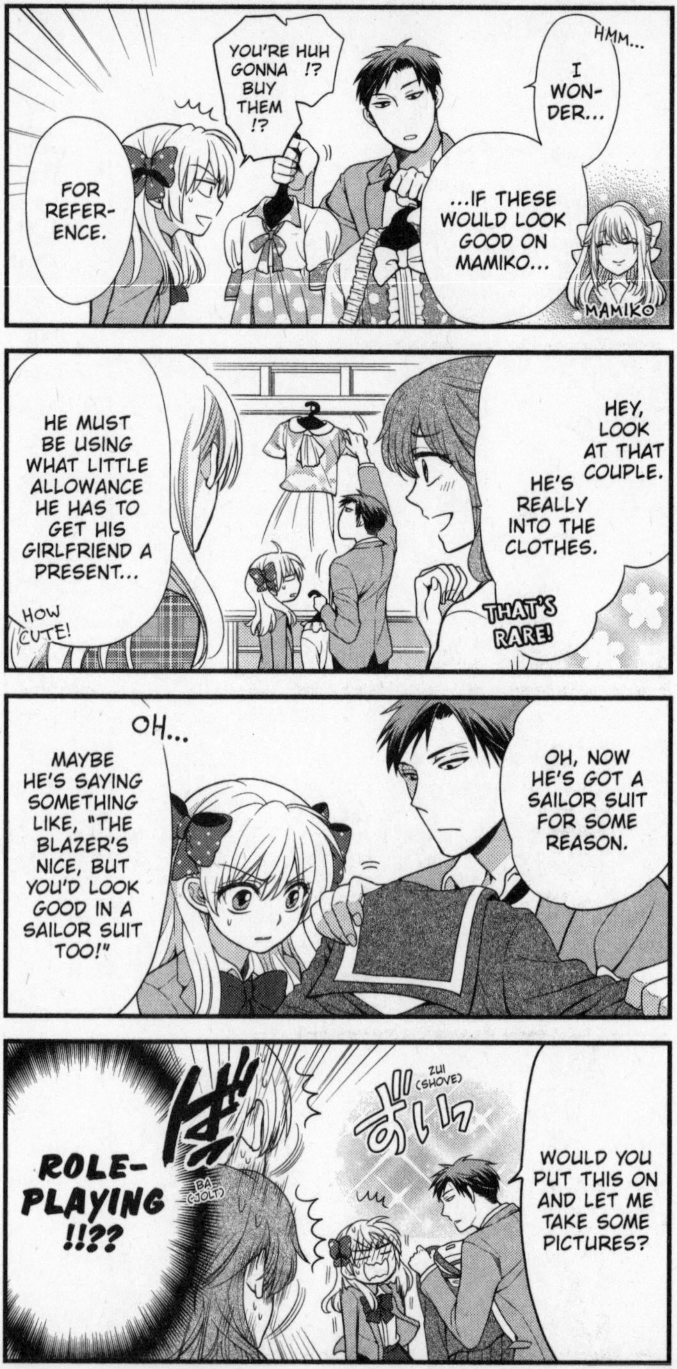
HMM...
I WONDER...
...IF THESE WOULD LOOK GOOD ON MAMIKO...
MAMIKO
YOU'RE GONNA BUY THEM!?
HUH!?
FOR REFERENCE.
HEY, LOOK AT THAT COUPLE.
HE'S REALLY INTO THE CLOTHES.
THAT'S RARE!
HE MUST BE USING WHAT LITTLE ALLOWANCE HE HAS TO GET HIS GIRLFRIEND A PRESENT...
HOW CUTE!
OH, NOW HE'S GOT A SAILOR SUIT FOR SOME REASON.
OH...
MAYBE HE'S SAYING SOMETHING LIKE, "THE BLAZER'S NICE, BUT YOU'D LOOK GOOD IN A SAILOR SUIT TOO!"
WOULD YOU PUT THIS ON AND LET ME TAKE SOME PICTURES?
ZUI (SHOVE)
BA (JOLT)
ROLE-PLAYING!!??

THE WORRIES OF AN ADOLESCENT BOY

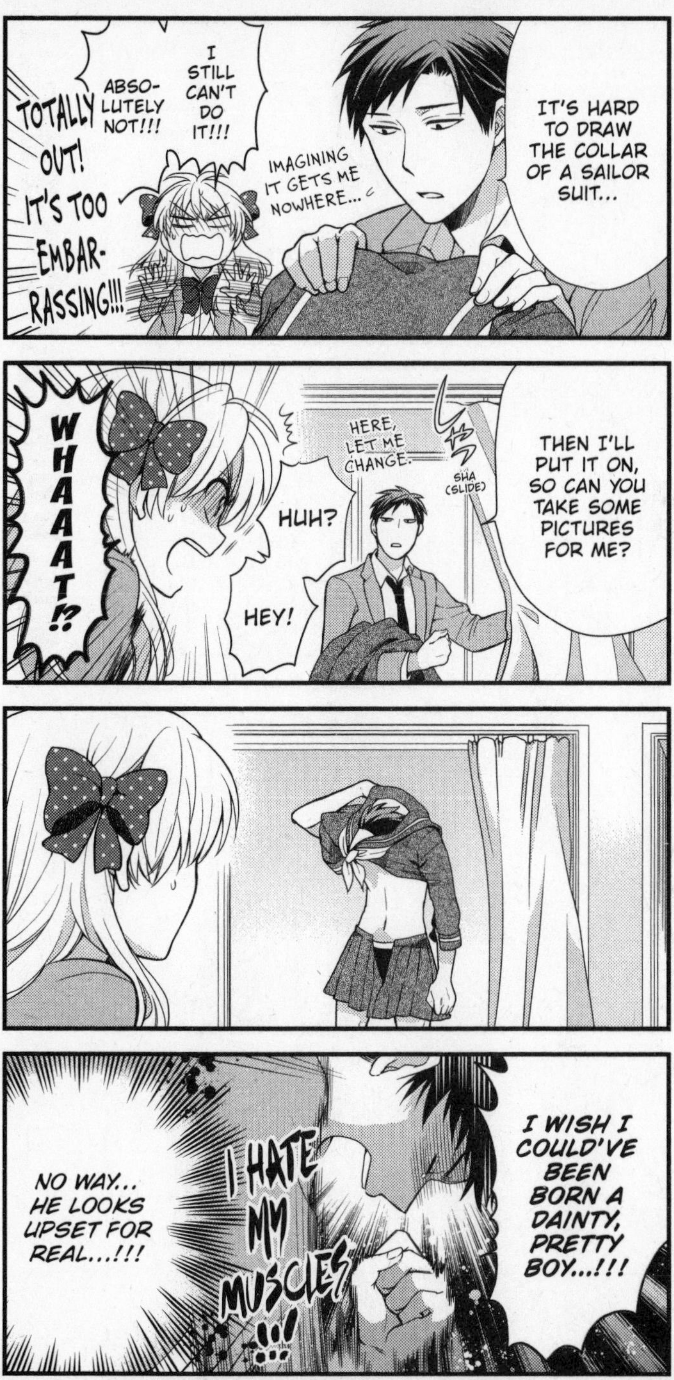
IT'S HARD TO DRAW THE COLLAR OF A SAILOR SUIT...
IMAGINING IT GETS ME NOWHERE...
I STILL CAN'T DO IT!!!
ABSO-LUTELY NOT!!!
TOTALLY OUT! IT'S TOO EMBAR-RASSING!!!
THEN I'LL PUT IT ON, SO CAN YOU TAKE SOME PICTURES FOR ME?
SHA (SLIDE)
HERE, LET ME CHANGE.
HUH?
HEY!
WHAAAAT!?
I WISH I COULD'VE BEEN BORN A DAINTY, PRETTY BOY...!!!
I HATE MY MUSCLES!!!
NO WAY... HE LOOKS UPSET FOR REAL...!!!

IN THE DOLL DEPARTMENT

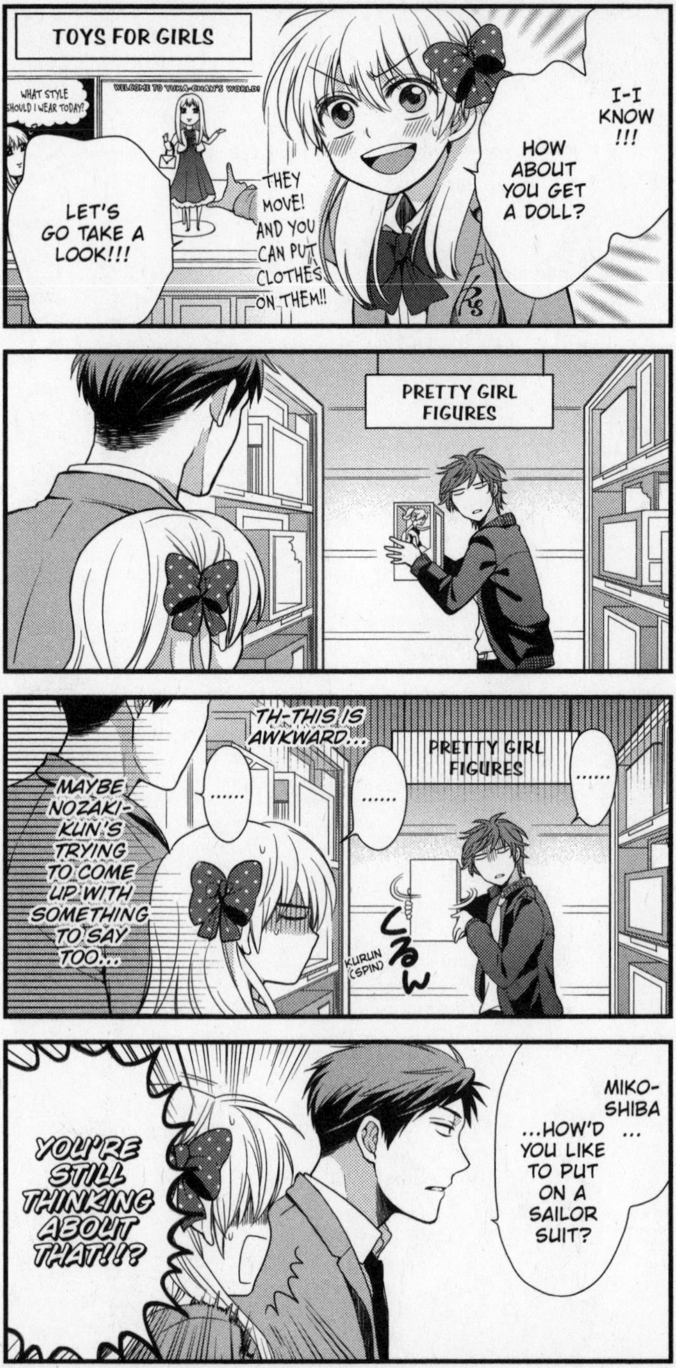
I-I KNOW!!!
HOW ABOUT YOU GET A DOLL?
TOYS FOR GIRLS
THEY MOVE! AND YOU CAN PUT CLOTHES ON THEM!!
WELCOME TO YUKA-CHAN'S WORLD!
WHAT STYLE SHOULD I WEAR TODAY?
LET'S GO TAKE A LOOK!!!
PRETTY GIRL FIGURES
......
PRETTY GIRL FIGURES
TH-THIS IS AWKWARD...
......
......
MAYBE NOZAKI-KUN'S TRYING TO COME UP WITH SOMETHING TO SAY TOO...
くるん
KURUN (SPIN)
MIKO-SHIBA ... ...HOW'D YOU LIKE TO PUT ON A SAILOR SUIT?
YOU'RE STILL THINKING ABOUT THAT!!?

AN ALL-AGES FIGURE

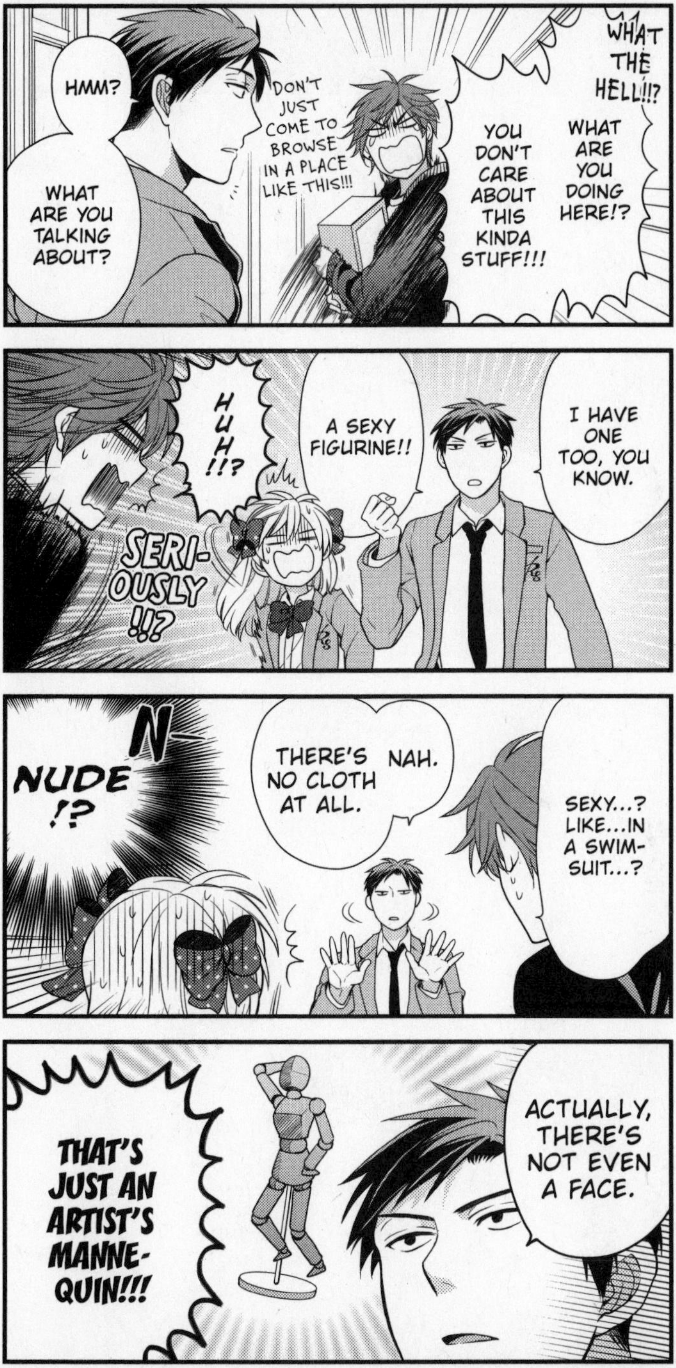
WHAT THE HELL!!?
WHAT ARE YOU DOING HERE!?
YOU DON'T CARE ABOUT THIS KINDA STUFF!!!
DON'T JUST COME TO BROWSE IN A PLACE LIKE THIS!!!
HMM?
WHAT ARE YOU TALKING ABOUT?
I HAVE ONE TOO, YOU KNOW.
A SEXY FIGURINE!!
HUH!!?
SERI-OUSLY!!?
SEXY...? LIKE...IN A SWIM-SUIT...?
NAH.
THERE'S NO CLOTH AT ALL.
N-NUDE!?
ACTUALLY, THERE'S NOT EVEN A FACE.
THAT'S JUST AN ARTIST'S MANNE-QUIN!!!

LOVE FOR A DOLL

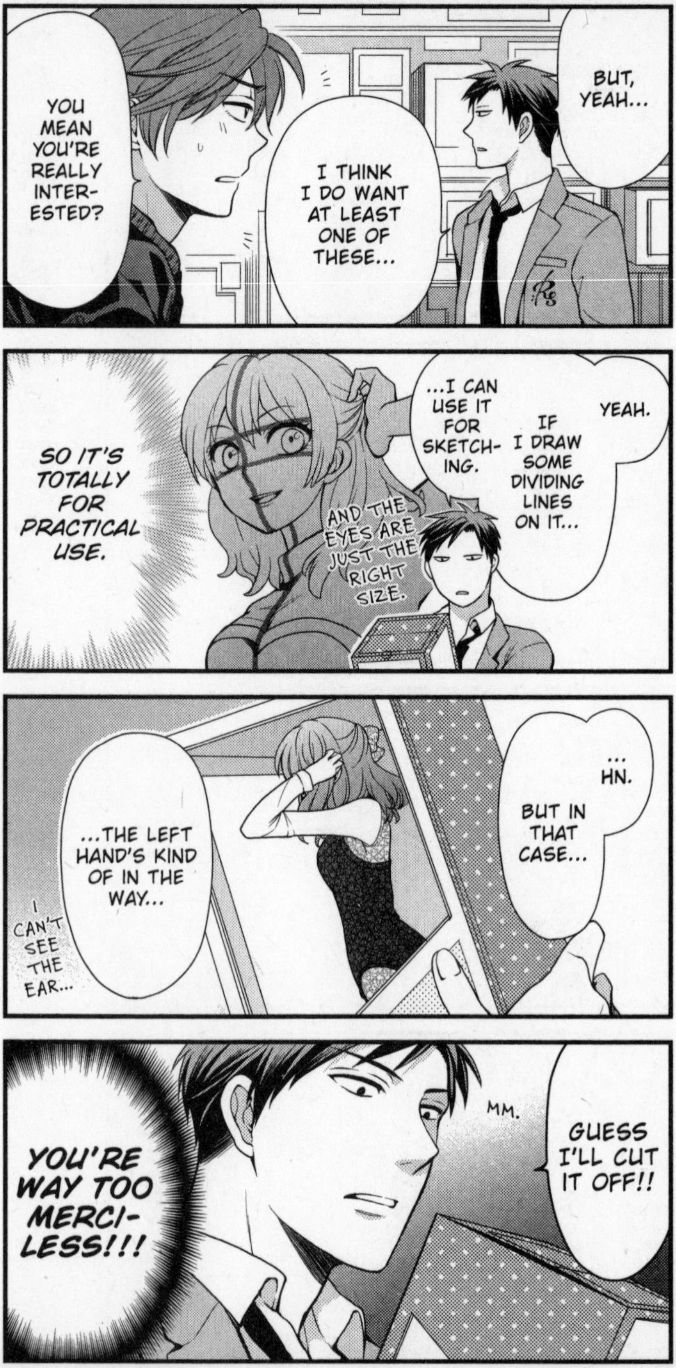
BUT, YEAH...
I THINK I DO WANT AT LEAST ONE OF THESE...
YOU MEAN YOU'RE REALLY INTERESTED?
YEAH.
IF I DRAW SOME DIVIDING LINES ON IT...
...I CAN USE IT FOR SKETCH-ING.
AND THE EYES ARE JUST THE RIGHT SIZE.
SO IT'S TOTALLY FOR PRACTICAL USE.
... HN.
BUT IN THAT CASE...
...THE LEFT HAND'S KIND OF IN THE WAY...
I CAN'T SEE THE EAR...
GUESS I'LL CUT IT OFF!!
MM.
YOU'RE WAY TOO MERCI-LESS!!!

WHEN GIVEN A CHOICE

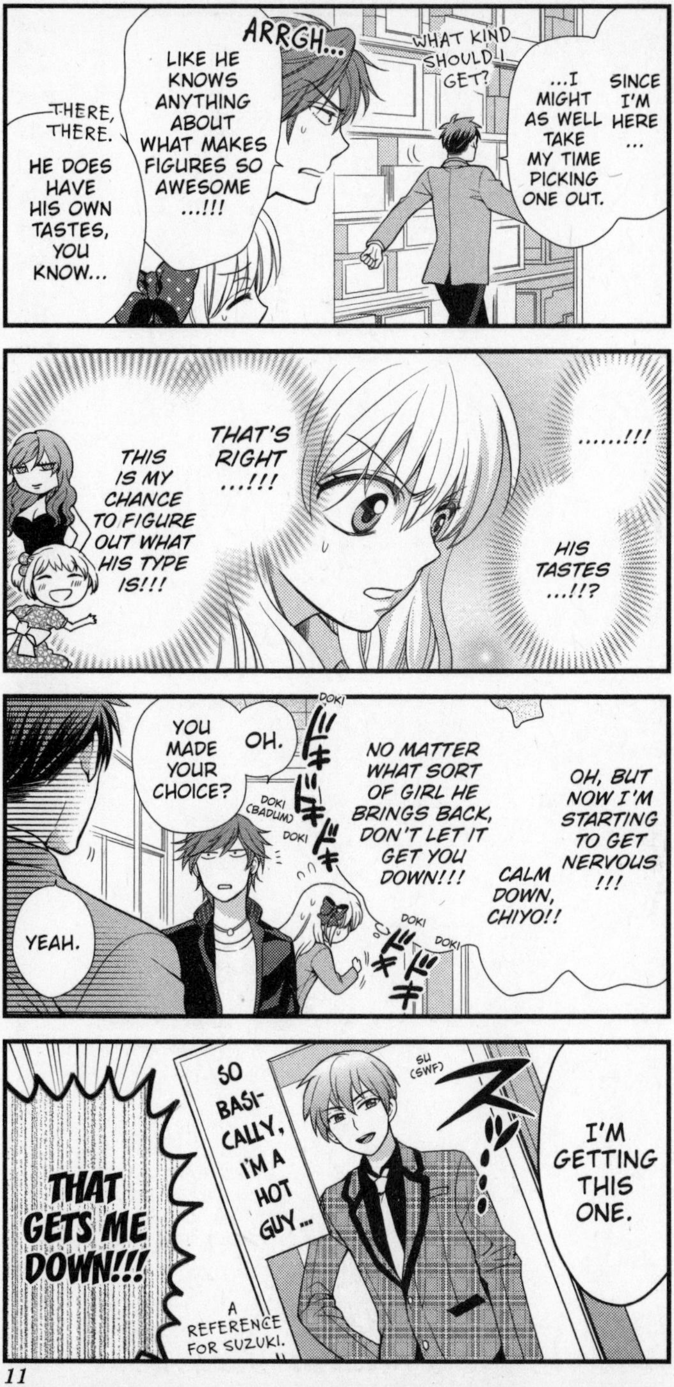

SINCE I'M HERE ...
...I MIGHT AS WELL TAKE MY TIME PICKING ONE OUT.
WHAT KIND SHOULD I GET?
ARRGH...
LIKE HE KNOWS ANYTHING ABOUT WHAT MAKES FIGURES SO AWESOME ...!!!
THERE, THERE.
HE DOES HAVE HIS OWN TASTES, YOU KNOW...
......!!!
HIS TASTES ...!!?
THAT'S RIGHT ...!!!
THIS IS MY CHANCE TO FIGURE OUT WHAT HIS TYPE IS!!!
OH, BUT NOW I'M STARTING TO GET NERVOUS !!!
CALM DOWN, CHIYO!!
NO MATTER WHAT SORT OF GIRL HE BRINGS BACK, DON'T LET IT GET YOU DOWN!!!
DOKI DOKI
DOKI (BADUM) DOKI
DOKI DOKI
OH.
YOU MADE YOUR CHOICE?
YEAH.
I'M GETTING THIS ONE.
SU (SWF)
SO BASI-CALLY, I'M A HOT GUY...
THAT GETS ME DOWN!!!
A REFERENCE FOR SUZUKI.

THE HIERARCHY OF ART SUPPLIES

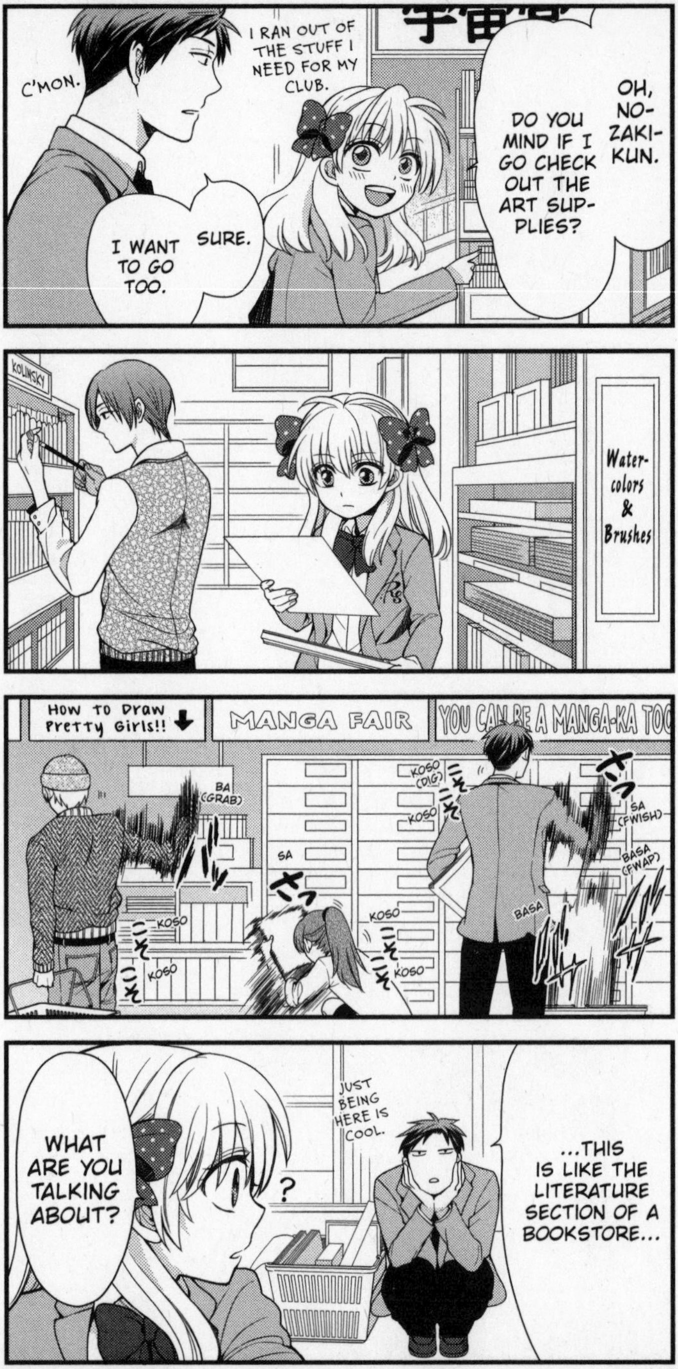
OH, NO-ZAKI-KUN.
DO YOU MIND IF I GO CHECK OUT THE ART SUP-PLIES?
I RAN OUT OF THE STUFF I NEED FOR MY CLUB.
SURE.
I WANT TO GO TOO.
C'MON.
Water-colors & Brushes
KOLINSKY
YOU CAN BE A MANGA-KA TOO
MANGA FAIR
How to Draw Pretty Girls!! ↓
さっ
SA (FWISH)
BASA (FWAP)
BASA
KOSO (DIG)
こそこそ
KOSO
KOSO
こそこそ
KOSO
さっ
SA
BA (GRAB)
こそこそ
KOSO
KOSO
...THIS IS LIKE THE LITERATURE SECTION OF A BOOKSTORE...
JUST BEING HERE IS COOL.
?
WHAT ARE YOU TALKING ABOUT?

"IT'S MY HOBBY"

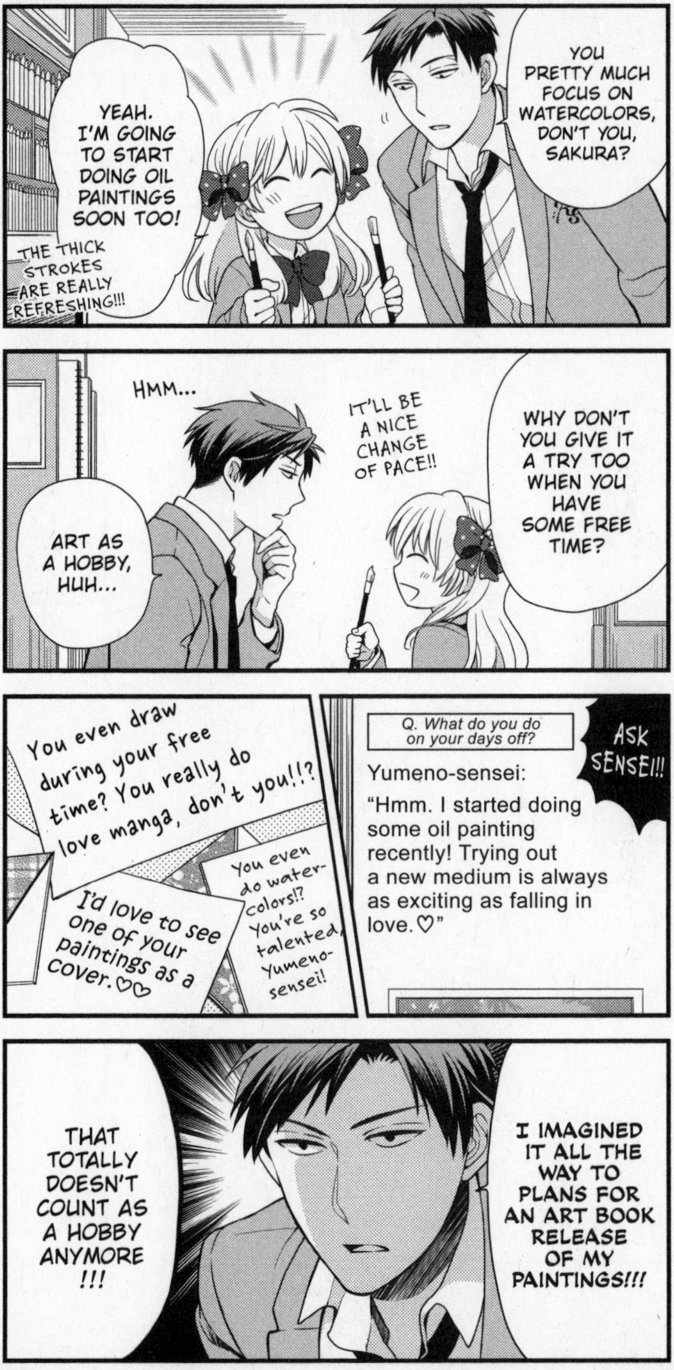
YOU PRETTY MUCH FOCUS ON WATERCOLORS, DON'T YOU, SAKURA?
YEAH. I'M GOING TO START DOING OIL PAINTINGS SOON TOO!
THE THICK STROKES ARE REALLY REFRESHING!!!
WHY DON'T YOU GIVE IT A TRY TOO WHEN YOU HAVE SOME FREE TIME?
IT'LL BE A NICE CHANGE OF PACE!!
HMM...
ART AS A HOBBY, HUH...
ASK SENSEI!!!
Q. What do you do on your days off?
Yumeno-sensei:
"Hmm. I started doing some oil painting recently! Trying out a new medium is always as exciting as falling in love.♡"
You even draw during your free time? You really do love manga, don't you!!?
You even do water-colors!? You're so talented, Yumeno-sensei!
I'd love to see one of your paintings as a cover.♡♡
I IMAGINED IT ALL THE WAY TO PLANS FOR AN ART BOOK RELEASE OF MY PAINTINGS!!!
THAT TOTALLY DOESN'T COUNT AS A HOBBY ANYMORE!!!

WHEN YOU'RE NOT HERE

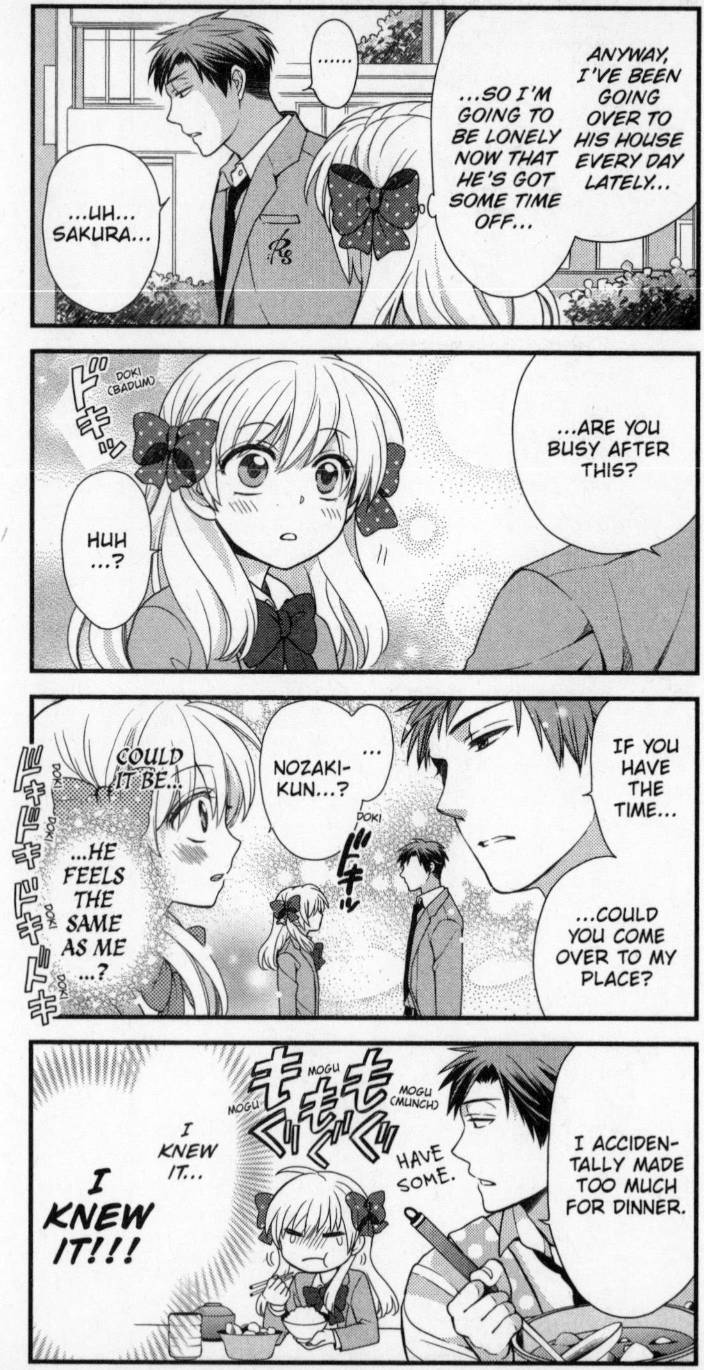
ANYWAY, I'VE BEEN GOING OVER TO HIS HOUSE EVERY DAY LATELY...
...SO I'M GOING TO BE LONELY NOW THAT HE'S GOT SOME TIME OFF...
......
...UH... SAKURA...
...ARE YOU BUSY AFTER THIS?
ドキッ
DOKI (BADUM)
HUH ...?
IF YOU HAVE THE TIME...
...COULD YOU COME OVER TO MY PLACE?
ドキッ
DOKI
... NOZAKI-KUN...?
COULD IT BE...
...HE FEELS THE SAME AS ME ...?
ドキドキドキドキ
DOKI DOKI DOKI DOKI
I ACCIDENTALLY MADE TOO MUCH FOR DINNER.
HAVE SOME.
もぐもぐもぐ
MOGU (MUNCH) MOGU MOGU
I KNEW IT...
I KNEW IT!!!

CARRYING OUT HIS ORIGINAL PLAN

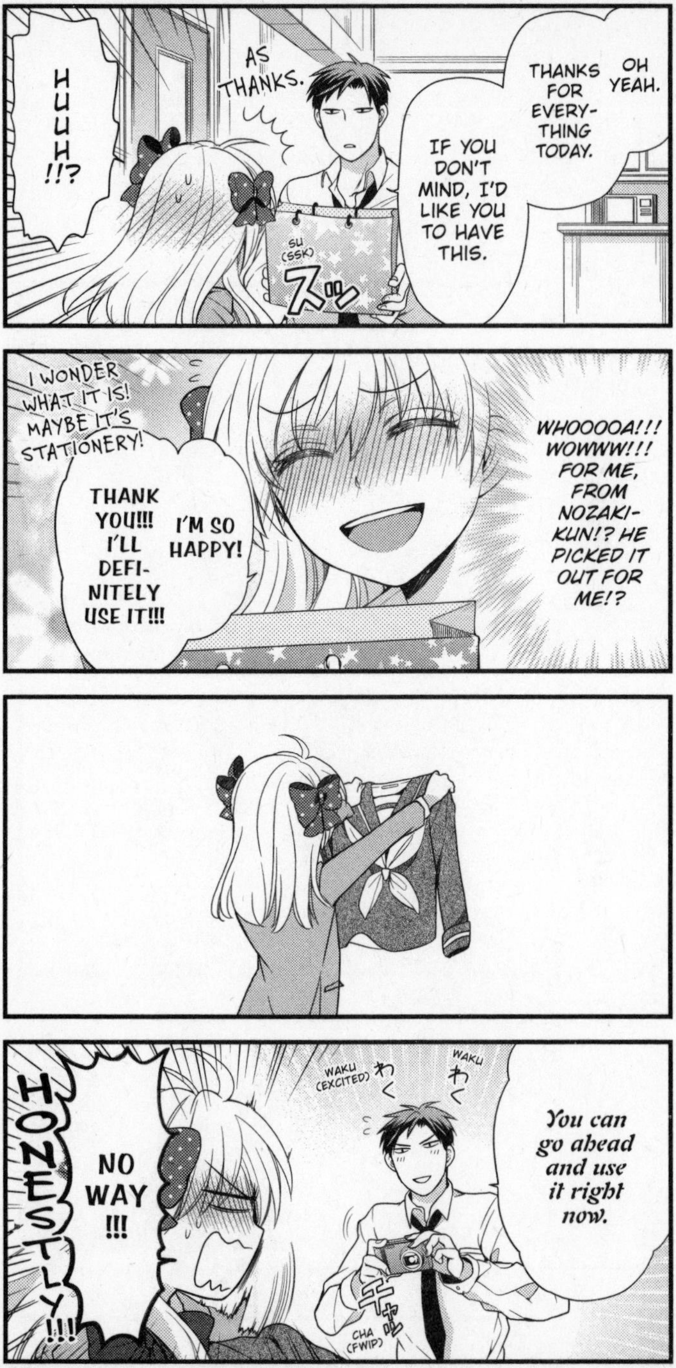
OH YEAH.
THANKS FOR EVERY-THING TODAY.
IF YOU DON'T MIND, I'D LIKE YOU TO HAVE THIS.
SU (SSK)
スッ
AS THANKS.
HUUUH!!?
WHOOOOA!!! WOWWW!!! FOR ME, FROM NOZAKI-KUN!? HE PICKED IT OUT FOR ME!?
I'M SO HAPPY!
THANK YOU!!! I'LL DEFI-NITELY USE IT!!!
I WONDER WHAT IT IS! MAYBE IT'S STATIONERY!
You can go ahead and use it right now.
WAKU
わく
WAKU (EXCITED)
わく
CHA (FWIP)
キャッ
NO WAY !!!
HONESTLY!!!

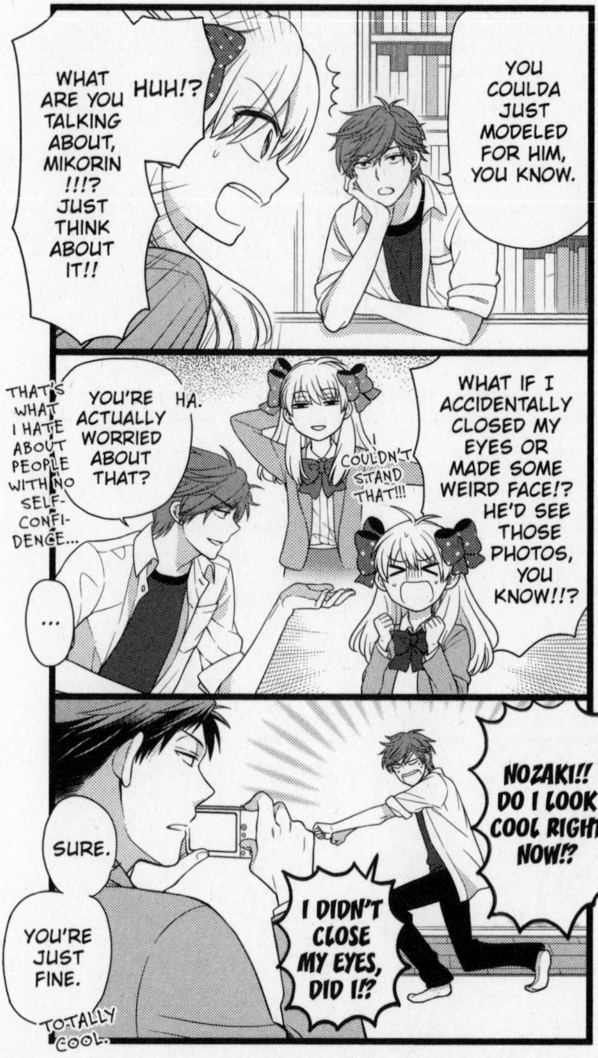
YOU COULDA JUST MODELED FOR HIM, YOU KNOW.
HUH!?
WHAT ARE YOU TALKING ABOUT, MIKORIN!!!? JUST THINK ABOUT IT!!
WHAT IF I ACCIDENTALLY CLOSED MY EYES OR MADE SOME WEIRD FACE!? HE'D SEE THOSE PHOTOS, YOU KNOW!!?
I COULDN'T STAND THAT!!!
HA.
YOU'RE ACTUALLY WORRIED ABOUT THAT?
THAT'S WHAT I HATE ABOUT PEOPLE WITH NO SELF-CONFIDENCE...
...
NOZAKI!! DO I LOOK COOL RIGHT NOW!?
I DIDN'T CLOSE MY EYES, DID I!?
SURE.
YOU'RE JUST FINE.
TOTALLY COOL.

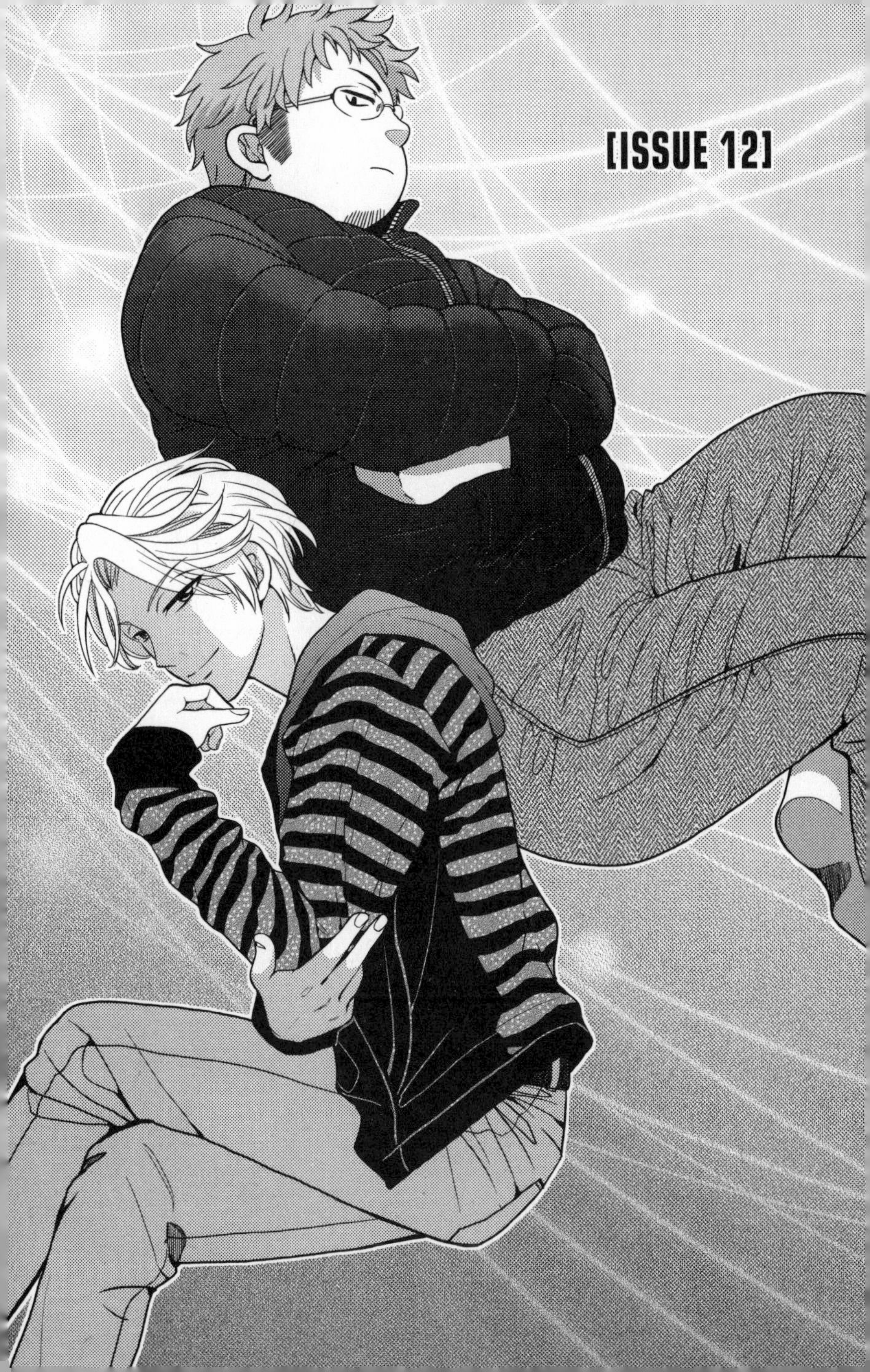
[ISSUE 12]

EXCITING PLANS

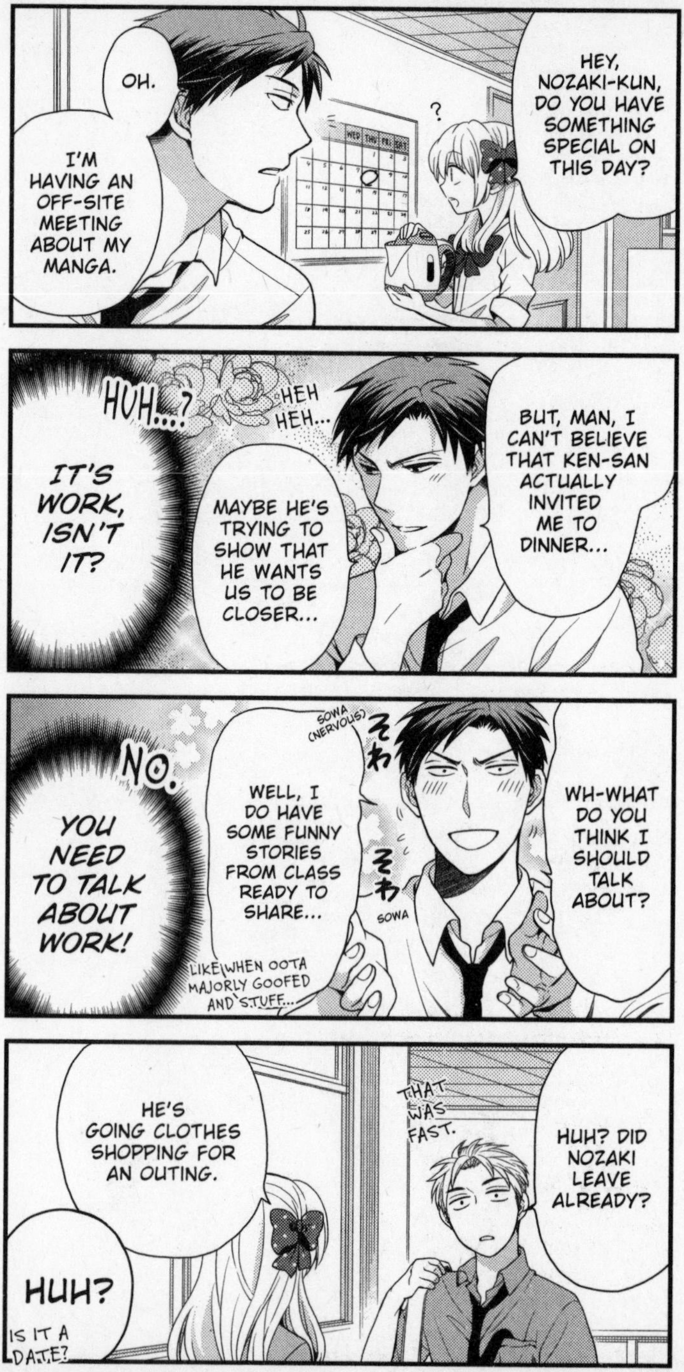
HEY, NOZAKI-KUN, DO YOU HAVE SOMETHING SPECIAL ON THIS DAY?
?
OH.
I'M HAVING AN OFF-SITE MEETING ABOUT MY MANGA.
BUT, MAN, I CAN'T BELIEVE THAT KEN-SAN ACTUALLY INVITED ME TO DINNER...
HEH HEH...
MAYBE HE'S TRYING TO SHOW THAT HE WANTS US TO BE CLOSER...
HUH...?
IT'S WORK, ISN'T IT?
WH-WHAT DO YOU THINK I SHOULD TALK ABOUT?
そわ
SOWA (NERVOUS)
そわ
SOWA
WELL, I DO HAVE SOME FUNNY STORIES FROM CLASS READY TO SHARE...
LIKE WHEN OOTA MAJORLY GOOFED AND STUFF...
NO.
YOU NEED TO TALK ABOUT WORK!
HUH? DID NOZAKI LEAVE ALREADY?
THAT WAS FAST.
HE'S GOING CLOTHES SHOPPING FOR AN OUTING.
HUH?
IS IT A DATE?

TEXT HOARDING

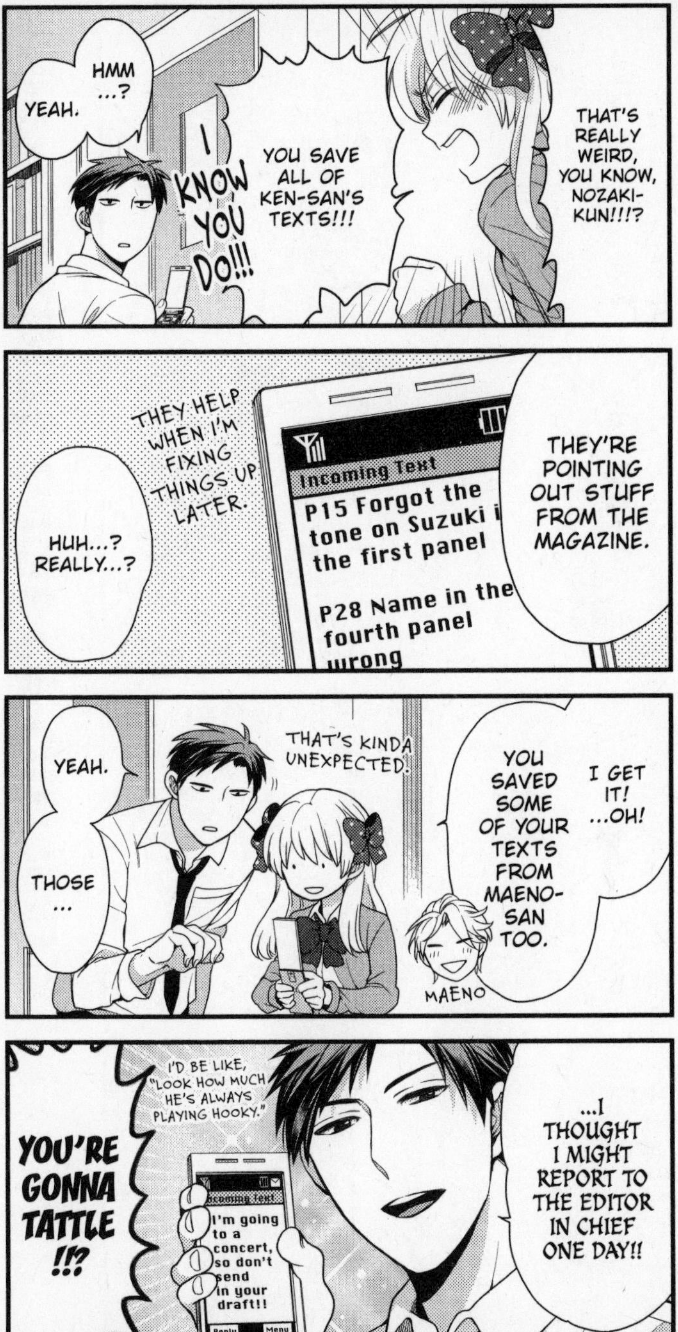

THAT'S REALLY WEIRD, YOU KNOW, NOZAKI-KUN!!!?
YOU SAVE ALL OF KEN-SAN'S TEXTS!!!
I KNOW YOU DO!!!
HMM ...? YEAH.
THEY'RE POINTING OUT STUFF FROM THE MAGAZINE.
Incoming Text
P15 Forgot the tone on Suzuki i the first panel
P28 Name in the fourth panel wrong
THEY HELP WHEN I'M FIXING THINGS UP LATER.
HUH...? REALLY...?
I GET IT! ...OH!
YOU SAVED SOME OF YOUR TEXTS FROM MAENO-SAN TOO.
MAENO
THAT'S KINDA UNEXPECTED.
YEAH.
THOSE ...
...I THOUGHT I MIGHT REPORT TO THE EDITOR IN CHIEF ONE DAY!!
I'D BE LIKE, "LOOK HOW MUCH HE'S ALWAYS PLAYING HOOKY."
Incoming Text
I'm going to a concert, so don't send in your draft!!
Reply
Menu
YOU'RE GONNA TATTLE!!?

A NEVER-ENDING GAME OF OLD MAID

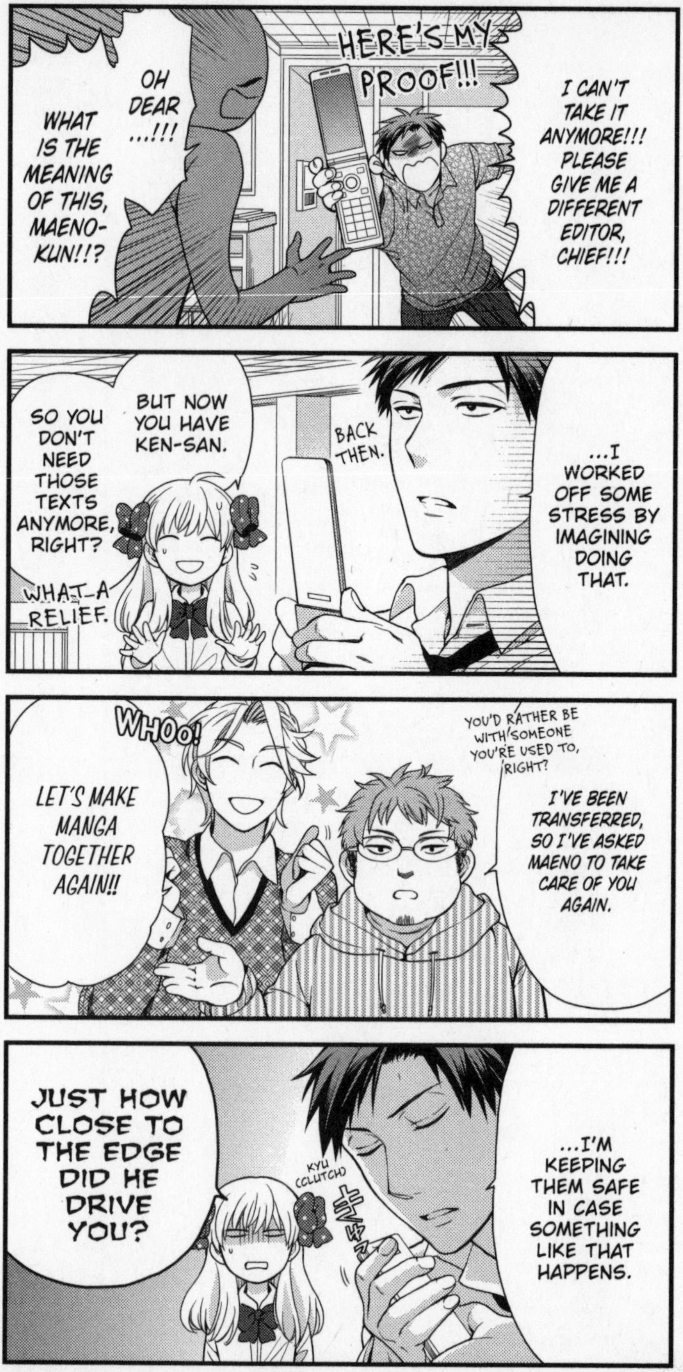
HERE'S MY PROOF!!!
I CAN'T TAKE IT ANYMORE!!! PLEASE GIVE ME A DIFFERENT EDITOR, CHIEF!!!
OH DEAR ...!!!
WHAT IS THE MEANING OF THIS, MAENO-KUN!!?
...I WORKED OFF SOME STRESS BY IMAGINING DOING THAT.
BACK THEN.
BUT NOW YOU HAVE KEN-SAN.
SO YOU DON'T NEED THOSE TEXTS ANYMORE, RIGHT?
WHAT A RELIEF.
I'VE BEEN TRANSFERRED, SO I'VE ASKED MAENO TO TAKE CARE OF YOU AGAIN.
YOU'D RATHER BE WITH SOMEONE YOU'RE USED TO, RIGHT?
WHOo!
LET'S MAKE MANGA TOGETHER AGAIN!!
...I'M KEEPING THEM SAFE IN CASE SOMETHING LIKE THAT HAPPENS.
KYU (CLUTCH)
JUST HOW CLOSE TO THE EDGE DID HE DRIVE YOU?

SPECIFIC ADVICE

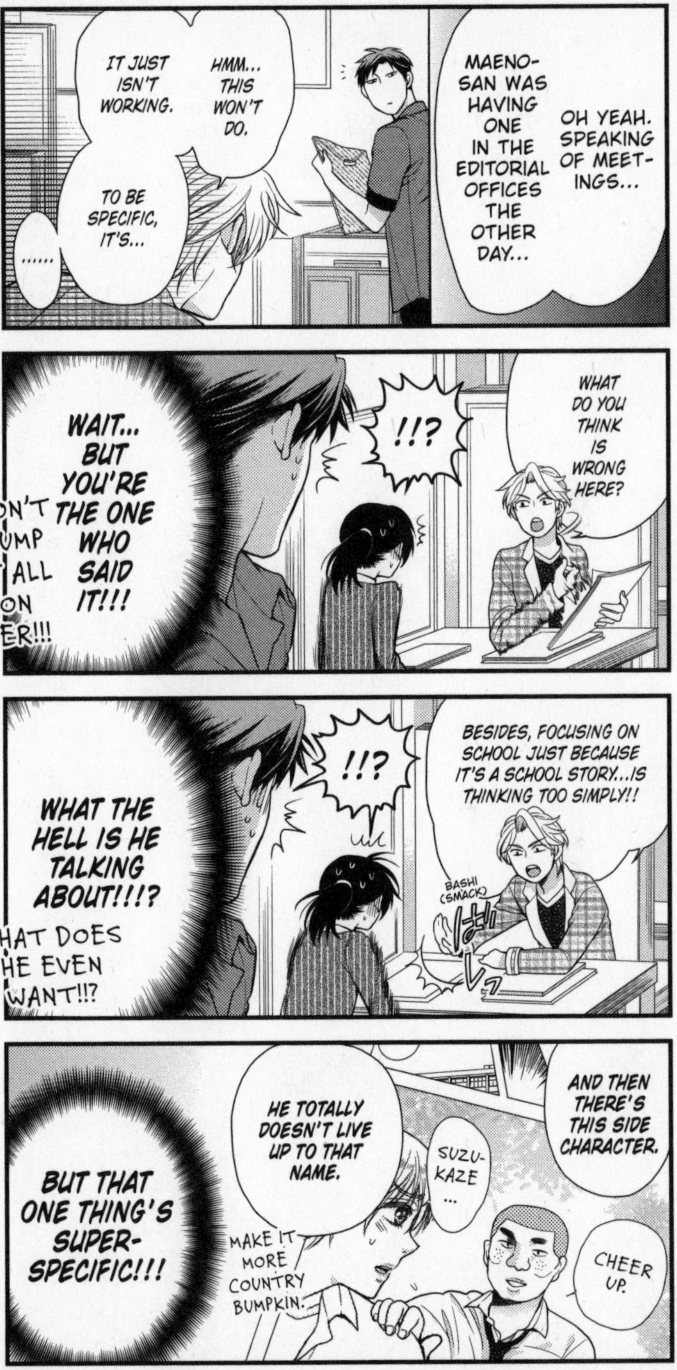
OH YEAH. SPEAKING OF MEET-INGS...
MAENO-SAN WAS HAVING ONE IN THE EDITORIAL OFFICES THE OTHER DAY...
HMM... THIS WON'T DO.
IT JUST ISN'T WORKING.
TO BE SPECIFIC, IT'S...
......
WHAT DO YOU THINK IS WRONG HERE?
!!?
WAIT... BUT YOU'RE THE ONE WHO SAID IT!!!
DON'T DUMP IT ALL ON HER!!!
BESIDES, FOCUSING ON SCHOOL JUST BECAUSE IT'S A SCHOOL STORY...IS THINKING TOO SIMPLY!!
!!?
BASHI (SMACK)
WHAT THE HELL IS HE TALKING ABOUT!!!?
WHAT DOES HE EVEN WANT!!?
AND THEN THERE'S THIS SIDE CHARACTER.
SUZU-KAZE ...
HE TOTALLY DOESN'T LIVE UP TO THAT NAME.
CHEER UP.
MAKE IT MORE COUNTRY BUMPKIN.
BUT THAT ONE THING'S SUPER-SPECIFIC!!!

A MATURING NEWBIE

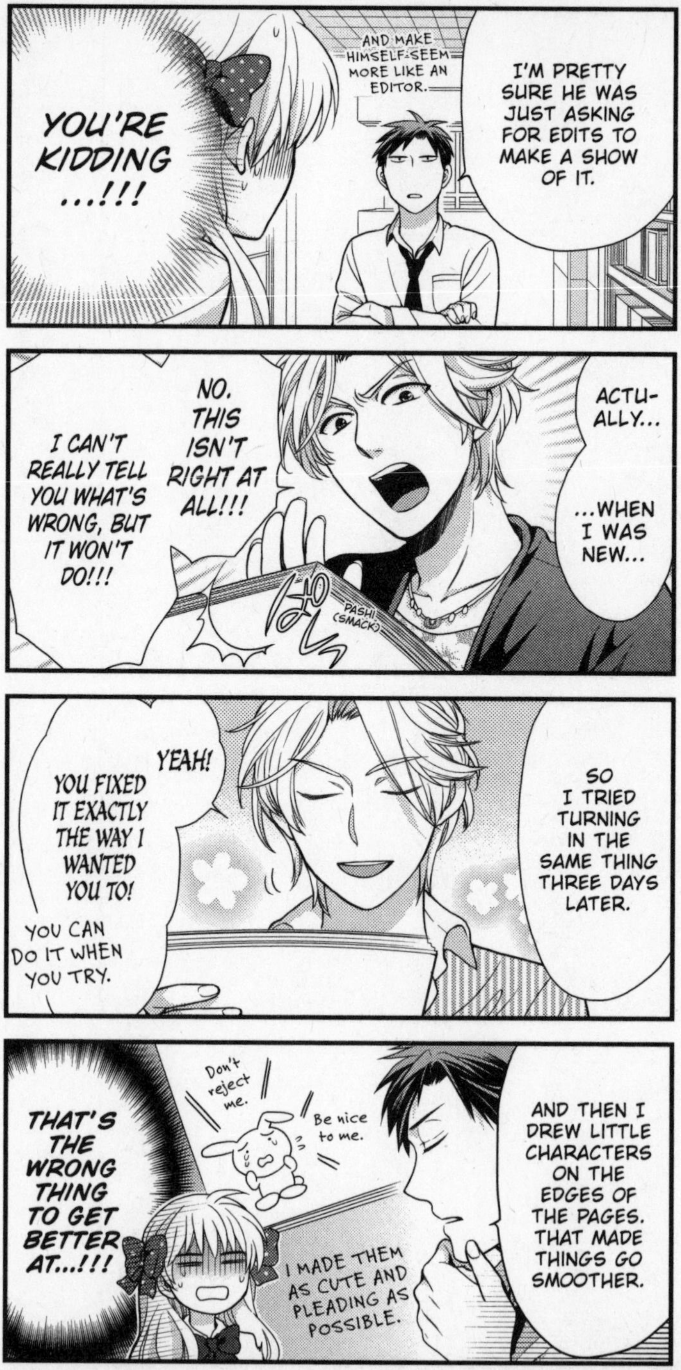
I'M PRETTY SURE HE WAS JUST ASKING FOR EDITS TO MAKE A SHOW OF IT.
AND MAKE HIMSELF SEEM MORE LIKE AN EDITOR.
YOU'RE KIDDING ...!!!
ACTU-ALLY...
...WHEN I WAS NEW...
NO. THIS ISN'T RIGHT AT ALL!!!
I CAN'T REALLY TELL YOU WHAT'S WRONG, BUT IT WON'T DO!!!
PASHI (SMACK)
SO I TRIED TURNING IN THE SAME THING THREE DAYS LATER.
YEAH!
YOU FIXED IT EXACTLY THE WAY I WANTED YOU TO!
YOU CAN DO IT WHEN YOU TRY.
AND THEN I DREW LITTLE CHARACTERS ON THE EDGES OF THE PAGES. THAT MADE THINGS GO SMOOTHER.
Be nice to me.
Don't reject me.
I MADE THEM AS CUTE AND PLEADING AS POSSIBLE.
THAT'S THE WRONG THING TO GET BETTER AT...!!!

TODAY'S TOPIC OF CONVERSATION

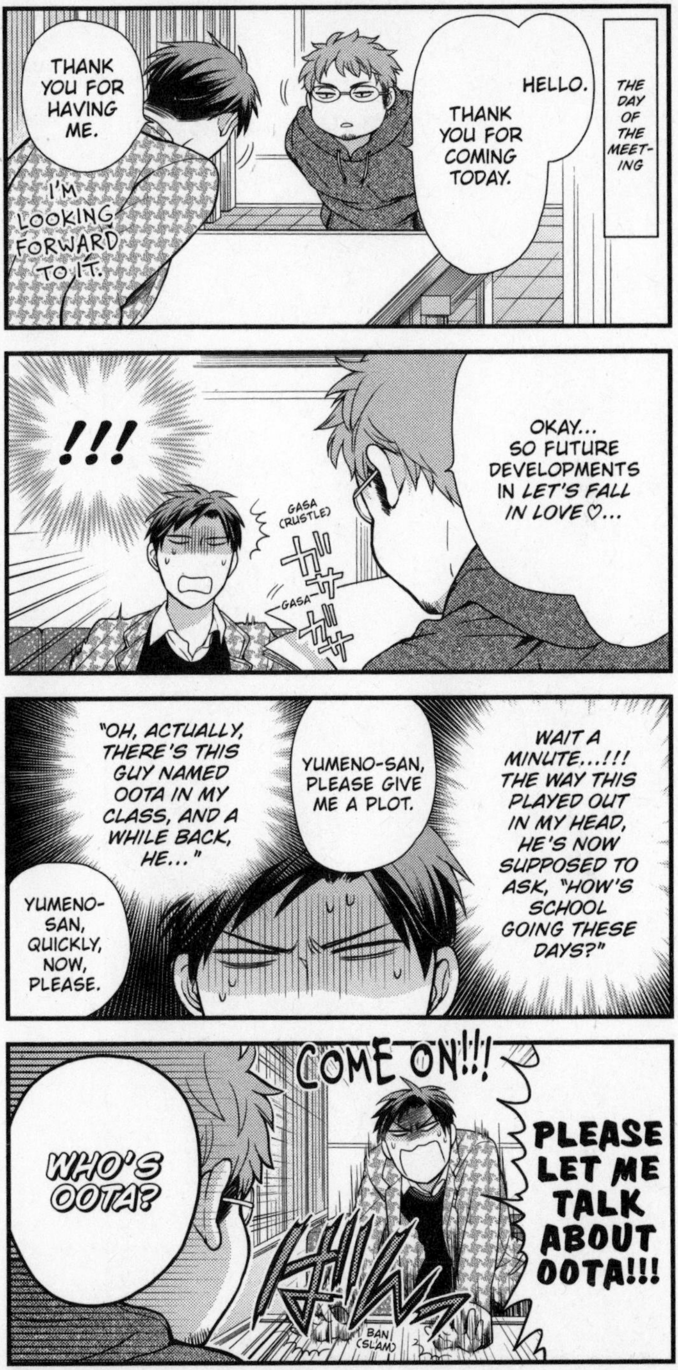
THE DAY OF THE MEETING
HELLO. THANK YOU FOR COMING TODAY.
THANK YOU FOR HAVING ME.
I'M LOOKING FORWARD TO IT.
OKAY... SO FUTURE DEVELOPMENTS IN LET'S FALL IN LOVE♡...
GASA (RUSTLE)
GASA
!!!
WAIT A MINUTE...!!! THE WAY THIS PLAYED OUT IN MY HEAD, HE'S NOW SUPPOSED TO ASK, "HOW'S SCHOOL GOING THESE DAYS?"
YUMENO-SAN, PLEASE GIVE ME A PLOT.
"OH, ACTUALLY, THERE'S THIS GUY NAMED OOTA IN MY CLASS, AND A WHILE BACK, HE..."
YUMENO-SAN, QUICKLY, NOW, PLEASE.
COME ON!!!
PLEASE LET ME TALK ABOUT OOTA!!!
BAN (SLAM)
WHO'S OOTA?

CHARACTER CONCEPT

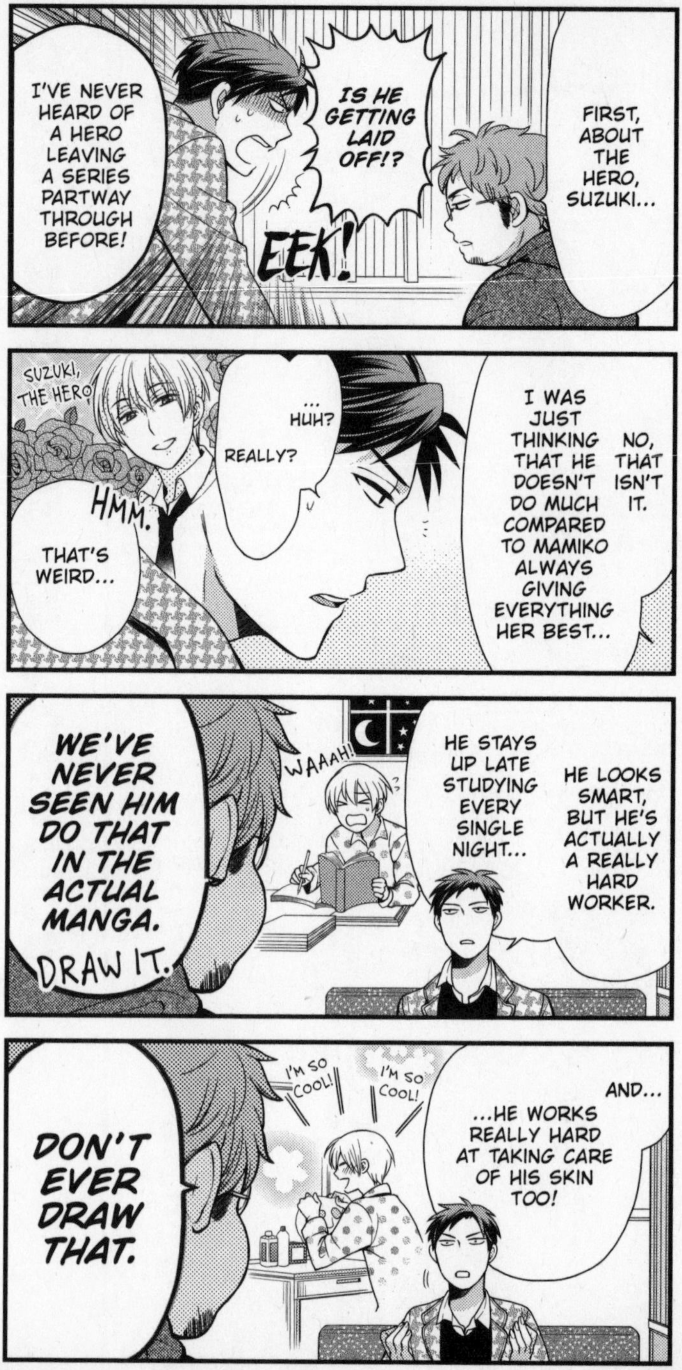
FIRST, ABOUT THE HERO, SUZUKI...
IS HE GETTING LAID OFF!?
EEK!
I'VE NEVER HEARD OF A HERO LEAVING A SERIES PARTWAY THROUGH BEFORE!
NO, THAT ISN'T IT.
I WAS JUST THINKING THAT HE DOESN'T DO MUCH COMPARED TO MAMIKO ALWAYS GIVING EVERYTHING HER BEST...
... HUH?
REALLY?
SUZUKI, THE HERO?
HMM.
THAT'S WEIRD...
HE LOOKS SMART, BUT HE'S ACTUALLY A REALLY HARD WORKER.
HE STAYS UP LATE STUDYING EVERY SINGLE NIGHT...
WAAAH!
WE'VE NEVER SEEN HIM DO THAT IN THE ACTUAL MANGA.
DRAW IT.
AND...
...HE WORKS REALLY HARD AT TAKING CARE OF HIS SKIN TOO!
I'M SO COOL!
I'M SO COOL!
DON'T EVER DRAW THAT.

A REFRESHING HOLIDAY

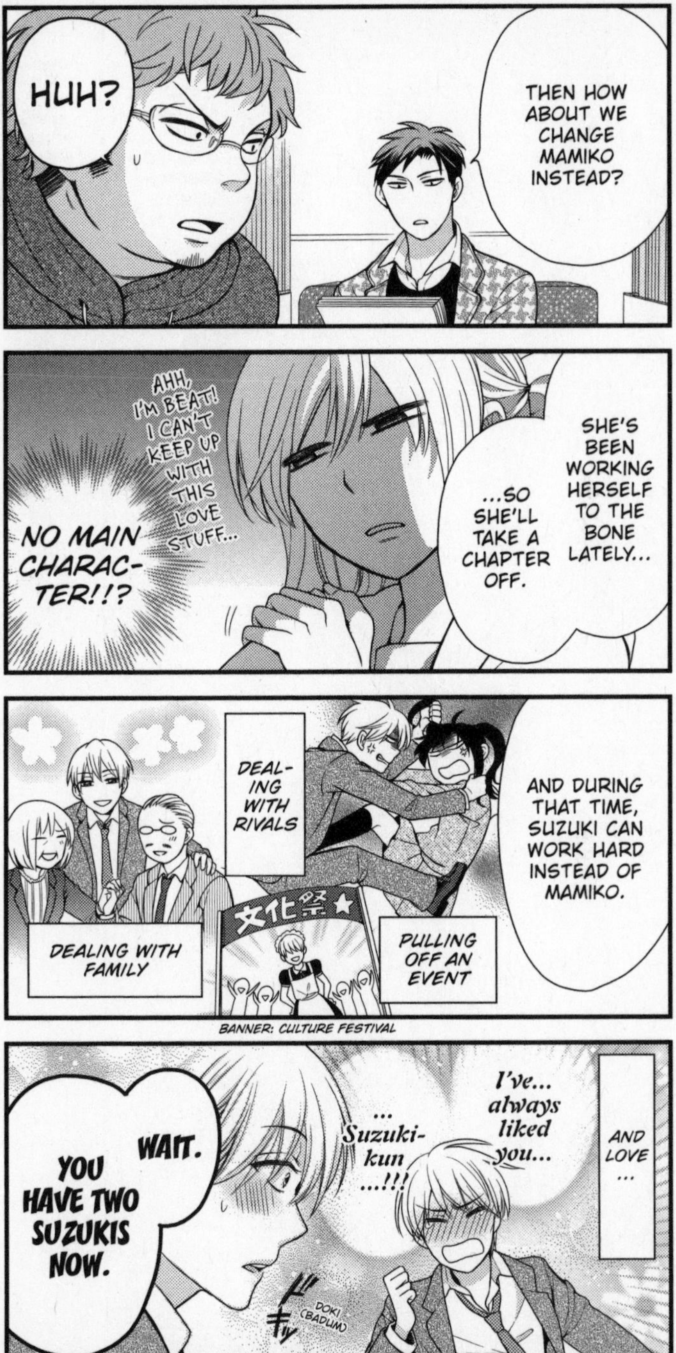
THEN HOW ABOUT WE CHANGE MAMIKO INSTEAD?
HUH?
SHE'S BEEN WORKING HERSELF TO THE BONE LATELY...
...SO SHE'LL TAKE A CHAPTER OFF.
AHH, I'M BEAT! I CAN'T KEEP UP WITH THIS LOVE STUFF...
NO MAIN CHARACTER!!?
AND DURING THAT TIME, SUZUKI CAN WORK HARD INSTEAD OF MAMIKO.
DEALING WITH RIVALS
PULLING OFF AN EVENT
文化祭★
DEALING WITH FAMILY
BANNER: CULTURE FESTIVAL
AND LOVE ...
I've... always liked you...
... Suzuki-kun ...!!!
DOKI (BADUM)
WAIT.
YOU HAVE TWO SUZUKIS NOW.

A COMMON POSE

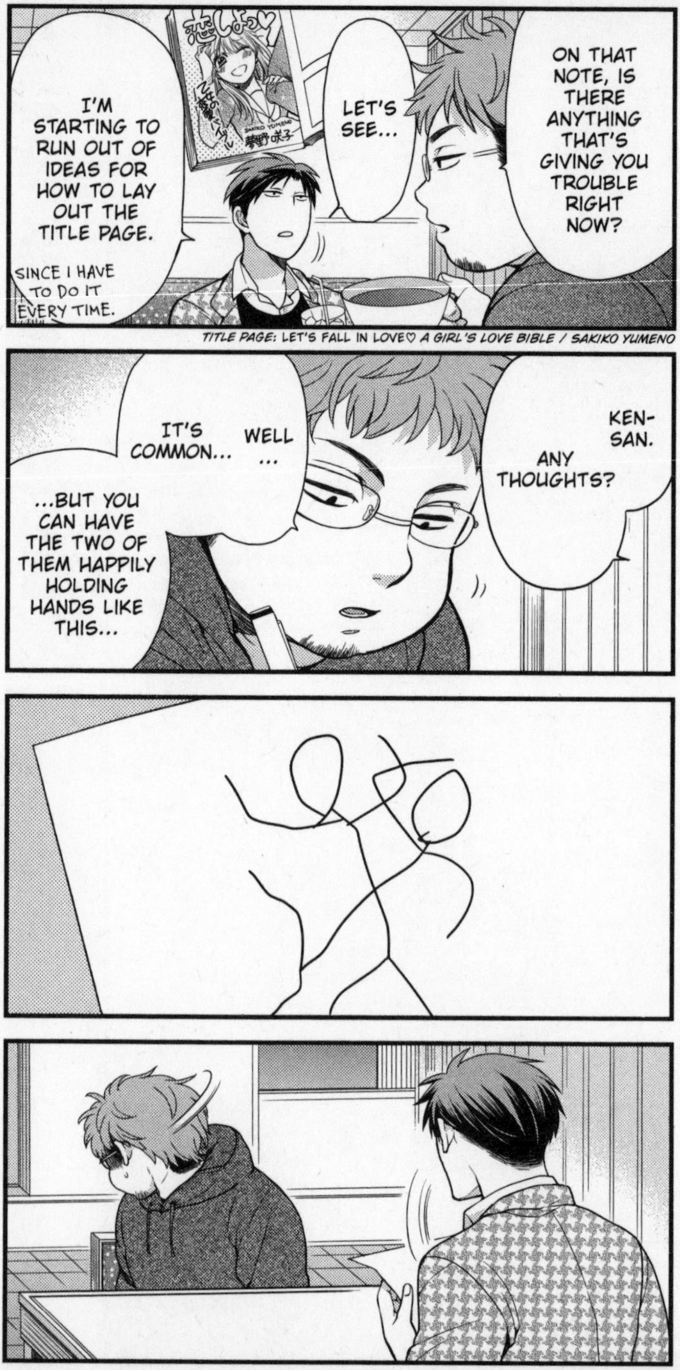

ON THAT NOTE, IS THERE ANYTHING THAT'S GIVING YOU TROUBLE RIGHT NOW?
LET'S SEE...
I'M STARTING TO RUN OUT OF IDEAS FOR HOW TO LAY OUT THE TITLE PAGE.
SINCE I HAVE TO DO IT EVERY TIME.
TITLE PAGE: LET'S FALL IN LOVE♡ A GIRL'S LOVE BIBLE / SAKIKO YUMENO
KEN-SAN.
ANY THOUGHTS?
WELL ...
IT'S COMMON...
...BUT YOU CAN HAVE THE TWO OF THEM HAPPILY HOLDING HANDS LIKE THIS...

MAYBE SF

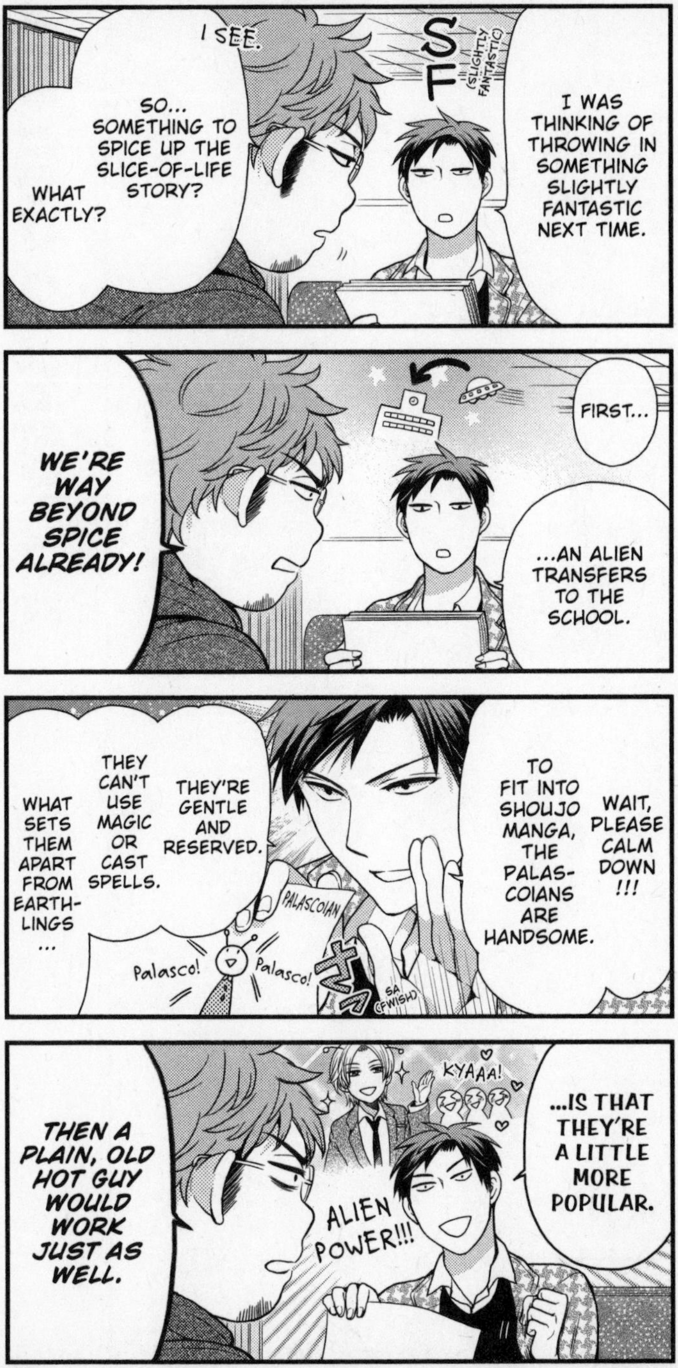
I WAS THINKING OF THROWING IN SOMETHING SLIGHTLY FANTASTIC NEXT TIME.
SF
(SLIGHTLY FANTASTIC)
I SEE.
SO... SOMETHING TO SPICE UP THE SLICE-OF-LIFE STORY?
WHAT EXACTLY?
FIRST...
...AN ALIEN TRANSFERS TO THE SCHOOL.
WE'RE WAY BEYOND SPICE ALREADY!
WAIT, PLEASE CALM DOWN!!!
TO FIT INTO SHOUJO MANGA, THE PALAS-COIANS ARE HANDSOME.
SA (FWISH)
PALASCOIAN
THEY'RE GENTLE AND RESERVED.
THEY CAN'T USE MAGIC OR CAST SPELLS.
WHAT SETS THEM APART FROM EARTH-LINGS...
Palasco!
Palasco!
KYAAA!
...IS THAT THEY'RE A LITTLE MORE POPULAR.
ALIEN POWER!!!
THEN A PLAIN, OLD HOT GUY WOULD WORK JUST AS WELL.

THE GOD OF LAUGHTER

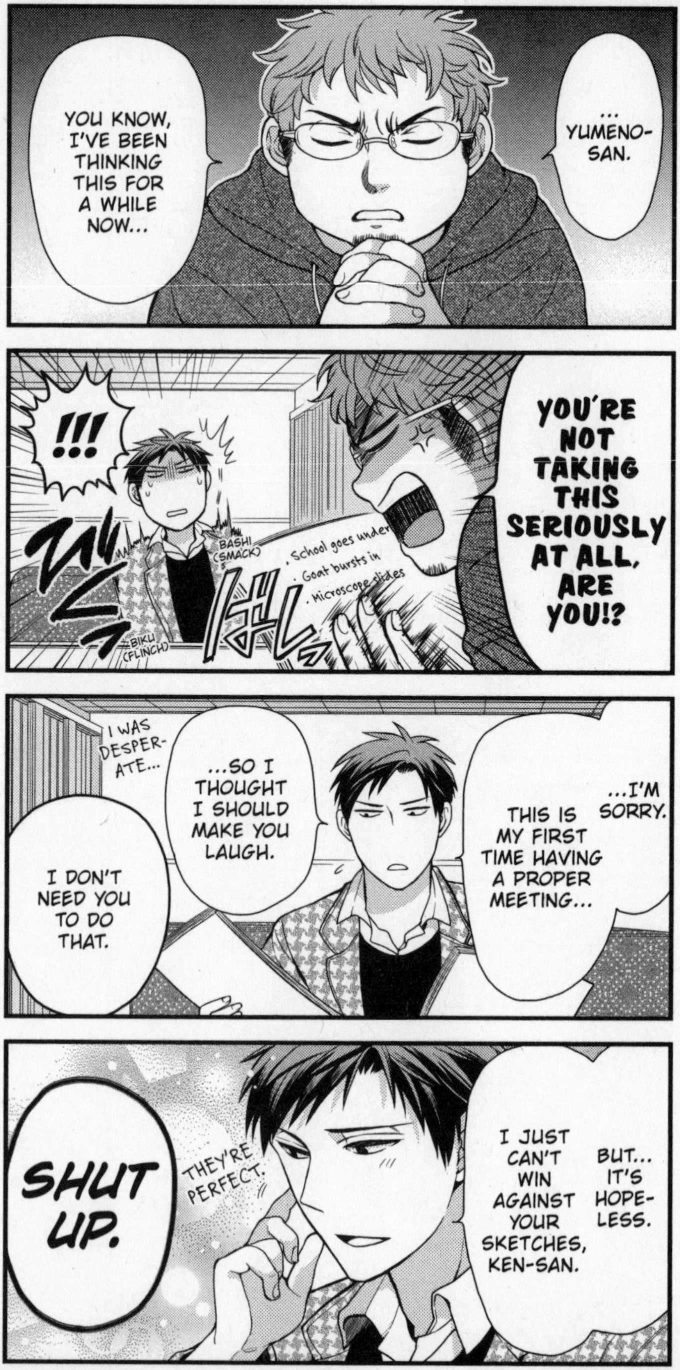
...YUMENO-SAN.
YOU KNOW, I'VE BEEN THINKING THIS FOR A WHILE NOW...
YOU'RE NOT TAKING THIS SERIOUSLY AT ALL, ARE YOU!?
· School goes under
· Goat bursts in
· Microscope slides
BASHI (SMACK)
!!!
BIKU (FLINCH)
...I'M SORRY.
THIS IS MY FIRST TIME HAVING A PROPER MEETING...
...SO I THOUGHT I SHOULD MAKE YOU LAUGH.
I WAS DESPERATE...
I DON'T NEED YOU TO DO THAT.
BUT... IT'S HOPELESS.
I JUST CAN'T WIN AGAINST YOUR SKETCHES, KEN-SAN.
THEY'RE PERFECT.
SHUT UP.

PRIMARY GOAL

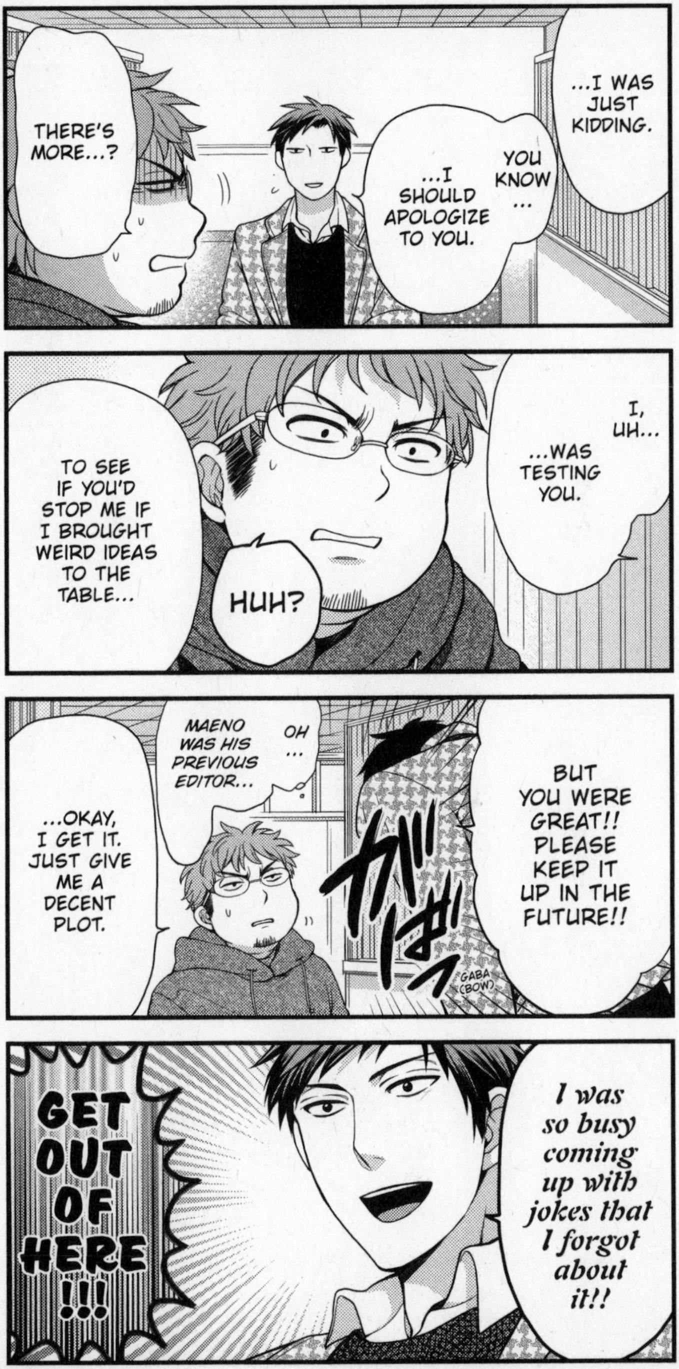

...I WAS JUST KIDDING.
YOU KNOW ...
...I SHOULD APOLOGIZE TO YOU.
THERE'S MORE...?
I, UH...
...WAS TESTING YOU.
TO SEE IF YOU'D STOP ME IF I BROUGHT WEIRD IDEAS TO THE TABLE...
HUH?
BUT YOU WERE GREAT!! PLEASE KEEP IT UP IN THE FUTURE!!
GABA (BOW)
OH ...
MAENO WAS HIS PREVIOUS EDITOR...
...OKAY, I GET IT. JUST GIVE ME A DECENT PLOT.
I was so busy coming up with jokes that I forgot about it!!
GET OUT OF HERE!!!

A SATISFYING RESULT

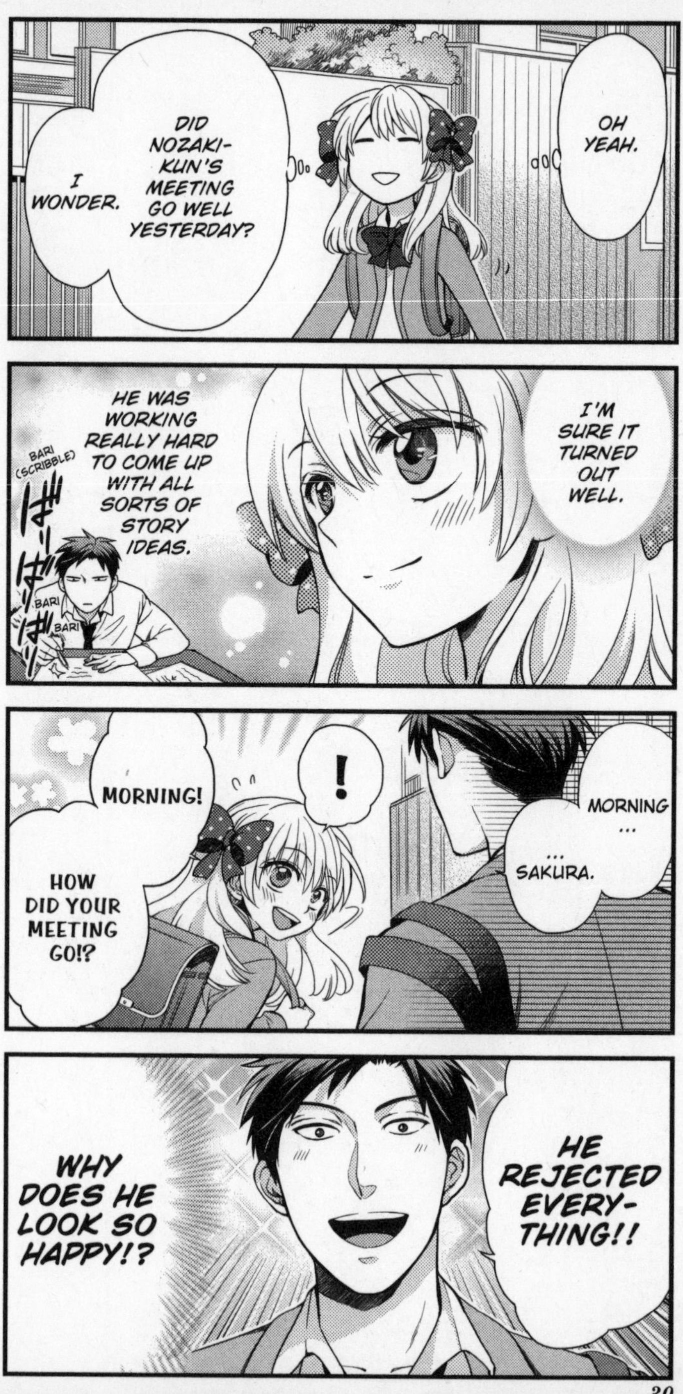
OH YEAH.
DID NOZAKI-KUN'S MEETING GO WELL YESTERDAY?
I WONDER.
I'M SURE IT TURNED OUT WELL.
HE WAS WORKING REALLY HARD TO COME UP WITH ALL SORTS OF STORY IDEAS.
BARI (SCRIBBLE)
BARI
BARI
MORNING ... ... SAKURA.
!
MORNING!
HOW DID YOUR MEETING GO!?
HE REJECTED EVERY-THING!!
WHY DOES HE LOOK SO HAPPY!?

FOR CRYING OUT LOUD. THAT WAS A USELESS MEET-ING...
HAAAH
OH?
MIYAMAE-KUN, YOU HAD A SIT-DOWN WITH YUMENO-SENSEI?
... WHOA!
WHAT'S THIS !!!?
I THINK YOU'RE ONTO SOMETHING HERE!
PALASCOIAN
Palasco!
Palas
IT LOOKS SUPER-INTEREST-ING!!!
......

ABOUT TONE

SCREEN TONE IS A PARTICULARLY USEFUL TOOL FOR SHOUJO MANGA. THERE ARE MANY TYPES AND MANY USES FOR HAIR, CLOTHES, AND EFFECTS!

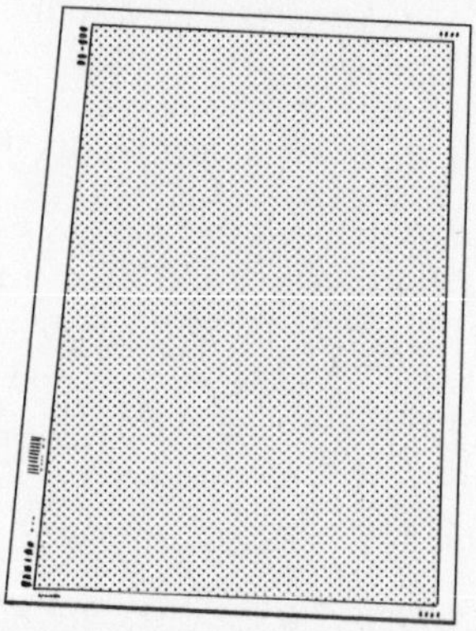

IT'S SOLD BAGGED LIKE THIS BY THE SHEET. EACH TONE HAS A NUMBER, AND BEFORE YOU KNOW IT, YOU REMEMBER MOST OF THEM. (EXAMPLES:) "NUMBER FORTY-ONE FOR SHADOWS ON CLOTHING." "THIS CHARACTER'S HAIR IS NUMBER TWENTY-SEVEN!" THERE ARE DIFFERENCES BETWEEN THE DIFFERENT COMPANIES, SO YOU CHOOSE THE ONES YOU PREFER, LIKE, "THIS ONE FOR CLOUDS!"

THERE ARE ALL SORTS OF DIFFERENT TYPES.

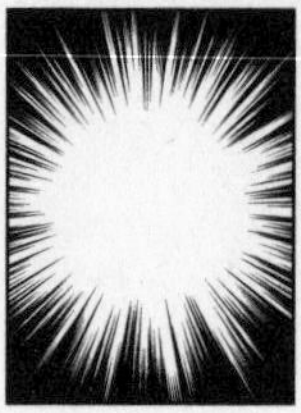

FLASHES
(FOR BACKGROUNDS AND SUCH)

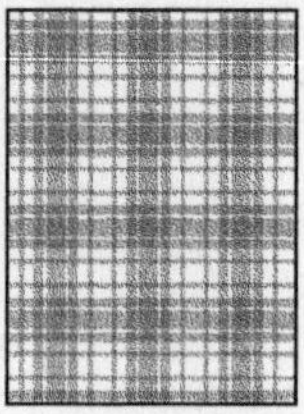

PATTERNS
(FOR DESIGNS ON CLOTHING AND SUCH)

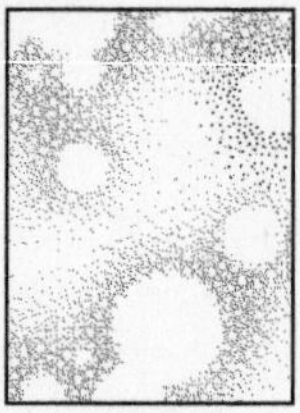

EFFECTS
(TO EXPRESS EMOTIONS)

HOW TO PUT IT ON

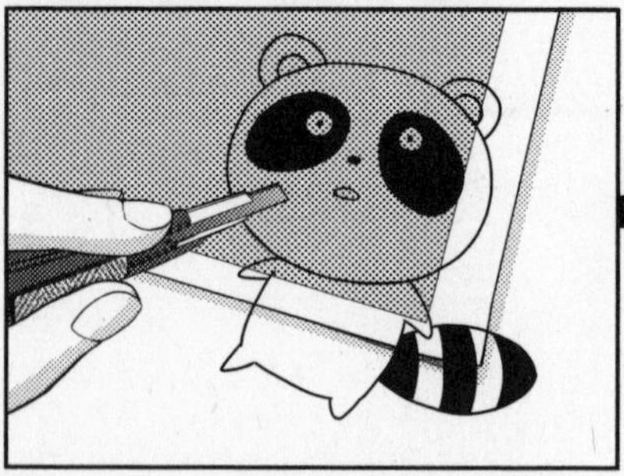

① PUT THE TONE OVER THE DRAWING WITH THE BACKING PAPER STILL ATTACHED. YOU CAN SEE THROUGH IT EVEN WITH THE BACKING THERE, SO USE A UTILITY KNIFE TO CUT THE TONE A LITTLE BIT BIGGER THAN THE DRAWING.

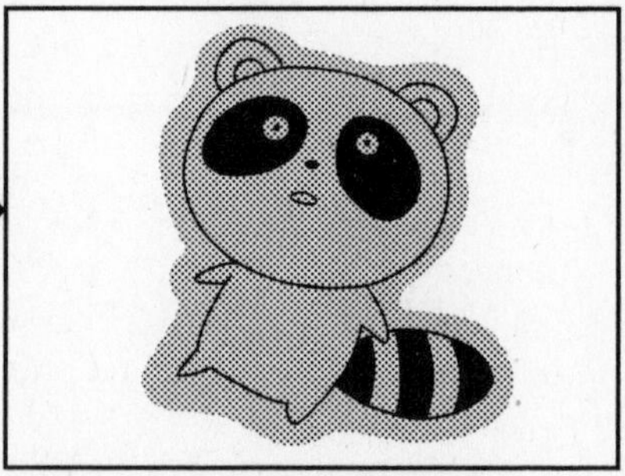

② PEEL THE TONE OFF OF THE BACKING PAPER AND PLACE IT GENTLY ATOP THE DRAWING. (TAKE CARE NOT TO LET ANY DUST GET UNDER THE TONE WHILE DOING THIS.)

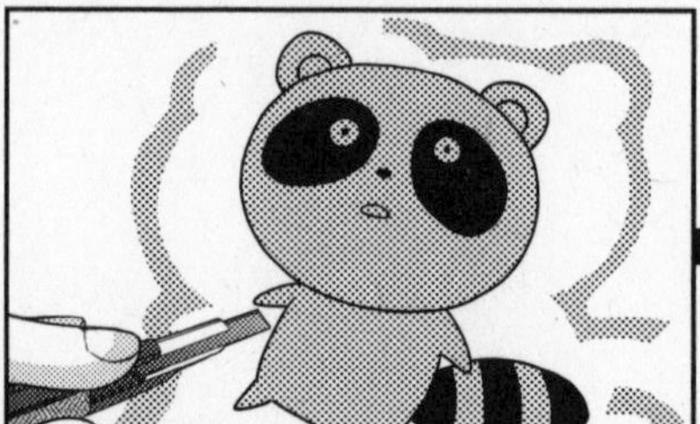

③ CUT THE EXCESS TONE AWAY WITH A UTILITY KNIFE. (AT THIS TIME, YOU CAN MAKE YOUR OWN DECISION WHETHER TO KEEP THE TRIMMED OFF BITS OF TONE TO USE AGAIN OR THROW THEM AWAY IF THEY'VE GOTTEN DIRTY.)

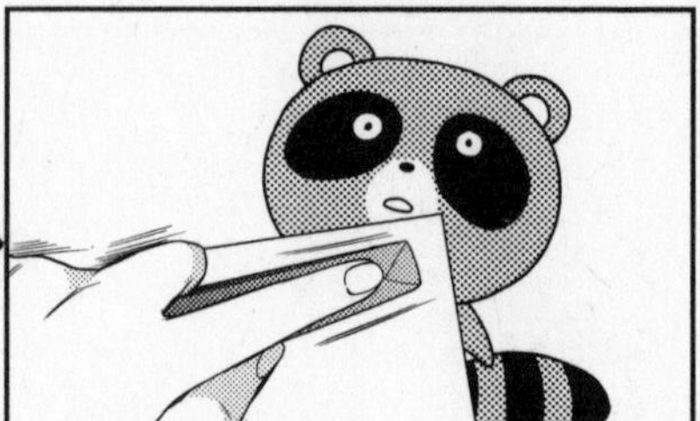

④ PUT A PIECE OF SCRAP PAPER OVER THE DRAWING AND RUB WITH A SCRAPER. (※ RUBBING THE TONE DIRECTLY WILL DAMAGE THE TONE.) THE TONE WILL PEEL OFF LATER IF YOU DON'T PRESS HARD ENOUGH, SO GO AT IT UNTIL YOUR HAND CRAMPS.

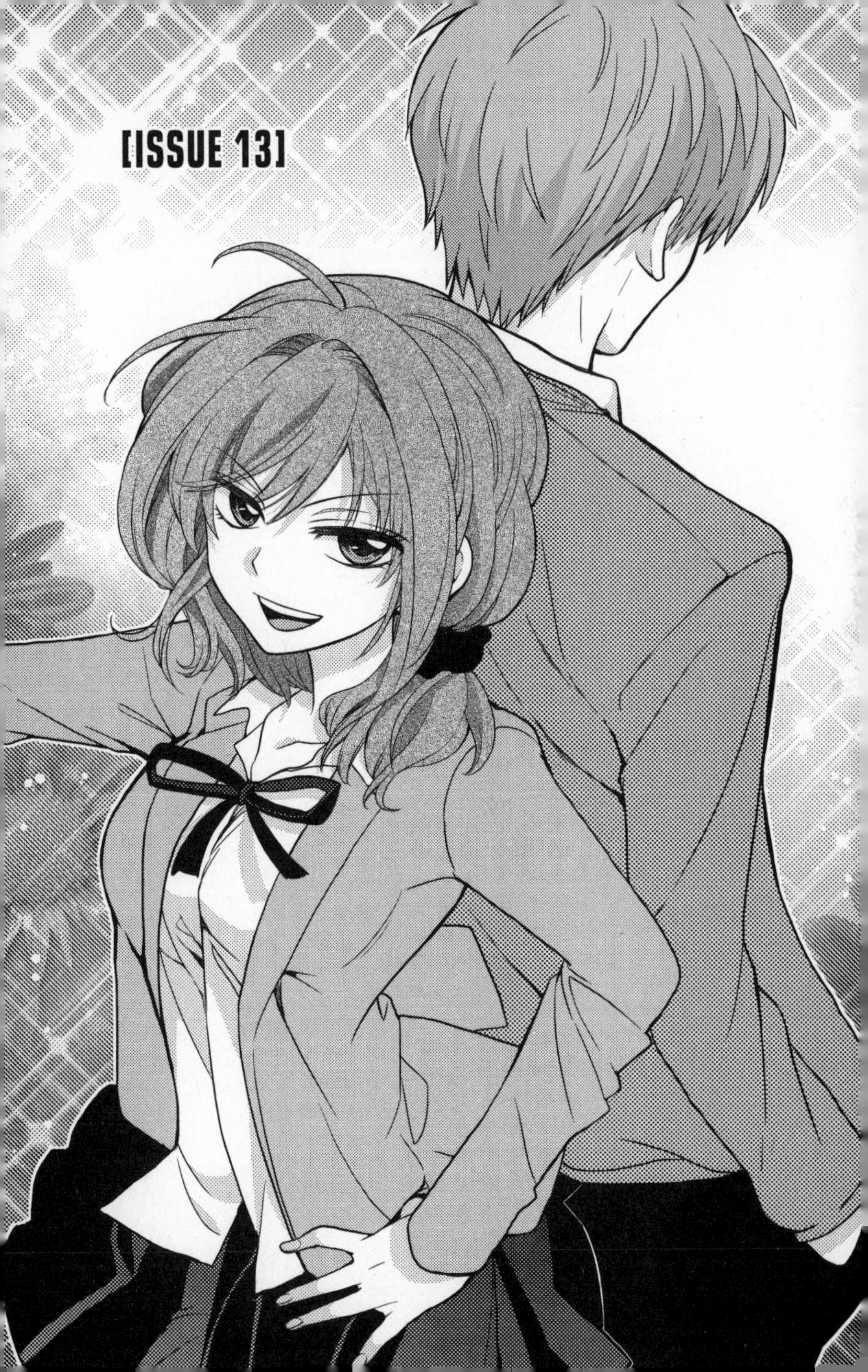
[ISSUE 13]

BGM

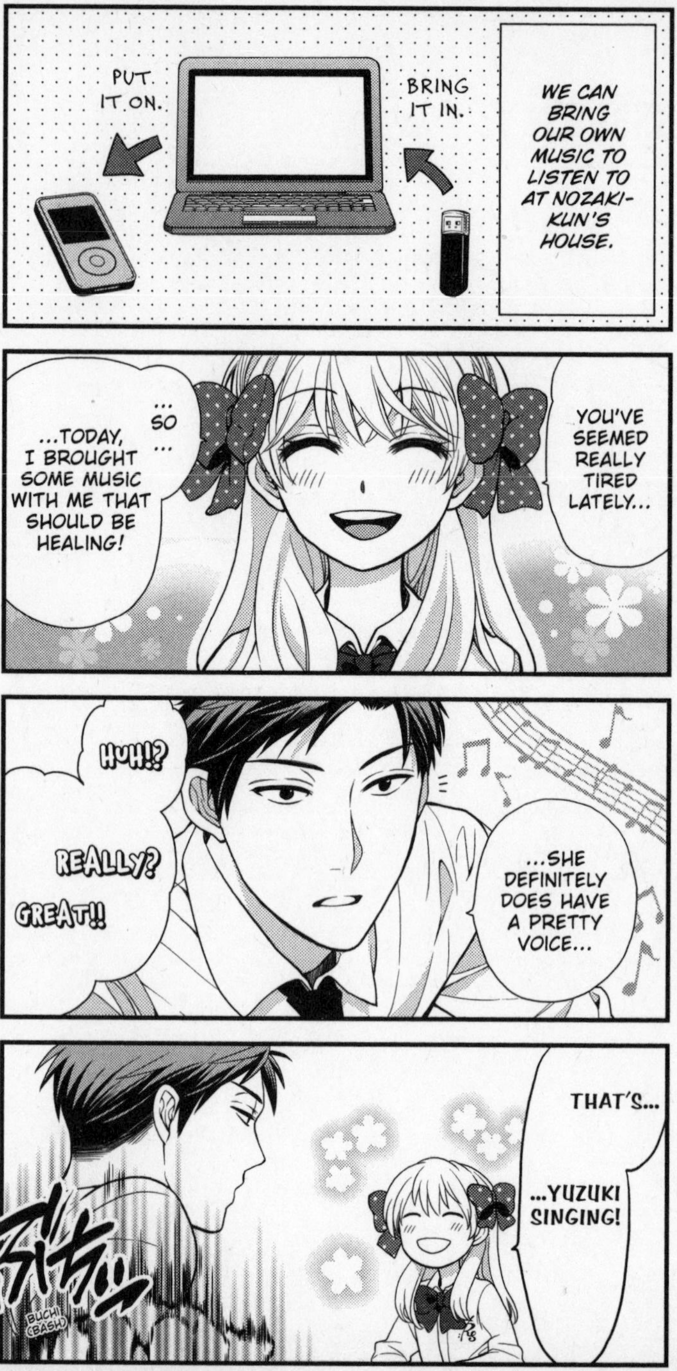
WE CAN BRING OUR OWN MUSIC TO LISTEN TO AT NOZAKI-KUN'S HOUSE.
BRING IT IN.
PUT IT ON.
YOU'VE SEEMED REALLY TIRED LATELY...
...SO...
...TODAY, I BROUGHT SOME MUSIC WITH ME THAT SHOULD BE HEALING!
...SHE DEFINITELY DOES HAVE A PRETTY VOICE...
HUH!?
REALLY?
GREAT!!
THAT'S...
...YUZUKI SINGING!
BUCHI (BASH)

THE POWER OF IMAGINATION

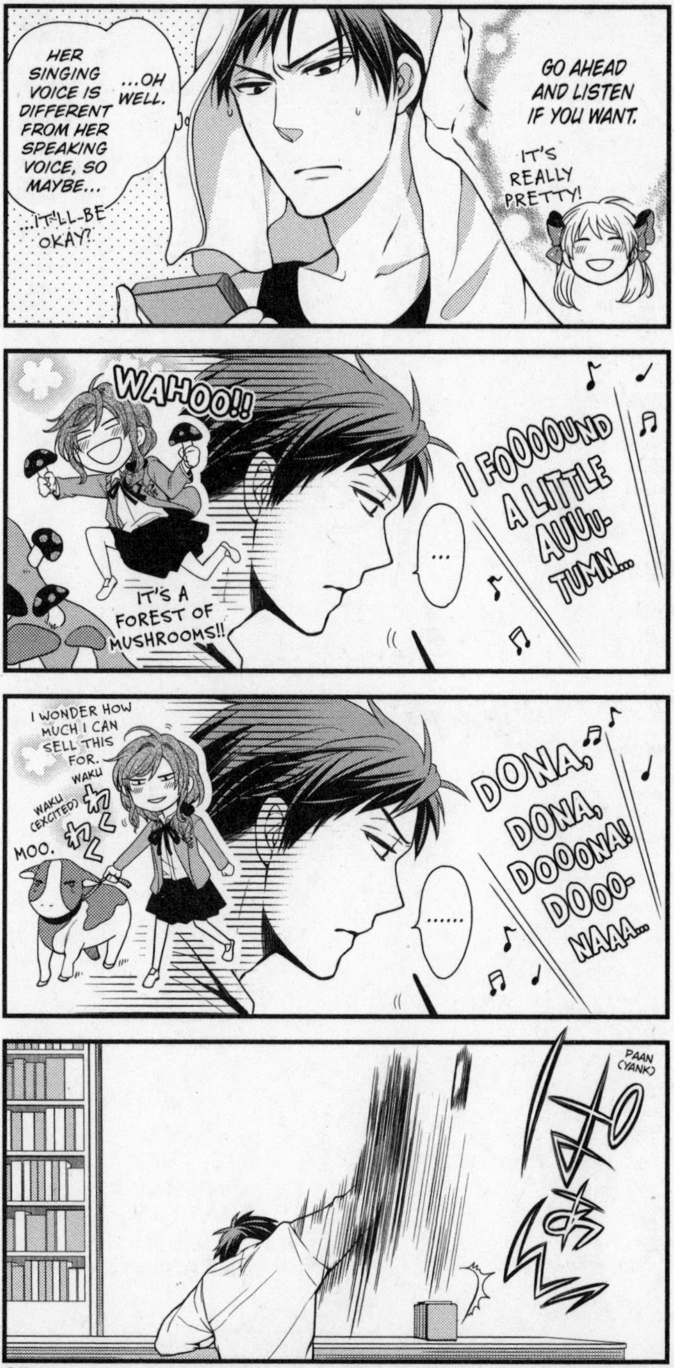
GO AHEAD AND LISTEN IF YOU WANT.
IT'S REALLY PRETTY!
...OH WELL.
HER SINGING VOICE IS DIFFERENT FROM HER SPEAKING VOICE, SO MAYBE...
...IT'LL BE OKAY?
I FOOOOUND A LITTLE AUUU-TUMN...
...
WAHOO!!
IT'S A FOREST OF MUSHROOMS!!
DONA, DONA, DOOONA! DOOO-NAAA...
......
I WONDER HOW MUCH I CAN SELL THIS FOR.
WAKU WAKU (EXCITED)
MOO.
PAAN (YANK)

A DREAMING BOY

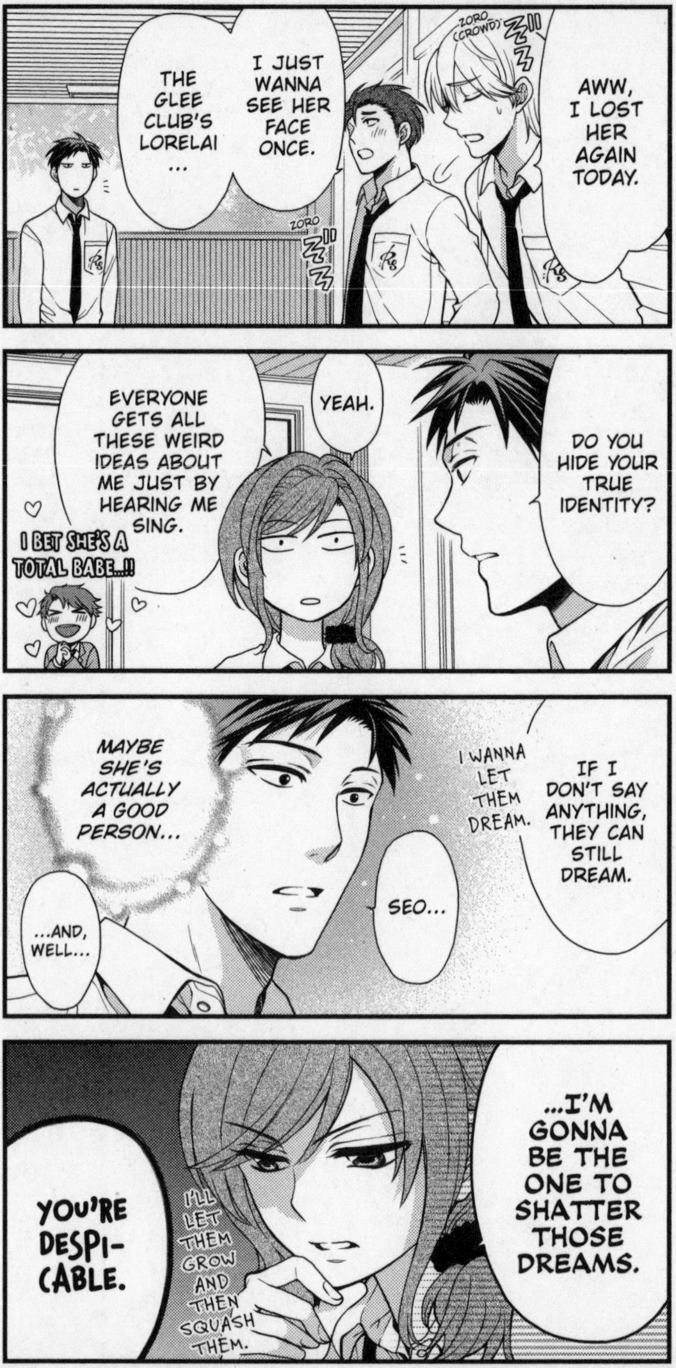

ZORO (CROWD)
AWW, I LOST HER AGAIN TODAY.
I JUST WANNA SEE HER FACE ONCE.
THE GLEE CLUB'S LORELAI ...
ZORO
DO YOU HIDE YOUR TRUE IDENTITY?
YEAH.
EVERYONE GETS ALL THESE WEIRD IDEAS ABOUT ME JUST BY HEARING ME SING.
I BET SHE'S A TOTAL BABE...!!
IF I DON'T SAY ANYTHING, THEY CAN STILL DREAM.
I WANNA LET THEM DREAM.
SEO...
MAYBE SHE'S ACTUALLY A GOOD PERSON...
...AND, WELL...
...I'M GONNA BE THE ONE TO SHATTER THOSE DREAMS.
I'LL LET THEM GROW AND THEN SQUASH THEM.
YOU'RE DESPICABLE.

THE REAL LORELAI

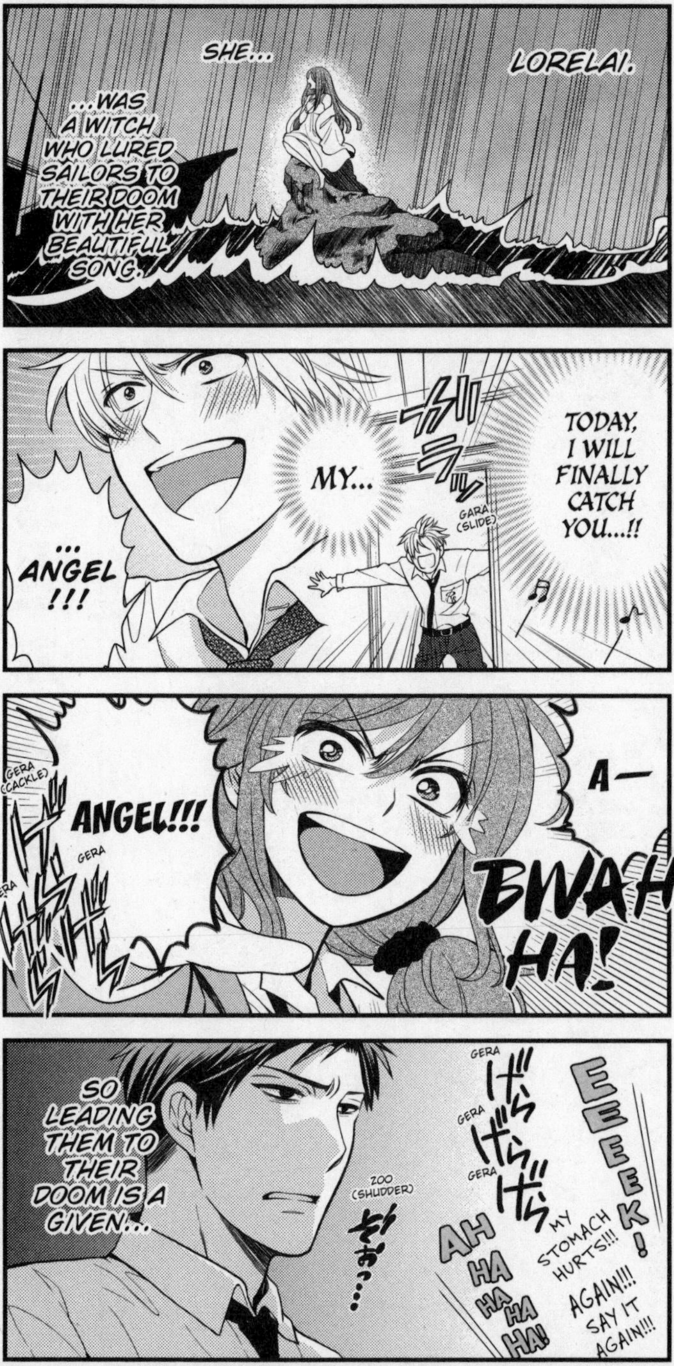
LORELAI.
SHE...
...WAS A WITCH WHO LURED SAILORS TO THEIR DOOM WITH HER BEAUTIFUL SONG.
TODAY, I WILL FINALLY CATCH YOU...!!
GARA (SLIDE)
MY...
...ANGEL!!!
A—
BWAH HA!
ANGEL!!!
GERA (CACKLE)
GERA
GERA
EEEEEK!
GERA
GERA
GERA
AGAIN!!! SAY IT AGAIN!!!
MY STOMACH HURTS!!!
AH HA HA HA HA HA!
ZOO (SHUDDER)
SO LEADING THEM TO THEIR DOOM IS A GIVEN...

HE PLAYED BASKETBALL IN JUNIOR HIGH

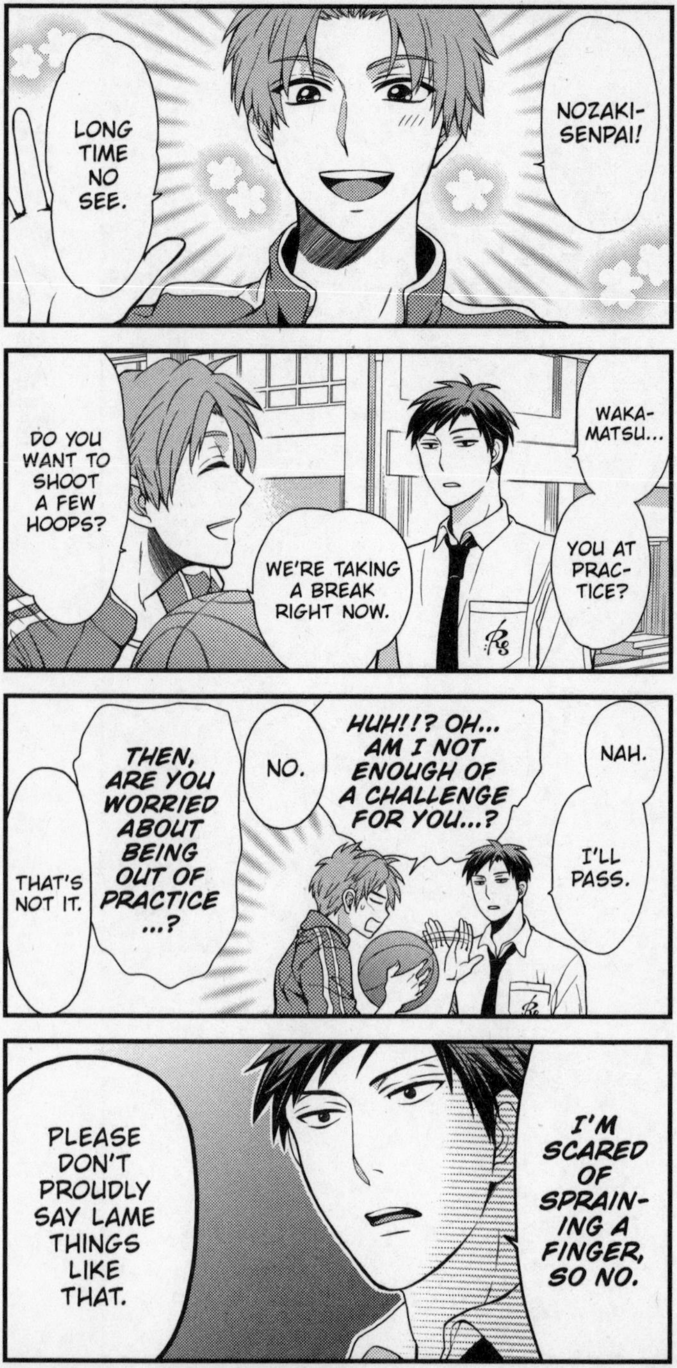
NOZAKI-SENPAI!
LONG TIME NO SEE.
WAKAMATSU...
YOU AT PRACTICE?
WE'RE TAKING A BREAK RIGHT NOW.
DO YOU WANT TO SHOOT A FEW HOOPS?
NAH.
I'LL PASS.
HUH!!? OH... AM I NOT ENOUGH OF A CHALLENGE FOR YOU...?
NO.
THEN, ARE YOU WORRIED ABOUT BEING OUT OF PRACTICE...?
THAT'S NOT IT.
I'M SCARED OF SPRAINING A FINGER, SO NO.
PLEASE DON'T PROUDLY SAY LAME THINGS LIKE THAT.

COOLNESS

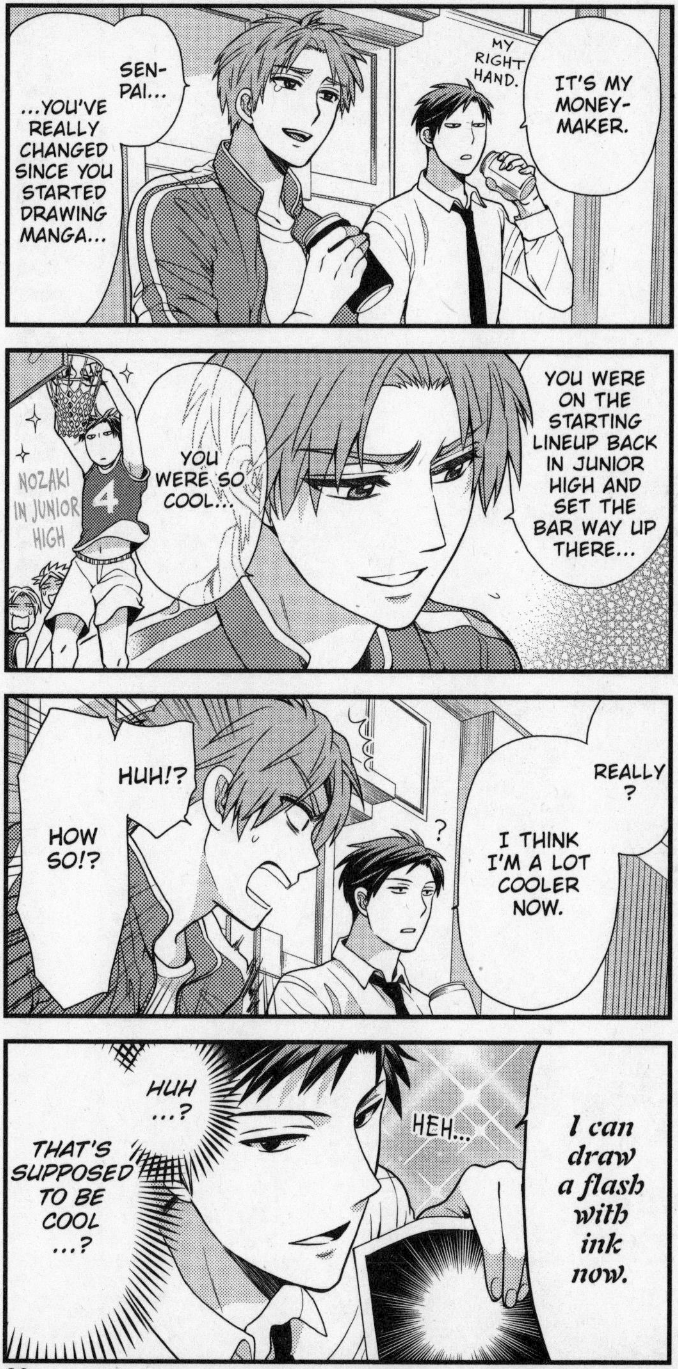

IT'S MY MONEY-MAKER.
MY RIGHT HAND.
SEN-PAI...
...YOU'VE REALLY CHANGED SINCE YOU STARTED DRAWING MANGA...
YOU WERE ON THE STARTING LINEUP BACK IN JUNIOR HIGH AND SET THE BAR WAY UP THERE...
YOU WERE SO COOL...
NOZAKI IN JUNIOR HIGH
REALLY?
I THINK I'M A LOT COOLER NOW.
?
HUH!?
HOW SO!?
I can draw a flash with ink now.
HEH...
HUH...?
THAT'S SUPPOSED TO BE COOL...?

COUNTLESS CASUALTIES

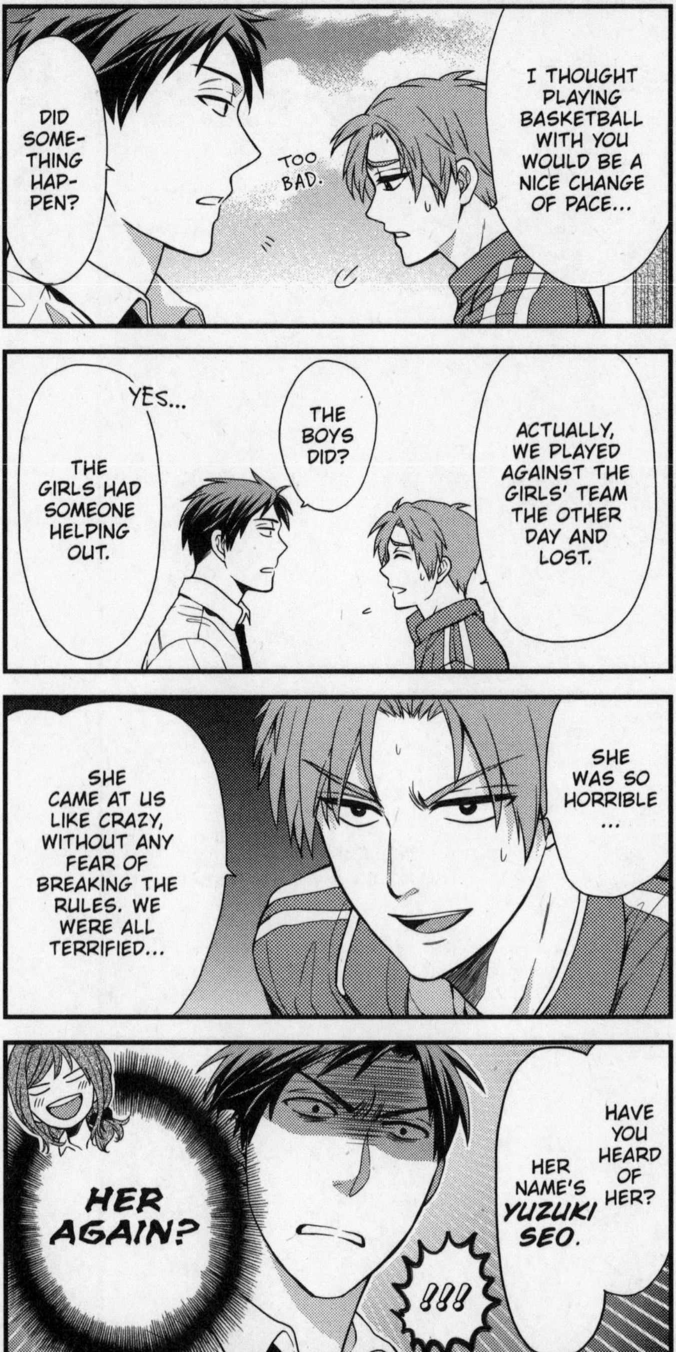

I THOUGHT PLAYING BASKETBALL WITH YOU WOULD BE A NICE CHANGE OF PACE...
TOO BAD.
DID SOMETHING HAPPEN?
ACTUALLY, WE PLAYED AGAINST THE GIRLS' TEAM THE OTHER DAY AND LOST.
THE BOYS DID?
YES...
THE GIRLS HAD SOMEONE HELPING OUT.
SHE WAS SO HORRIBLE...
SHE CAME AT US LIKE CRAZY, WITHOUT ANY FEAR OF BREAKING THE RULES. WE WERE ALL TERRIFIED...
HAVE YOU HEARD OF HER?
HER NAME'S YUZUKI SEO.
!!!
HER AGAIN?

A BATTLEFIELD WITH NOWHERE TO RUN

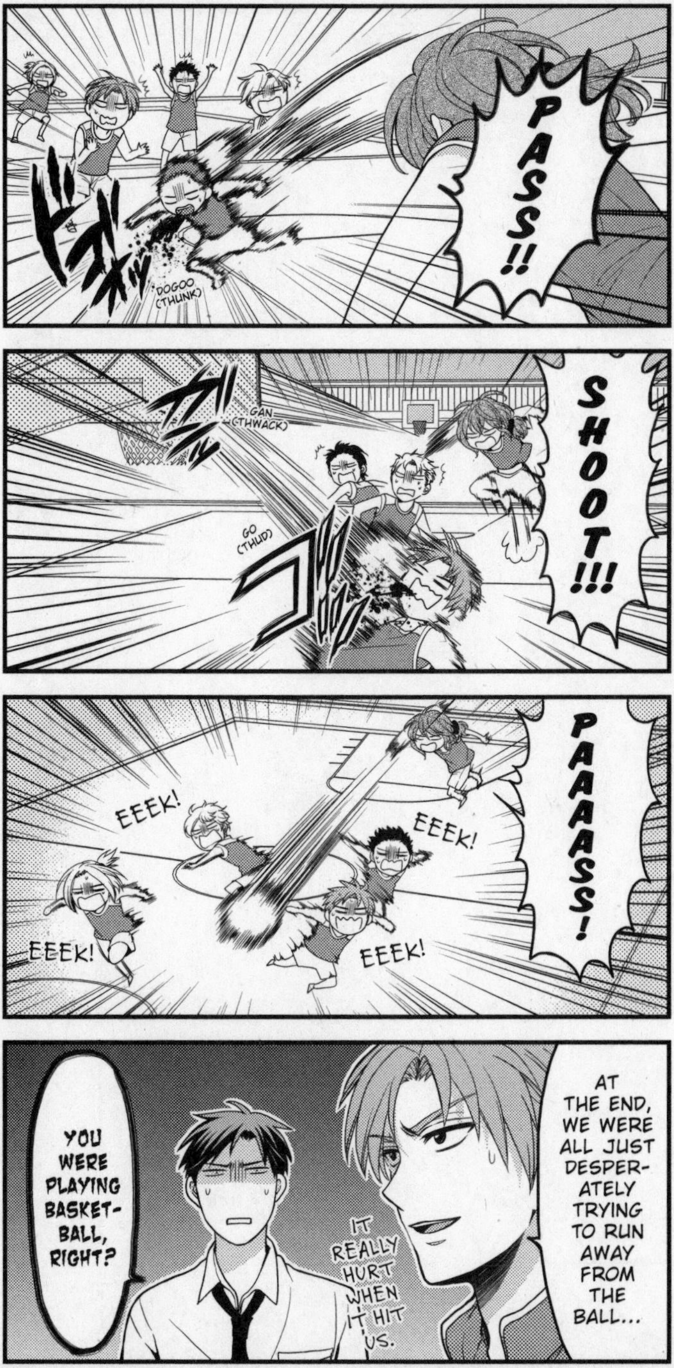
PASS!!
DOGOO (THUNK)
SHOOT!!!
GAN (THWACK)
GO (THUD)
PAAAASS!
EEEK!
EEEK!
EEEK!
EEEK!
AT THE END, WE WERE ALL JUST DESPERATELY TRYING TO RUN AWAY FROM THE BALL...
IT REALLY HURT WHEN IT HIT US.
YOU WERE PLAYING BASKETBALL, RIGHT?

NOZAKI-SENPAI'S KINDNESS

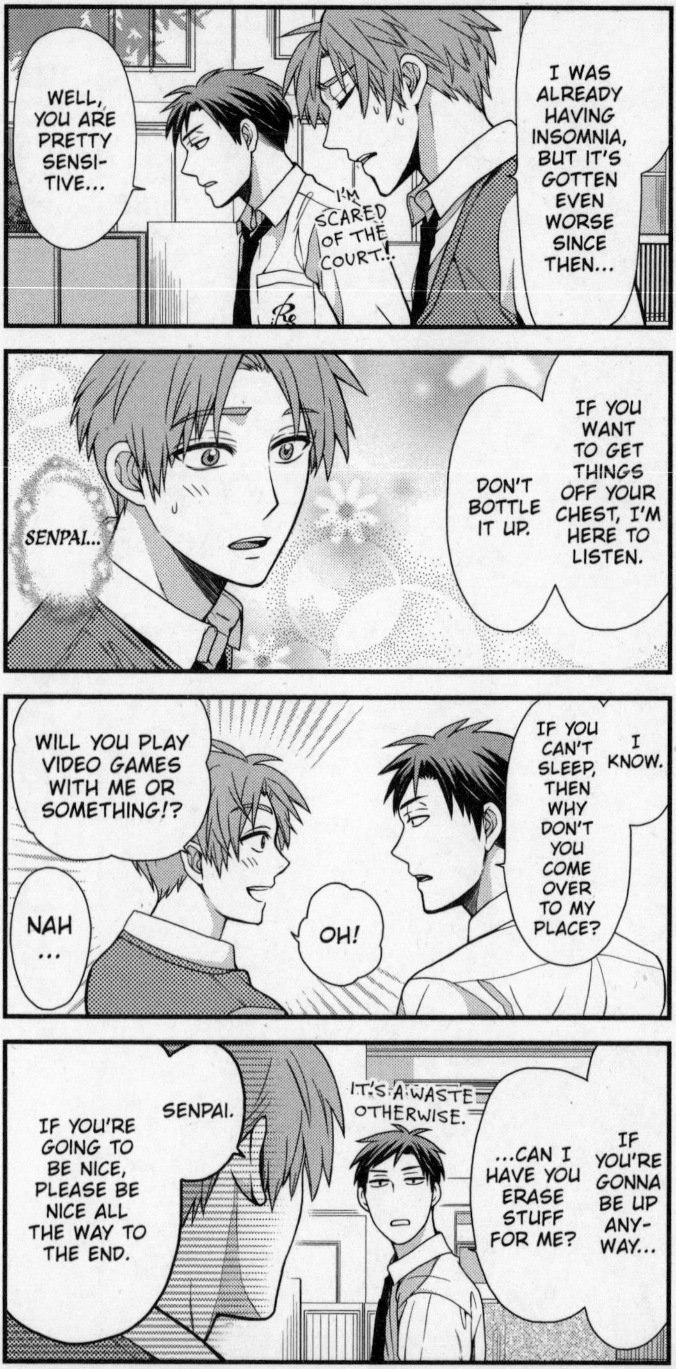
I WAS ALREADY HAVING INSOMNIA, BUT IT'S GOTTEN EVEN WORSE SINCE THEN...
I'M SCARED OF THE COURT...
WELL, YOU ARE PRETTY SENSI-TIVE...
IF YOU WANT TO GET THINGS OFF YOUR CHEST, I'M HERE TO LISTEN.
DON'T BOTTLE IT UP.
SENPAI...
I KNOW.
IF YOU CAN'T SLEEP, THEN WHY DON'T YOU COME OVER TO MY PLACE?
OH!
WILL YOU PLAY VIDEO GAMES WITH ME OR SOMETHING!?
NAH...
IF YOU'RE GONNA BE UP ANY-WAY...
...CAN I HAVE YOU ERASE STUFF FOR ME?
IT'S A WASTE OTHERWISE.
SENPAI.
IF YOU'RE GOING TO BE NICE, PLEASE BE NICE ALL THE WAY TO THE END.

WAKAMATSU-KUN, THE INSOMNIAC

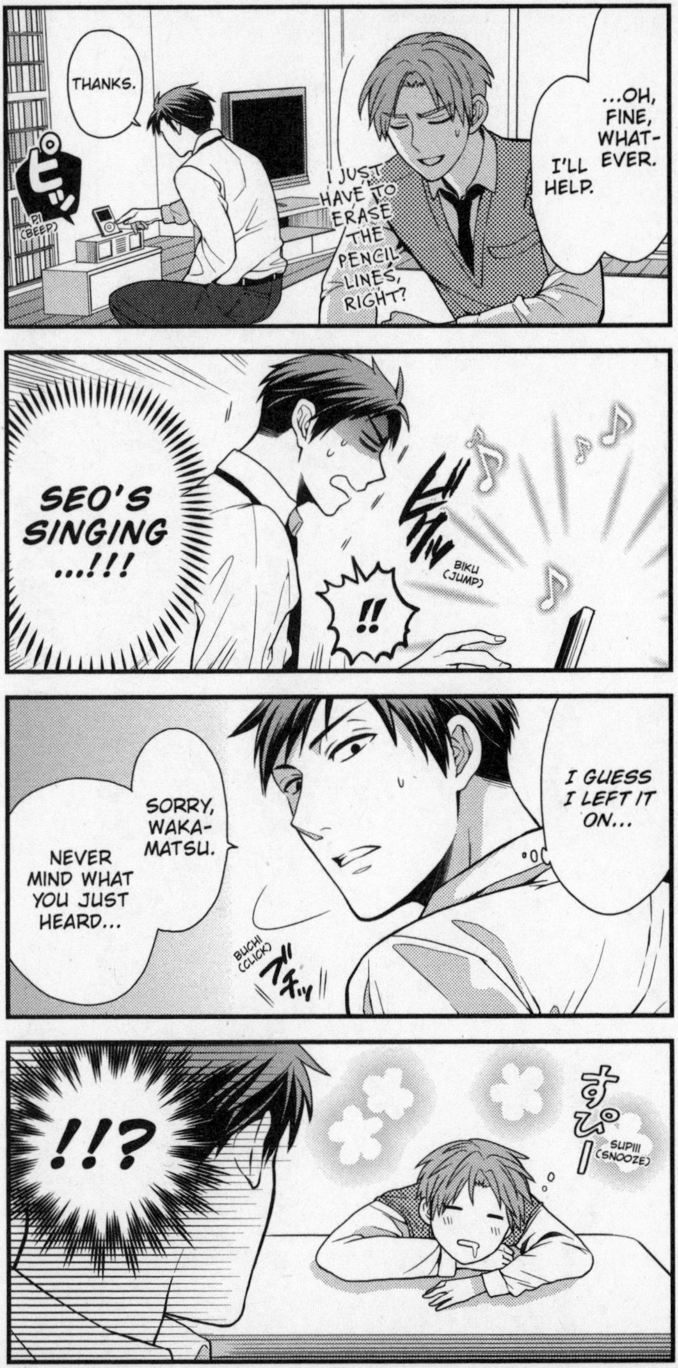
...OH, FINE, WHATEVER.
I'LL HELP.
I JUST HAVE TO ERASE THE PENCIL LINES, RIGHT?
THANKS.
ピッ
PI (BEEP)
BIKU (JUMP)
!!
SEO'S SINGING ...!!!
I GUESS I LEFT IT ON...
SORRY, WAKAMATSU.
NEVER MIND WHAT YOU JUST HEARD...
ブチッ
BUCHI (CLICK)
すぴー
SUPIII (SNOOZE)
!!?

A TROUBLED CONSCIENCE

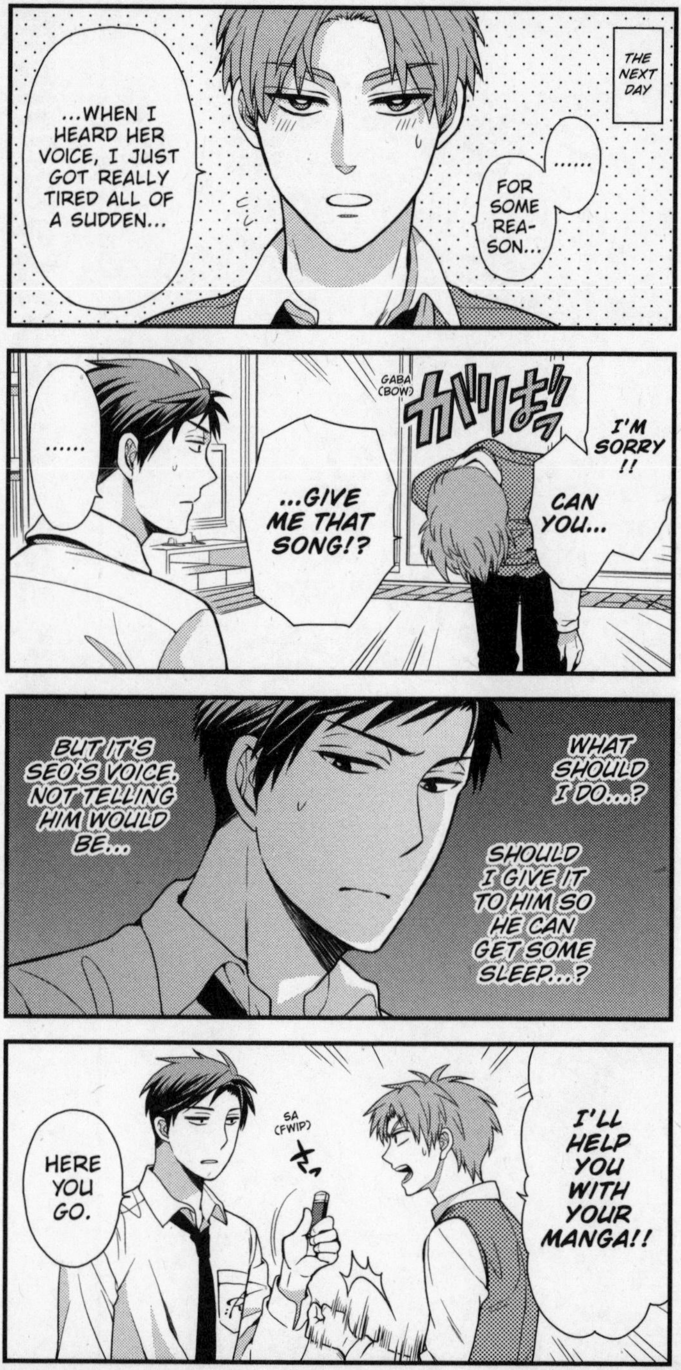
THE NEXT DAY
......
FOR SOME REA-SON...
...WHEN I HEARD HER VOICE, I JUST GOT REALLY TIRED ALL OF A SUDDEN...
I'M SORRY!!
GABA (BOW)
CAN YOU...
...GIVE ME THAT SONG!?
......
WHAT SHOULD I DO...?
SHOULD I GIVE IT TO HIM SO HE CAN GET SOME SLEEP...?
BUT IT'S SEO'S VOICE, NOT TELLING HIM WOULD BE...
I'LL HELP YOU WITH YOUR MANGA!!
SA (FWIP)
HERE YOU GO.

STAR-CROSSED LOVE

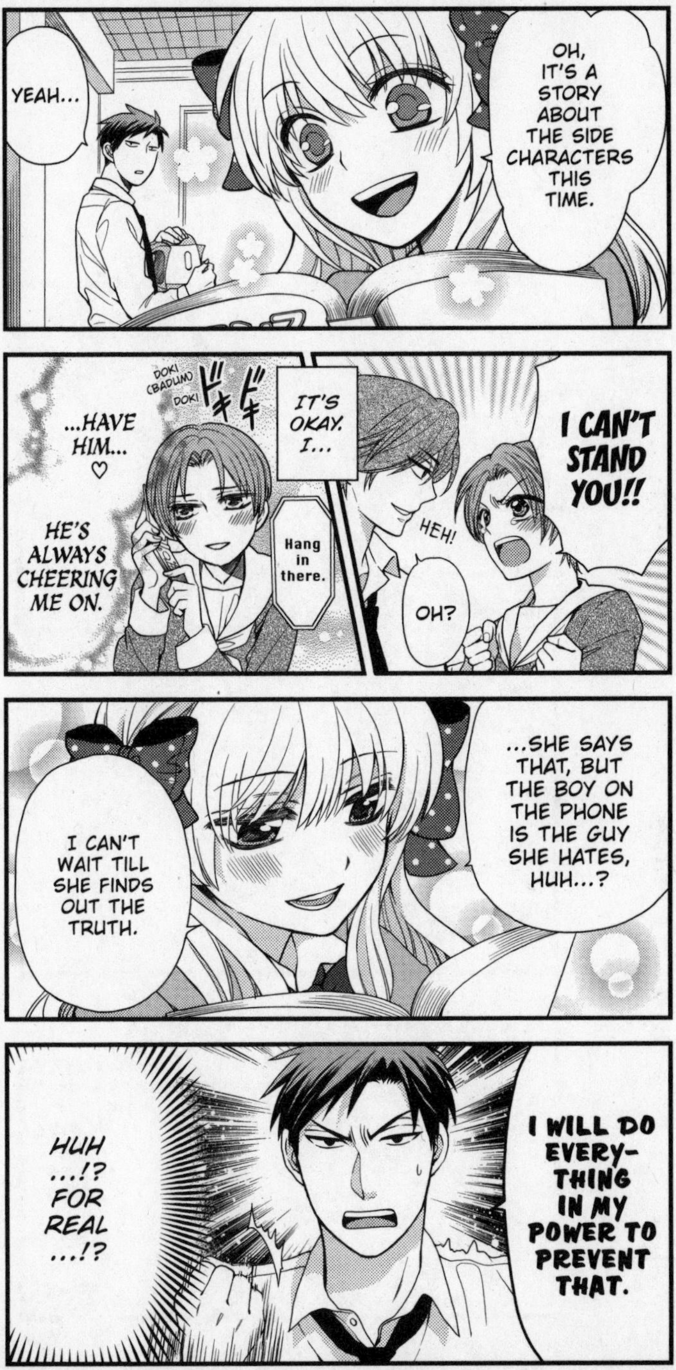
OH, IT'S A STORY ABOUT THE SIDE CHARACTERS THIS TIME.
YEAH...
I CAN'T STAND YOU!!
HEH!
OH?
IT'S OKAY. I...
DOKI (BADUM) DOKI
ドキドキ
...HAVE HIM... ♡
Hang in there.
HE'S ALWAYS CHEERING ME ON.
...SHE SAYS THAT, BUT THE BOY ON THE PHONE IS THE GUY SHE HATES, HUH...?
I CAN'T WAIT TILL SHE FINDS OUT THE TRUTH.
I WILL DO EVERY-THING IN MY POWER TO PREVENT THAT.
HUH ...!? FOR REAL ...!?

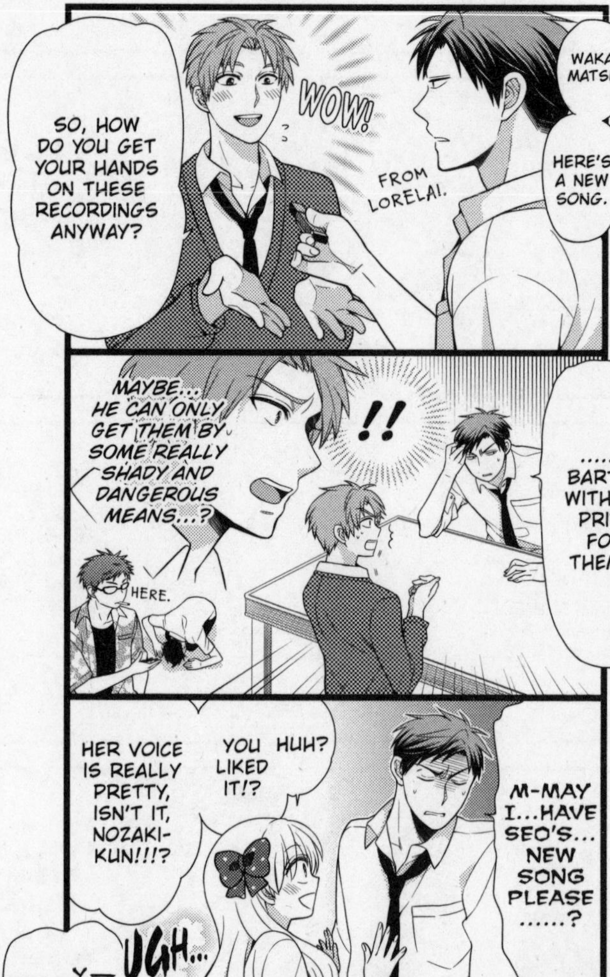
WAKA-MATSU.
HERE'S A NEW SONG.
FROM LORELAI.
WOW!
SO, HOW DO YOU GET YOUR HANDS ON THESE RECORDINGS ANYWAY?
......I BARTER WITH MY PRIDE FOR THEM...
!!
MAYBE... HE CAN ONLY GET THEM BY SOME REALLY SHADY AND DANGEROUS MEANS...?
HERE.
M-MAY I...HAVE SEO'S... NEW SONG PLEASE ......?
HUH? YOU LIKED IT!?
HER VOICE IS REALLY PRETTY, ISN'T IT, NOZAKI-KUN!!!?
UGH...
Y— YEAH...

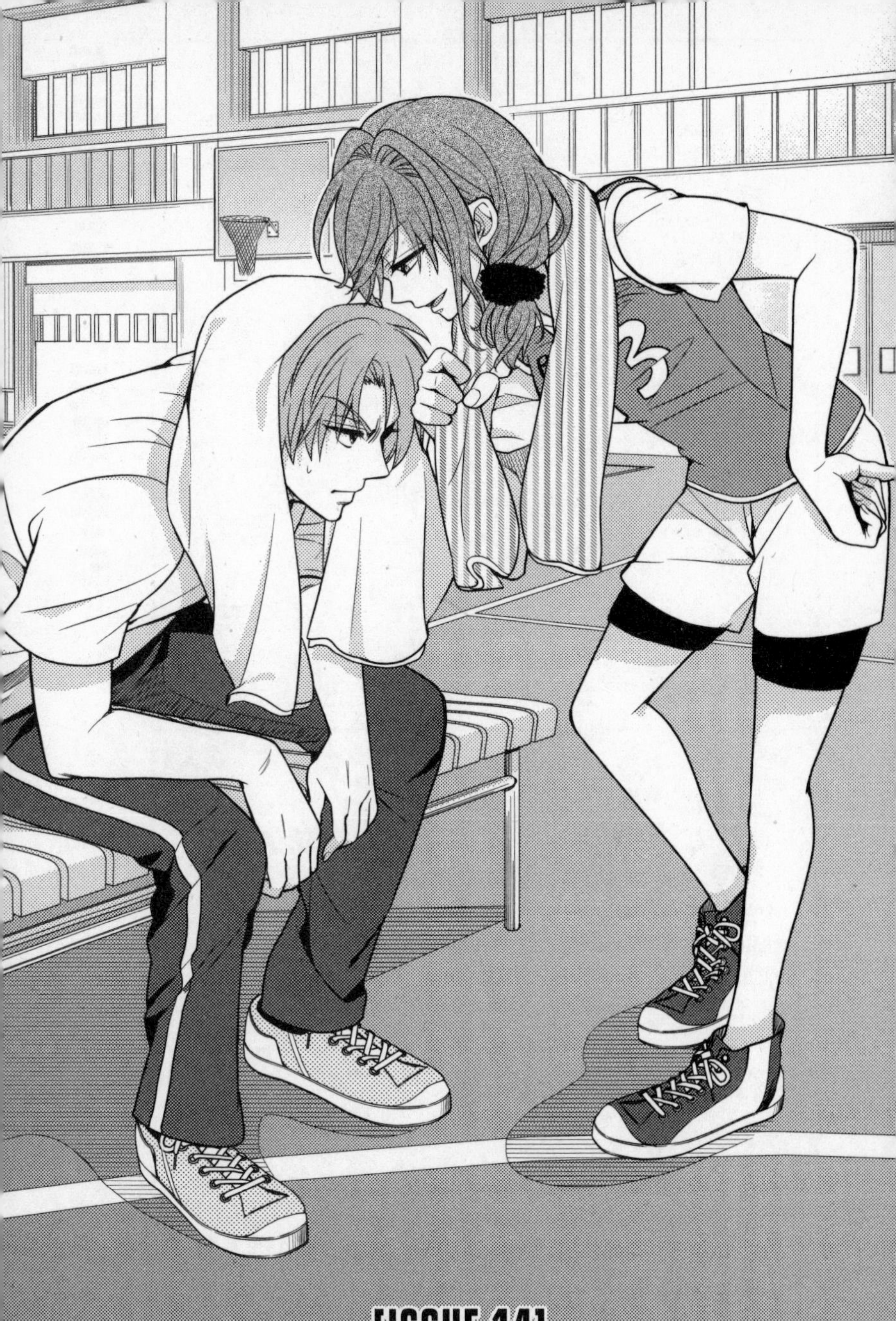

[ISSUE 14]

WHAT SHE GIVES HIM

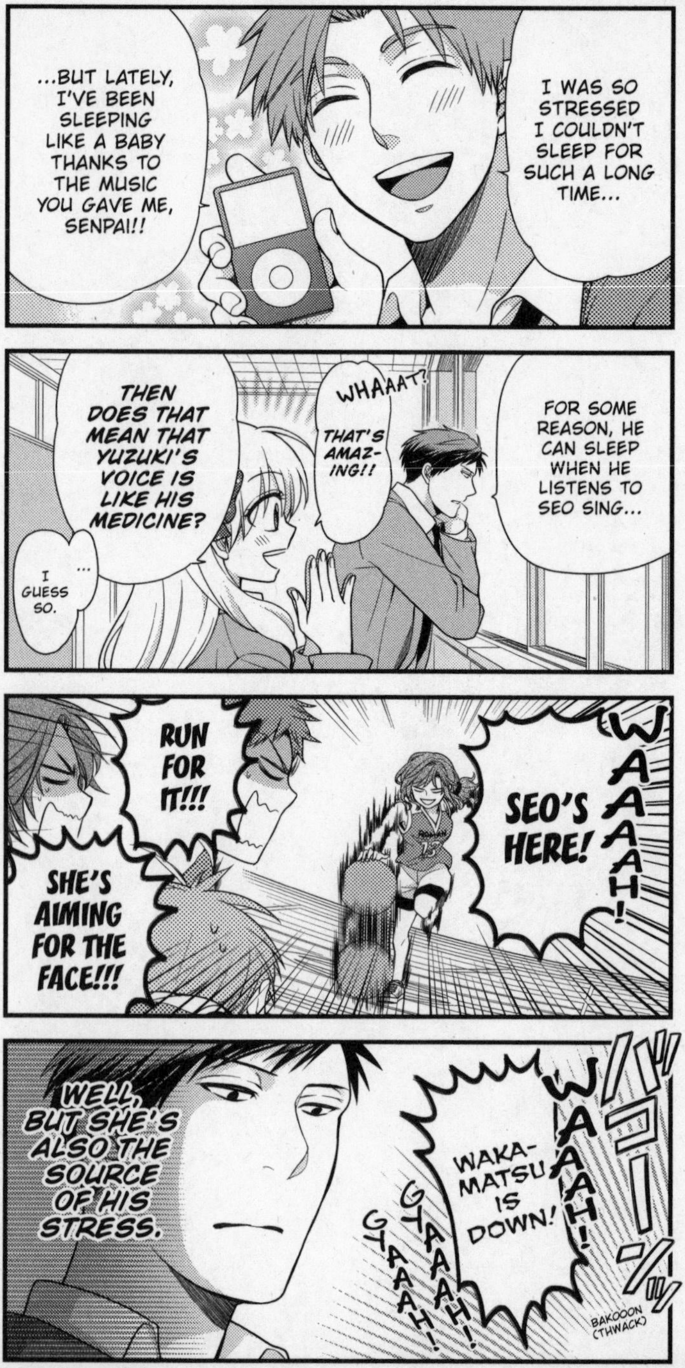
I WAS SO STRESSED I COULDN'T SLEEP FOR SUCH A LONG TIME...
...BUT LATELY, I'VE BEEN SLEEPING LIKE A BABY THANKS TO THE MUSIC YOU GAVE ME, SENPAI!!
FOR SOME REASON, HE CAN SLEEP WHEN HE LISTENS TO SEO SING...
WHAAAT?
THAT'S AMAZ-ING!!
THEN DOES THAT MEAN THAT YUZUKI'S VOICE IS LIKE HIS MEDICINE?
...
I GUESS SO.
WAAAAAH!
SEO'S HERE!
RUN FOR IT!!!
SHE'S AIMING FOR THE FACE!!!
BAKOOON (THWACK)
WAAAAH!
WAKA-MATSU IS DOWN!
GYAAAAH!
GYAAAAH!
WELL, BUT SHE'S ALSO THE SOURCE OF HIS STRESS.

THE BEST HE CAN DO TO FIGHT BACK

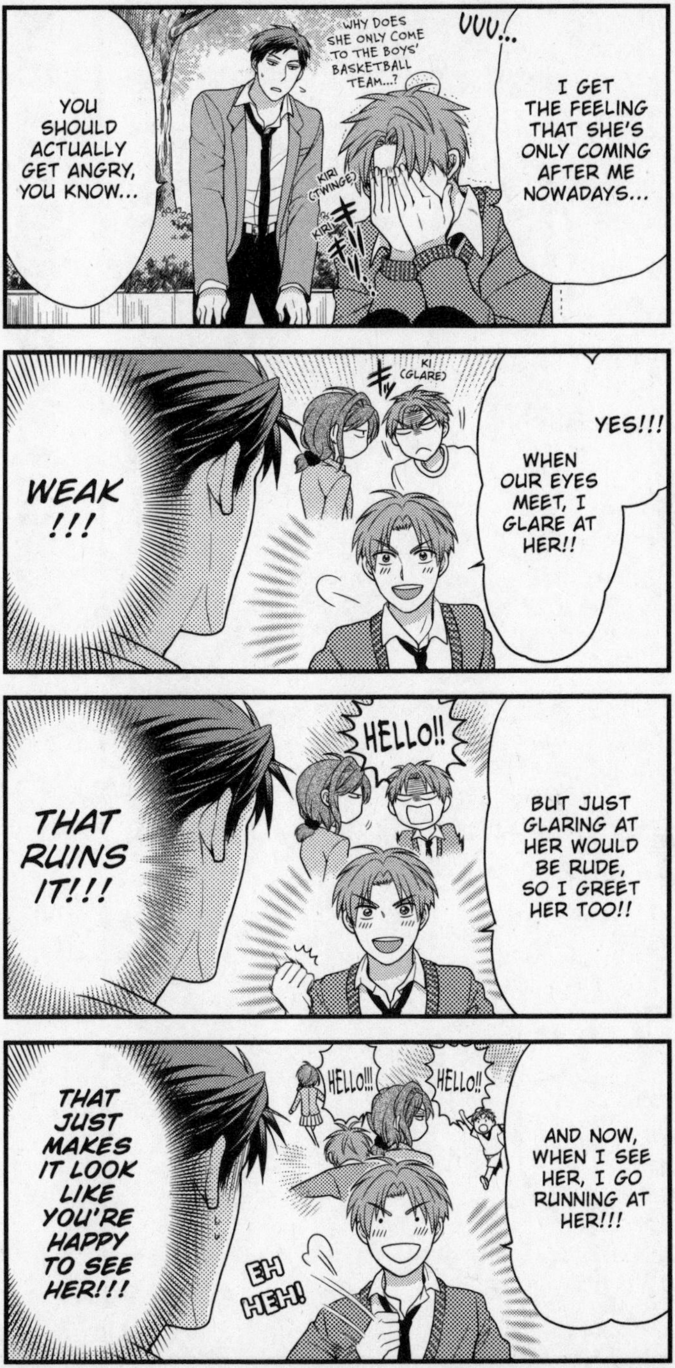
UUU...
I GET THE FEELING THAT SHE'S ONLY COMING AFTER ME NOWADAYS...
WHY DOES SHE ONLY COME TO THE BOYS' BASKETBALL TEAM...?
KIRI (TWINGE)
KIRI
YOU SHOULD ACTUALLY GET ANGRY, YOU KNOW...
YES!!!
WHEN OUR EYES MEET, I GLARE AT HER!!
KI (GLARE)
WEAK !!!
HELLO!!
BUT JUST GLARING AT HER WOULD BE RUDE, SO I GREET HER TOO!!
THAT RUINS IT!!!
HELLO!!
AND NOW, WHEN I SEE HER, I GO RUNNING AT HER!!!
HELLO!!!
EH HEH!
THAT JUST MAKES IT LOOK LIKE YOU'RE HAPPY TO SEE HER!!!

REFERENCE MATERIAL

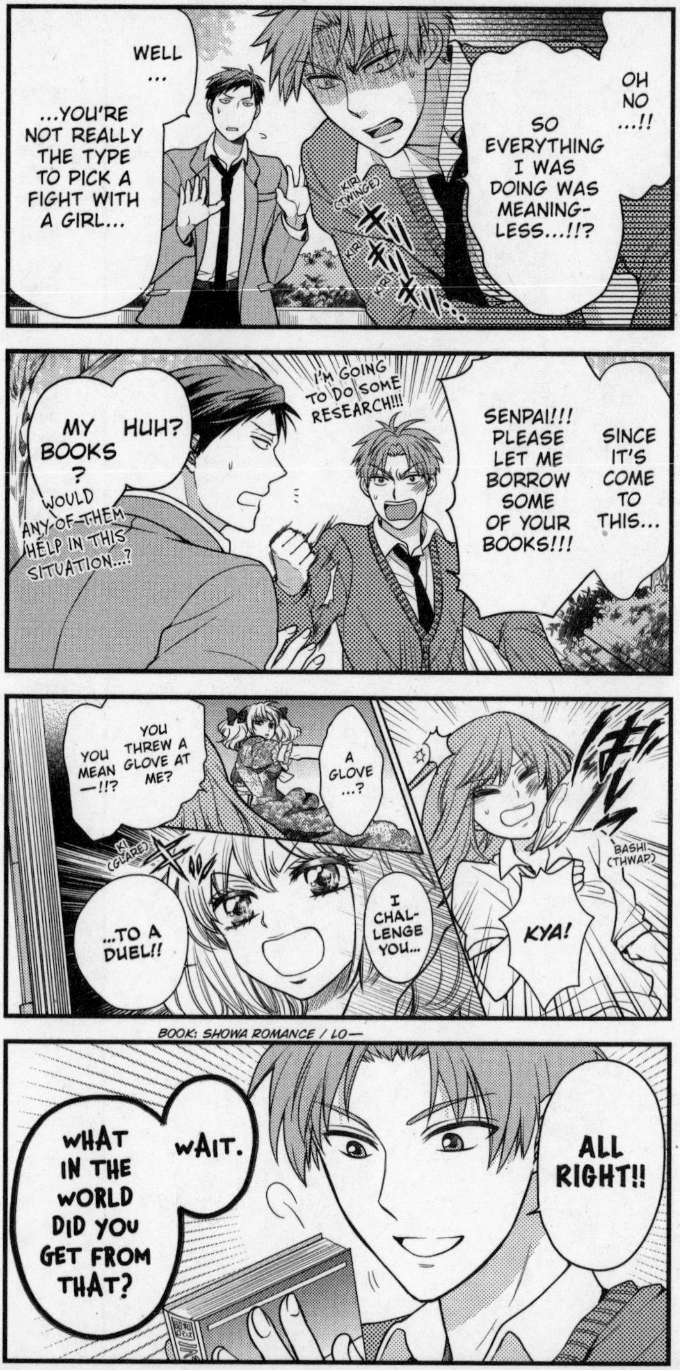
OH NO ...!!
SO EVERYTHING I WAS DOING WAS MEANING-LESS...!!?
KIRI (TWINGE)
KIRI
KIRI
WELL ...
...YOU'RE NOT REALLY THE TYPE TO PICK A FIGHT WITH A GIRL...
SINCE IT'S COME TO THIS...
SENPAI!!! PLEASE LET ME BORROW SOME OF YOUR BOOKS!!!
I'M GOING TO DO SOME RESEARCH!!!
HUH?
MY BOOKS?
WOULD ANY OF THEM HELP IN THIS SITUATION...?
BASHI (THWAP)
KYA!
A GLOVE ...?
YOU THREW A GLOVE AT ME?
YOU MEAN —!!?
KI (GLARE)
I CHAL-LENGE YOU...
...TO A DUEL!!
BOOK: SHOWA ROMANCE / LO—
ALL RIGHT!!
WAIT.
WHAT IN THE WORLD DID YOU GET FROM THAT?

MAKING A CHOICE

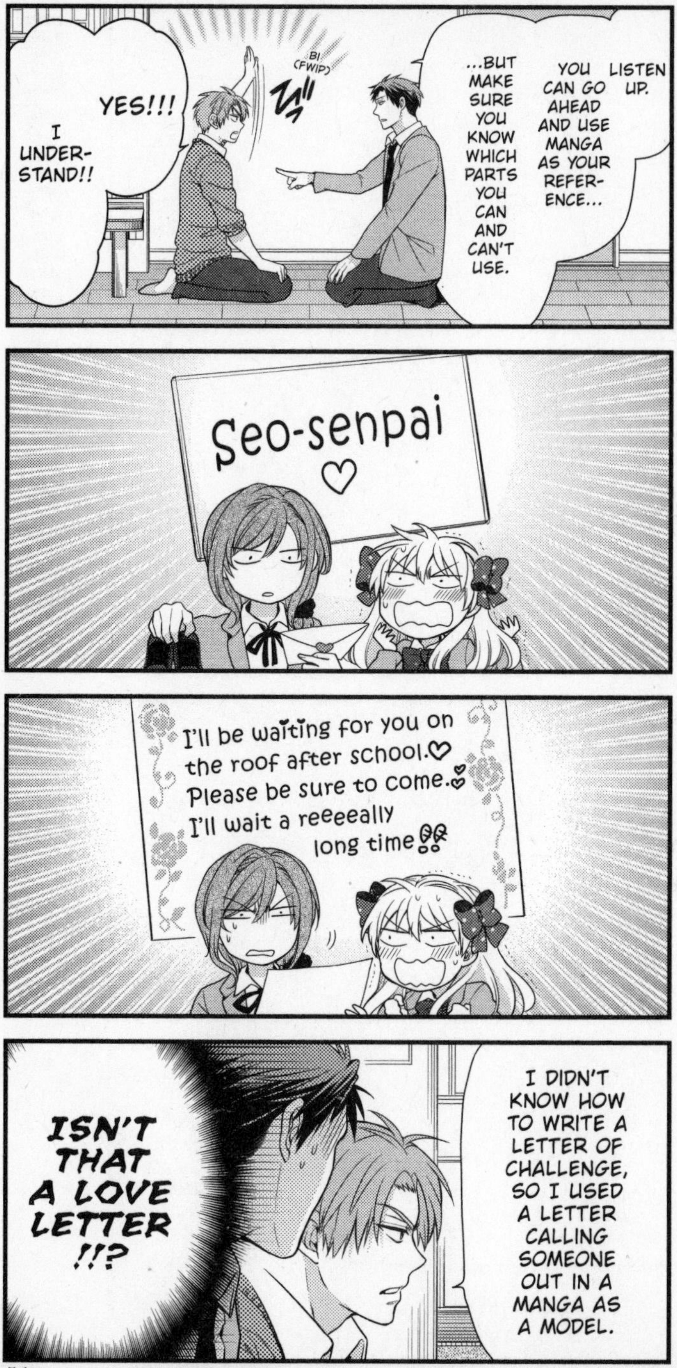
LISTEN UP.
YOU CAN GO AHEAD AND USE MANGA AS YOUR REFERENCE...
...BUT MAKE SURE YOU KNOW WHICH PARTS YOU CAN AND CAN'T USE.
BI (FWIP)
YES!!!
I UNDERSTAND!!
Seo-senpai ♡
I'll be waiting for you on the roof after school.♡ Please be sure to come. I'll wait a reeeeally long time!!
I DIDN'T KNOW HOW TO WRITE A LETTER OF CHALLENGE, SO I USED A LETTER CALLING SOMEONE OUT IN A MANGA AS A MODEL.
ISN'T THAT A LOVE LETTER!!?

WHY I CALLED YOU HERE

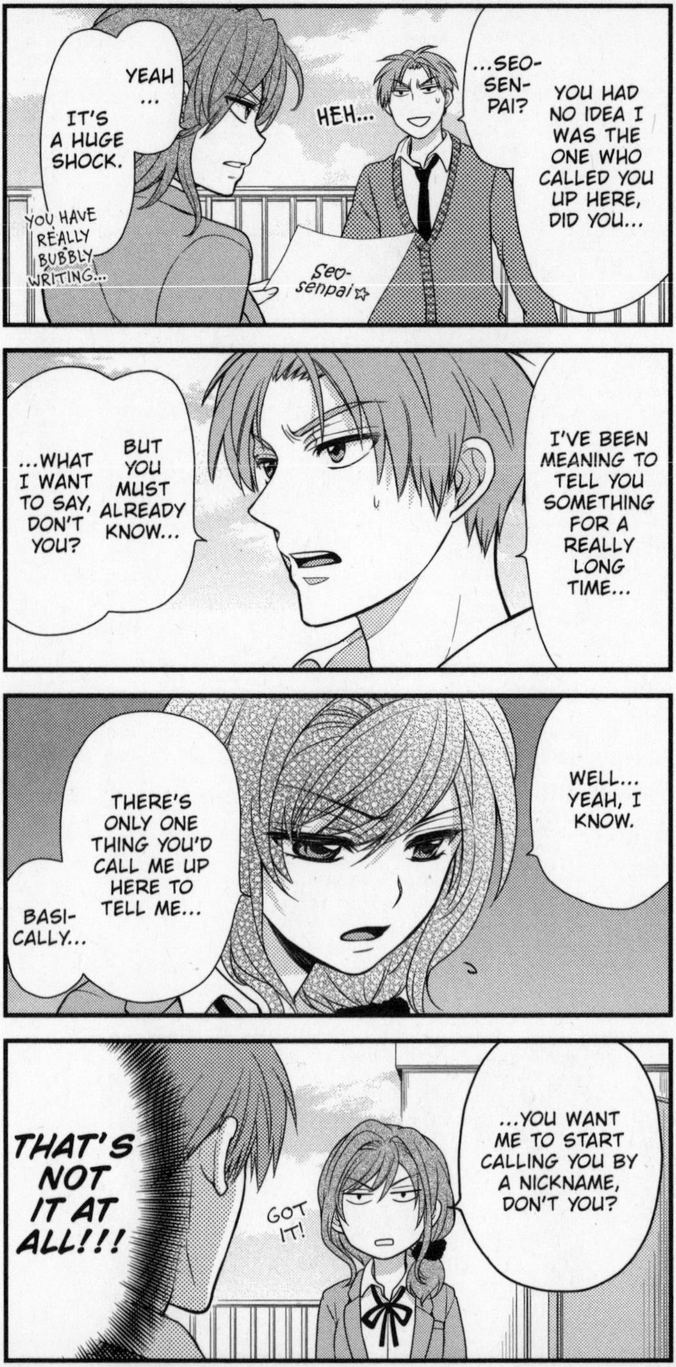

YOU HAD NO IDEA I WAS THE ONE WHO CALLED YOU UP HERE, DID YOU...
...SEO-SENPAI?
HEH...
YEAH... IT'S A HUGE SHOCK.
YOU HAVE REALLY BUBBLY WRITING...
Seo♡senpai☆
I'VE BEEN MEANING TO TELL YOU SOMETHING FOR A REALLY LONG TIME...
BUT YOU MUST ALREADY KNOW...
...WHAT I WANT TO SAY, DON'T YOU?
WELL... YEAH, I KNOW.
THERE'S ONLY ONE THING YOU'D CALL ME UP HERE TO TELL ME...
BASICALLY...
...YOU WANT ME TO START CALLING YOU BY A NICKNAME, DON'T YOU?
GOT IT!
THAT'S NOT IT AT ALL!!!

I TAKE IT ALL BACK × 2

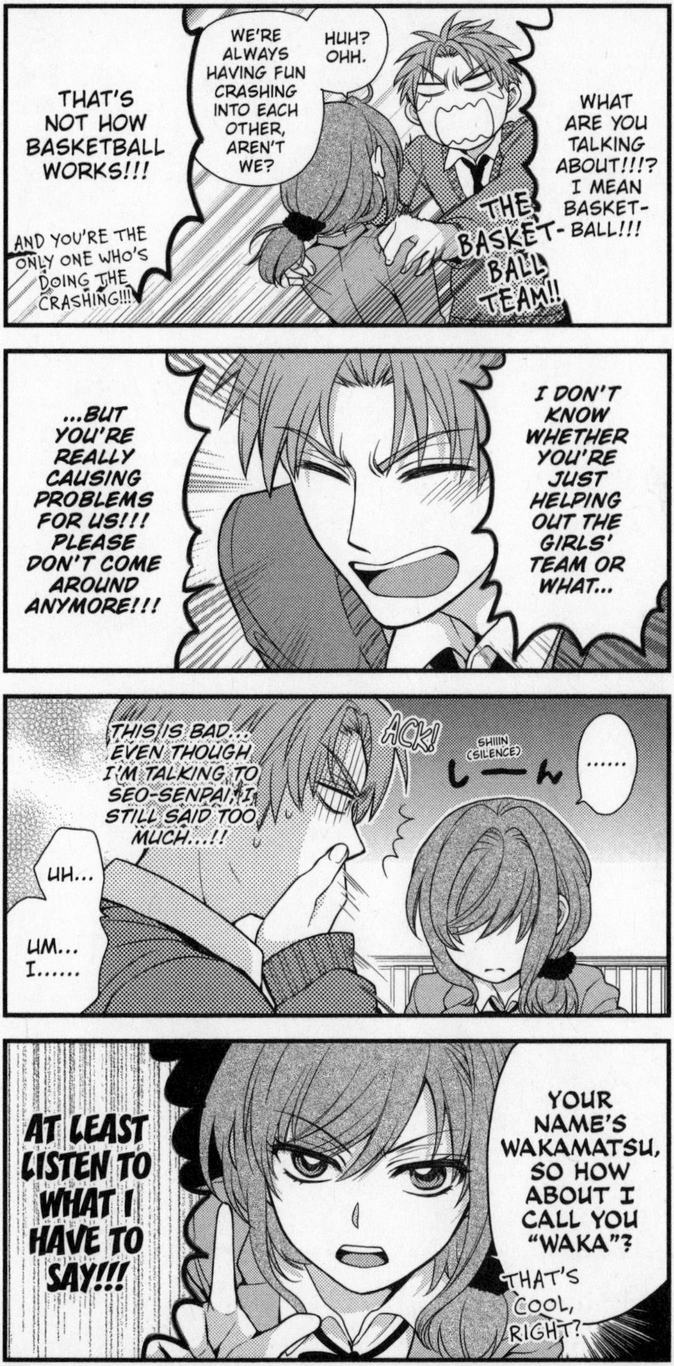

WHAT ARE YOU TALKING ABOUT!!!? I MEAN BASKET-BALL!!!
THE BASKET-BALL TEAM!!
HUH? OHH.
WE'RE ALWAYS HAVING FUN CRASHING INTO EACH OTHER, AREN'T WE?
THAT'S NOT HOW BASKETBALL WORKS!!!
AND YOU'RE THE ONLY ONE WHO'S DOING THE CRASHING!!!
I DON'T KNOW WHETHER YOU'RE JUST HELPING OUT THE GIRLS' TEAM OR WHAT...
...BUT YOU'RE REALLY CAUSING PROBLEMS FOR US!!! PLEASE DON'T COME AROUND ANYMORE!!!
......
SHIIIN (SILENCE)
しーん
ACK!
THIS IS BAD... EVEN THOUGH I'M TALKING TO SEO-SENPAI, I STILL SAID TOO MUCH...!!
UH...
UM... I......
YOUR NAME'S WAKAMATSU, SO HOW ABOUT I CALL YOU "WAKA"?
THAT'S COOL, RIGHT?
AT LEAST LISTEN TO WHAT I HAVE TO SAY!!!

JUST ME

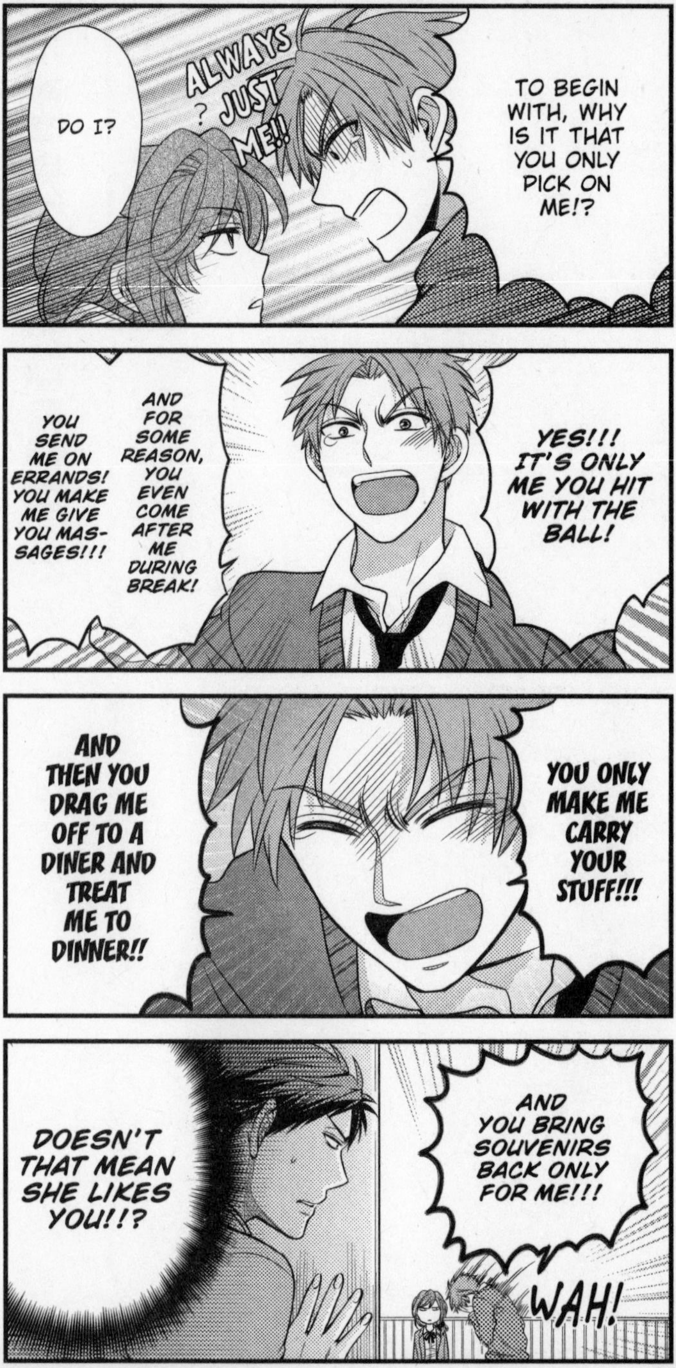

TO BEGIN WITH, WHY IS IT THAT YOU ONLY PICK ON ME!?
ALWAYS JUST ME!!
?
DO I?
YES!!! IT'S ONLY ME YOU HIT WITH THE BALL!
AND FOR SOME REASON, YOU EVEN COME AFTER ME DURING BREAK!
YOU SEND ME ON ERRANDS! YOU MAKE ME GIVE YOU MAS-SAGES!!!
YOU ONLY MAKE ME CARRY YOUR STUFF!!!
AND THEN YOU DRAG ME OFF TO A DINER AND TREAT ME TO DINNER!!
AND YOU BRING SOUVENIRS BACK ONLY FOR ME!!!
WAH!
DOESN'T THAT MEAN SHE LIKES YOU!!?

BEHOLD THE FRUITS OF MY RESEARCH!!

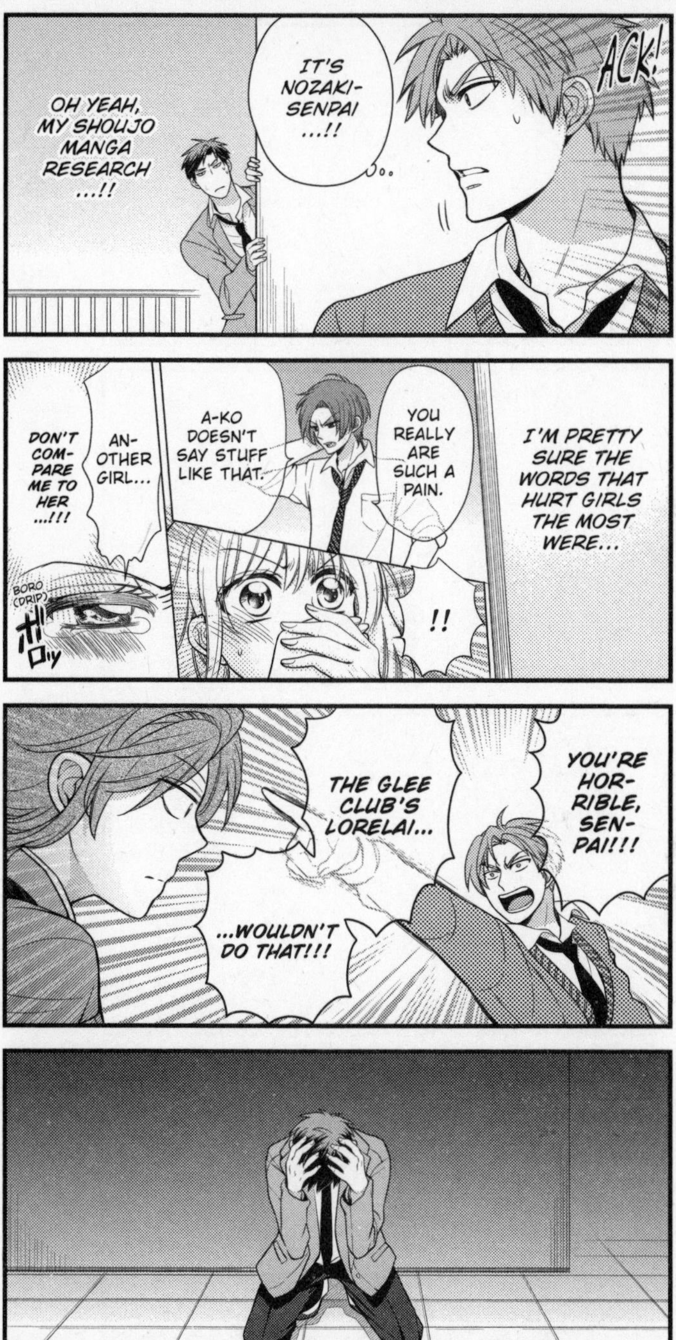
ACK!
IT'S NOZAKI-SENPAI...!!
OH YEAH, MY SHOUJO MANGA RESEARCH...!!
I'M PRETTY SURE THE WORDS THAT HURT GIRLS THE MOST WERE...
YOU REALLY ARE SUCH A PAIN.
A-KO DOESN'T SAY STUFF LIKE THAT.
!!
ANOTHER GIRL...
DON'T COMPARE ME TO HER...!!!
BORO (DRIP)
YOU'RE HORRIBLE, SENPAI!!!
THE GLEE CLUB'S LORELAI...
...WOULDN'T DO THAT!!!

THE SAD TRUTH

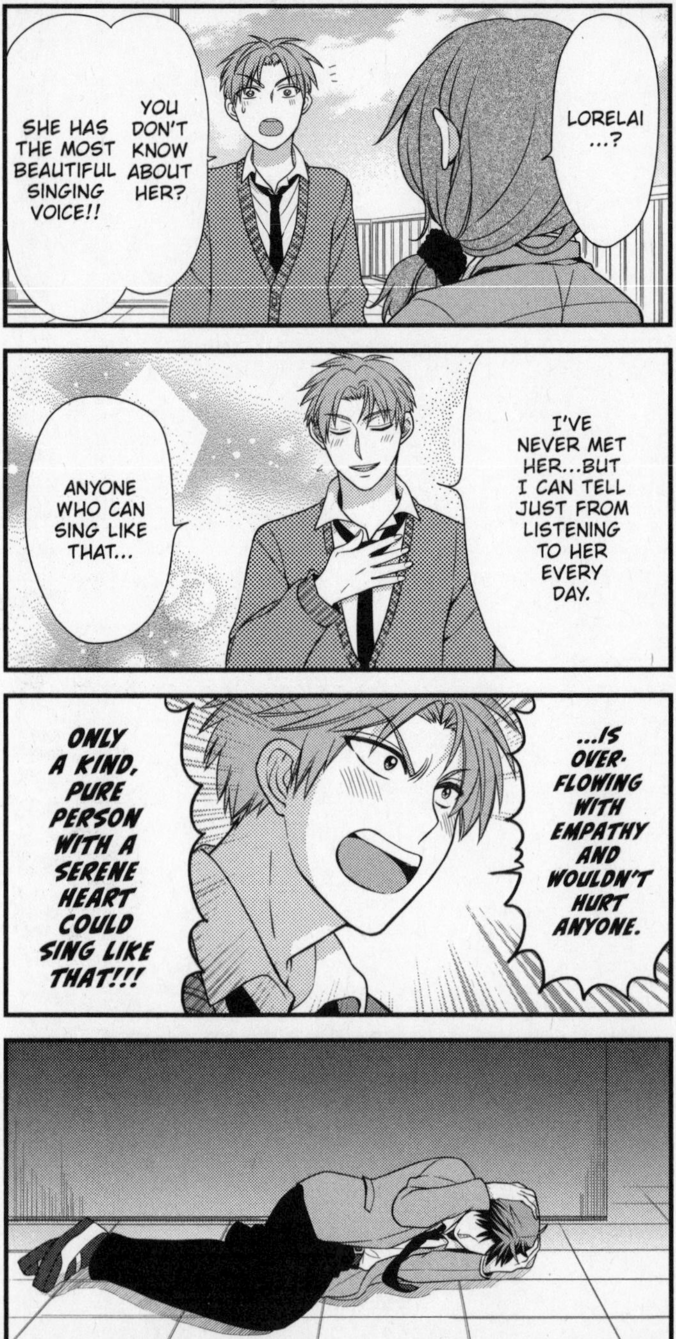
LORELAI ...?
YOU DON'T KNOW ABOUT HER?
SHE HAS THE MOST BEAUTIFUL SINGING VOICE!!
I'VE NEVER MET HER...BUT I CAN TELL JUST FROM LISTENING TO HER EVERY DAY.
ANYONE WHO CAN SING LIKE THAT...
...IS OVER-FLOWING WITH EMPATHY AND WOULDN'T HURT ANYONE.
ONLY A KIND, PURE PERSON WITH A SERENE HEART COULD SING LIKE THAT!!!

COMPARING HER TO ANOTHER GIRL

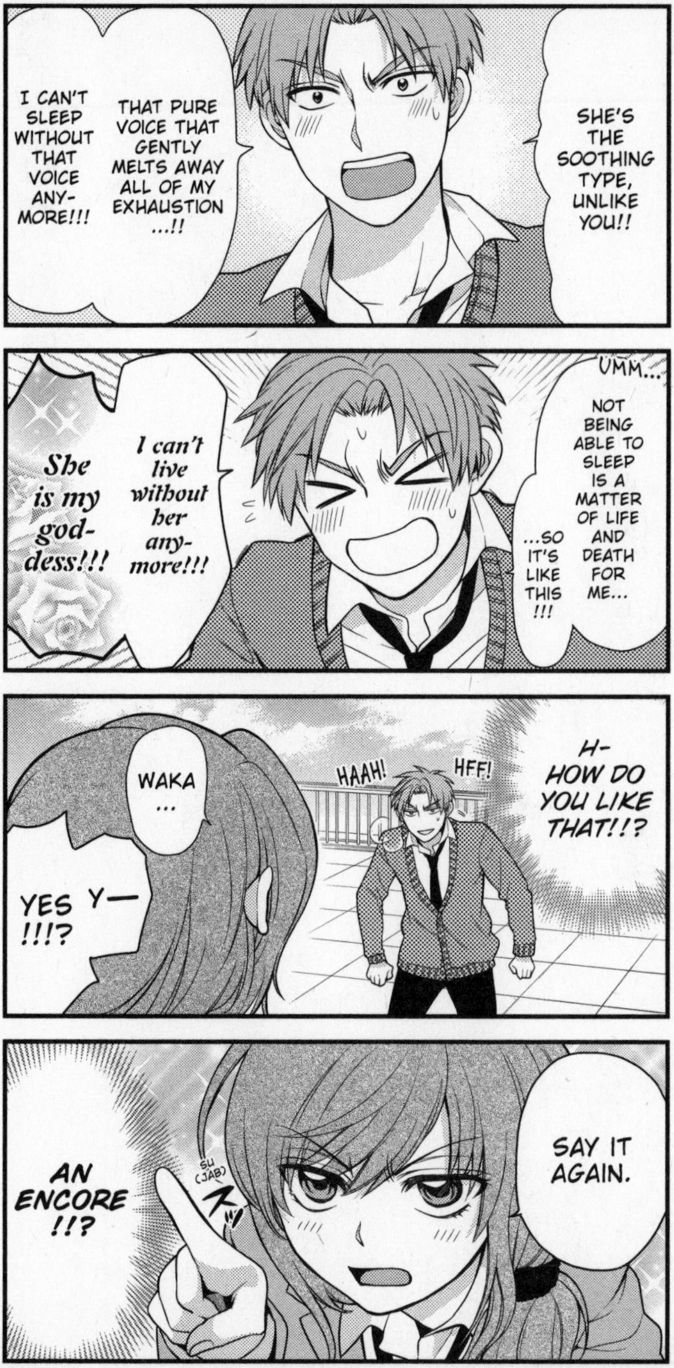
SHE'S THE SOOTHING TYPE, UNLIKE YOU!!
THAT PURE VOICE THAT GENTLY MELTS AWAY ALL OF MY EXHAUSTION ...!!
I CAN'T SLEEP WITHOUT THAT VOICE ANYMORE!!!
UMM...
NOT BEING ABLE TO SLEEP IS A MATTER OF LIFE AND DEATH FOR ME...
...SO IT'S LIKE THIS!!!
I can't live without her anymore!!!
She is my goddess!!!
H-HOW DO YOU LIKE THAT!!?
HFF!
HAAH!
WAKA...
YES Y—!!!?
SAY IT AGAIN.
SU (JAB)
AN ENCORE!!?

ONE LAST ASSAULT

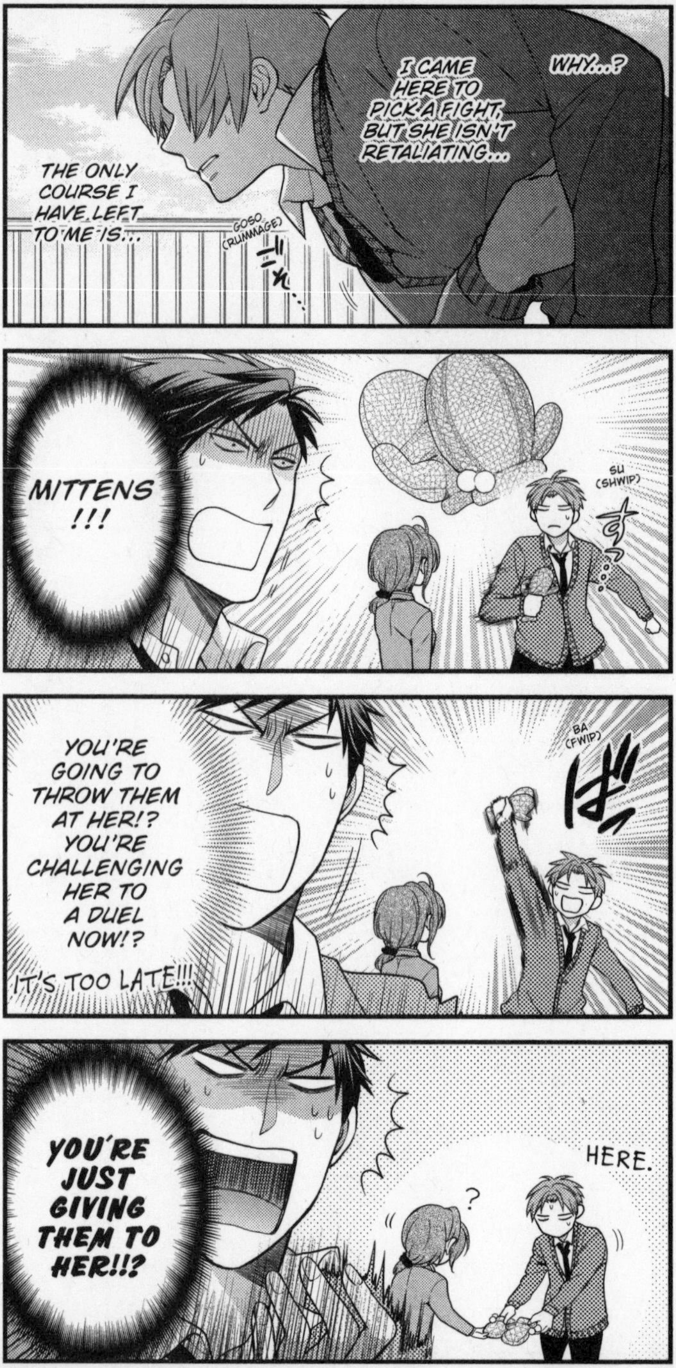
WHY...?
I CAME HERE TO PICK A FIGHT, BUT SHE ISN'T RETALIATING...
THE ONLY COURSE I HAVE LEFT TO ME IS...
GOSO (RUMMAGE)
SU (SHWIP)
MITTENS !!!
BA (FWIP)
YOU'RE GOING TO THROW THEM AT HER!? YOU'RE CHALLENGING HER TO A DUEL NOW!?
IT'S TOO LATE!!!
HERE.
?
YOU'RE JUST GIVING THEM TO HER!!?

TOTAL DEFEAT

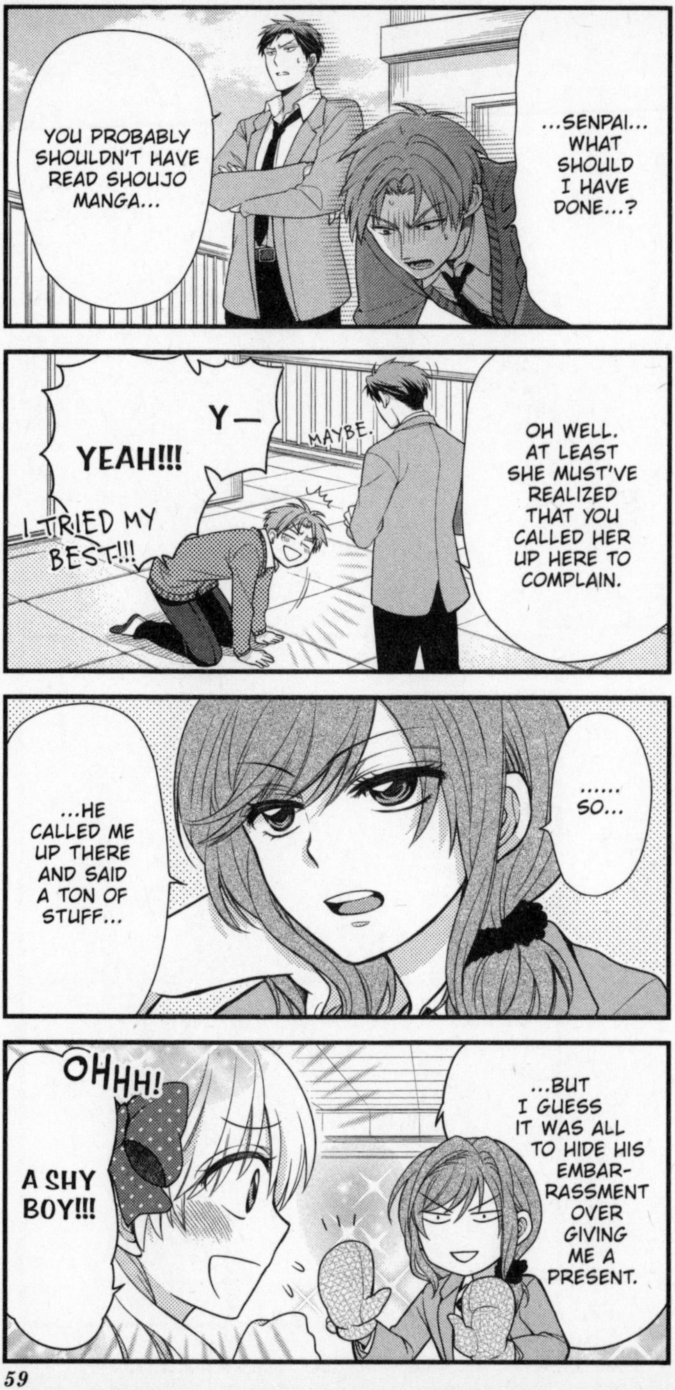
...SENPAI... WHAT SHOULD I HAVE DONE...?
YOU PROBABLY SHOULDN'T HAVE READ SHOUJO MANGA...
OH WELL. AT LEAST SHE MUST'VE REALIZED THAT YOU CALLED HER UP HERE TO COMPLAIN.
MAYBE.
Y— YEAH!!!
I TRIED MY BEST!!!
...... SO...
...HE CALLED ME UP THERE AND SAID A TON OF STUFF...
...BUT I GUESS IT WAS ALL TO HIDE HIS EMBARRASSMENT OVER GIVING ME A PRESENT.
OHHHH!
A SHY BOY!!!

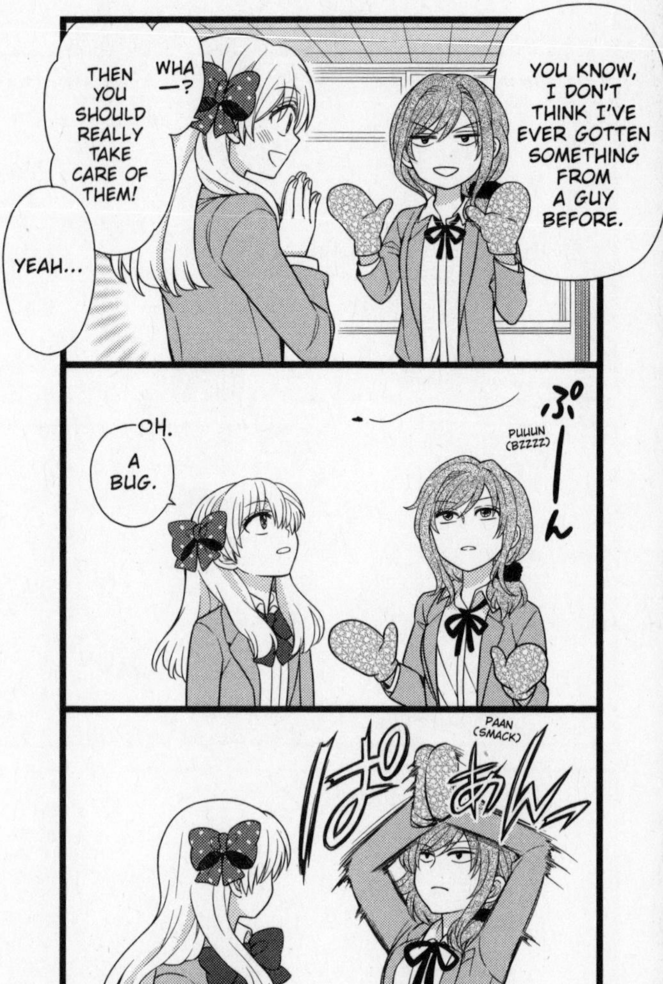
YOU KNOW, I DON'T THINK I'VE EVER GOTTEN SOMETHING FROM A GUY BEFORE.
WHA—?
THEN YOU SHOULD REALLY TAKE CARE OF THEM!
YEAH...
ぷーん
PUUUN (BZZZZ)
—OH. A BUG.
ぱあん
PAAN (SMACK)

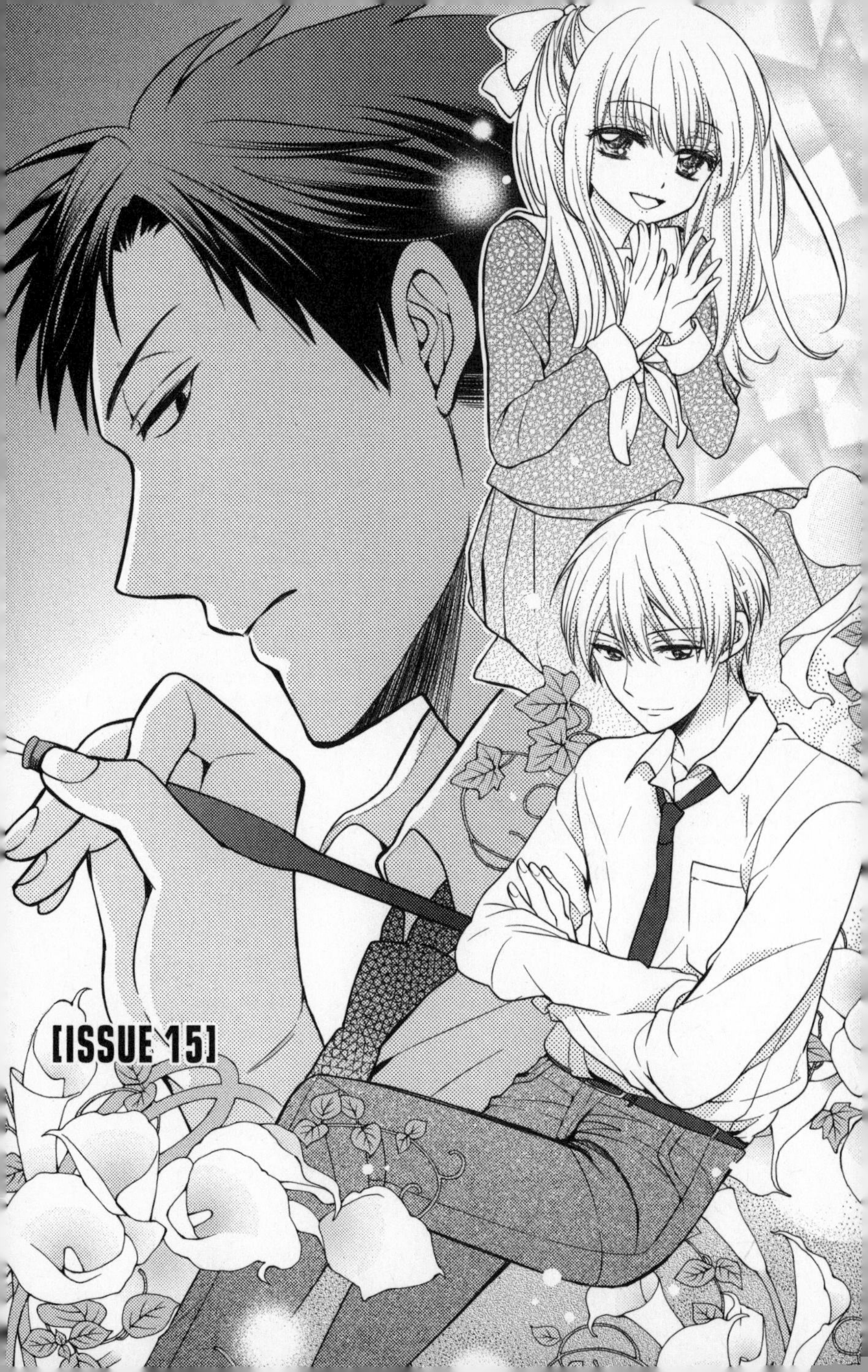
[ISSUE 15]

MAMIKO'S FEELINGS

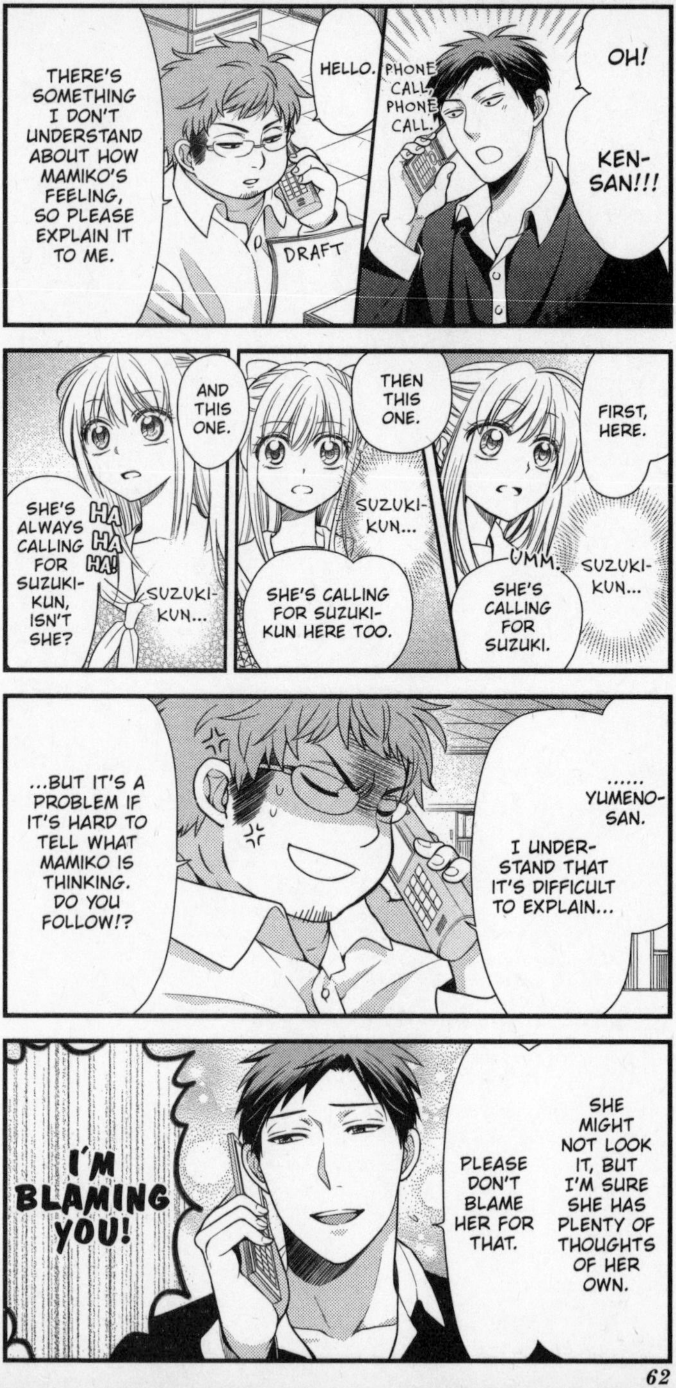
OH!
KEN-SAN!!!
PHONE CALL, PHONE CALL.
HELLO.
THERE'S SOMETHING I DON'T UNDERSTAND ABOUT HOW MAMIKO'S FEELING, SO PLEASE EXPLAIN IT TO ME.
DRAFT
FIRST, HERE.
SUZUKI-KUN...
UMM.
SHE'S CALLING FOR SUZUKI.
THEN THIS ONE.
SUZUKI-KUN...
SHE'S CALLING FOR SUZUKI-KUN HERE TOO.
AND THIS ONE.
SUZUKI-KUN...
HA HA HA!
SHE'S ALWAYS CALLING FOR SUZUKI-KUN, ISN'T SHE?
...... YUMENO-SAN.
I UNDERSTAND THAT IT'S DIFFICULT TO EXPLAIN...
...BUT IT'S A PROBLEM IF IT'S HARD TO TELL WHAT MAMIKO IS THINKING. DO YOU FOLLOW!?
SHE MIGHT NOT LOOK IT, BUT I'M SURE SHE HAS PLENTY OF THOUGHTS OF HER OWN.
PLEASE DON'T BLAME HER FOR THAT.
I'M BLAMING YOU!

PUT YOURSELF IN HER SHOES

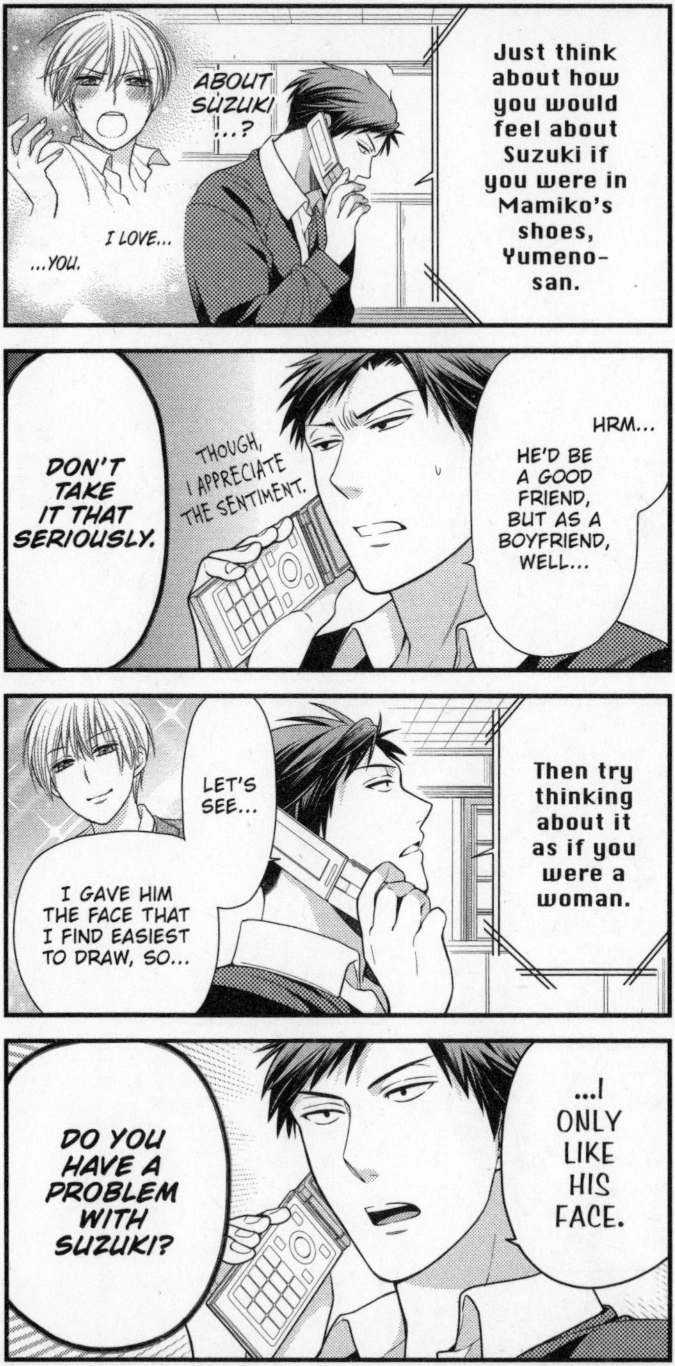
Just think about how you would feel about Suzuki if you were in Mamiko's shoes, Yumeno-san.
ABOUT SUZUKI ...?
I LOVE...
...YOU.
HRM...
HE'D BE A GOOD FRIEND, BUT AS A BOYFRIEND, WELL...
THOUGH, I APPRECIATE THE SENTIMENT.
DON'T TAKE IT THAT SERIOUSLY.
Then try thinking about it as if you were a woman.
LET'S SEE...
I GAVE HIM THE FACE THAT I FIND EASIEST TO DRAW, SO...
...I ONLY LIKE HIS FACE.
DO YOU HAVE A PROBLEM WITH SUZUKI?

MAMIKO'S WORLD

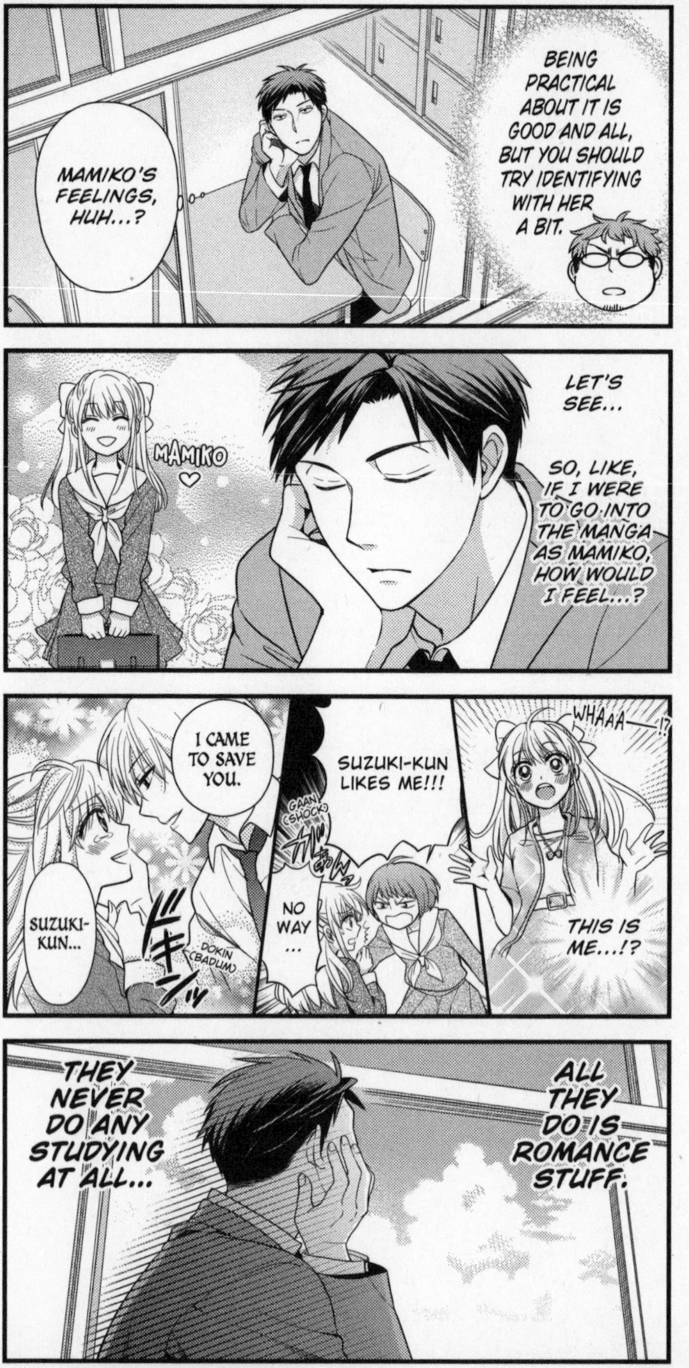
BEING PRACTICAL ABOUT IT IS GOOD AND ALL, BUT YOU SHOULD TRY IDENTIFYING WITH HER A BIT.
MAMIKO'S FEELINGS, HUH...?
LET'S SEE...
SO, LIKE, IF I WERE TO GO INTO THE MANGA AS MAMIKO, HOW WOULD I FEEL...?
MAMIKO ♥
WHAAA—!?
THIS IS ME...!?
SUZUKI-KUN LIKES ME!!!
GAAN (SHOCK)
NO WAY ...
I CAME TO SAVE YOU.
SUZUKI-KUN...
DOKIN (BADUM)
ALL THEY DO IS ROMANCE STUFF.
THEY NEVER DO ANY STUDYING AT ALL...

BECOMING☆MAMIKO

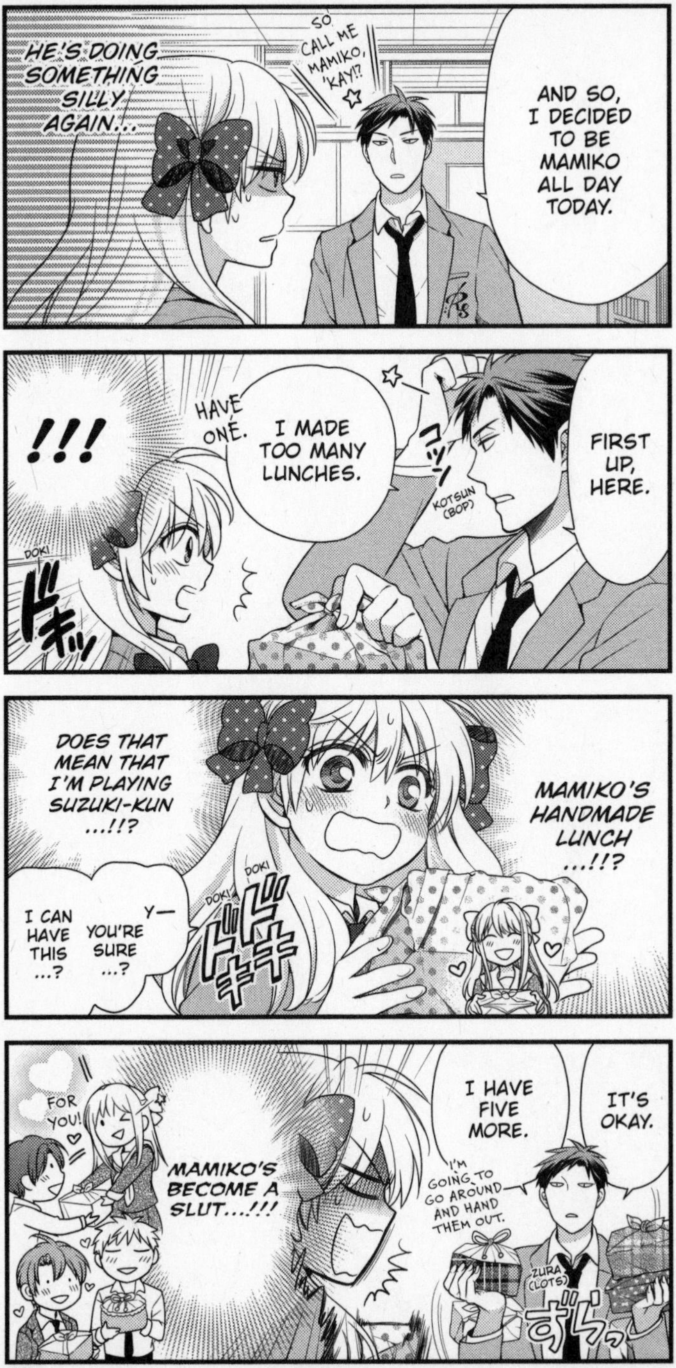

AND SO, I DECIDED TO BE MAMIKO ALL DAY TODAY.
SO CALL ME MAMIKO, 'KAY!? ☆
HE'S DOING SOMETHING SILLY AGAIN...
FIRST UP, HERE.
KOTSUN (BOP)
I MADE TOO MANY LUNCHES.
HAVE ONE.
!!!
DOKI
ドキッ
MAMIKO'S HANDMADE LUNCH ...!!?
DOKI DOKI
ドキドキ
DOES THAT MEAN THAT I'M PLAYING SUZUKI-KUN ...!!?
Y— YOU'RE SURE ...?
I CAN HAVE THIS ...?
IT'S OKAY.
I HAVE FIVE MORE.
I'M GOING TO GO AROUND AND HAND THEM OUT.
ZURA (LOTS)
ずらっ
MAMIKO'S BECOME A SLUT...!!!
FOR YOU!

DIG IN♡

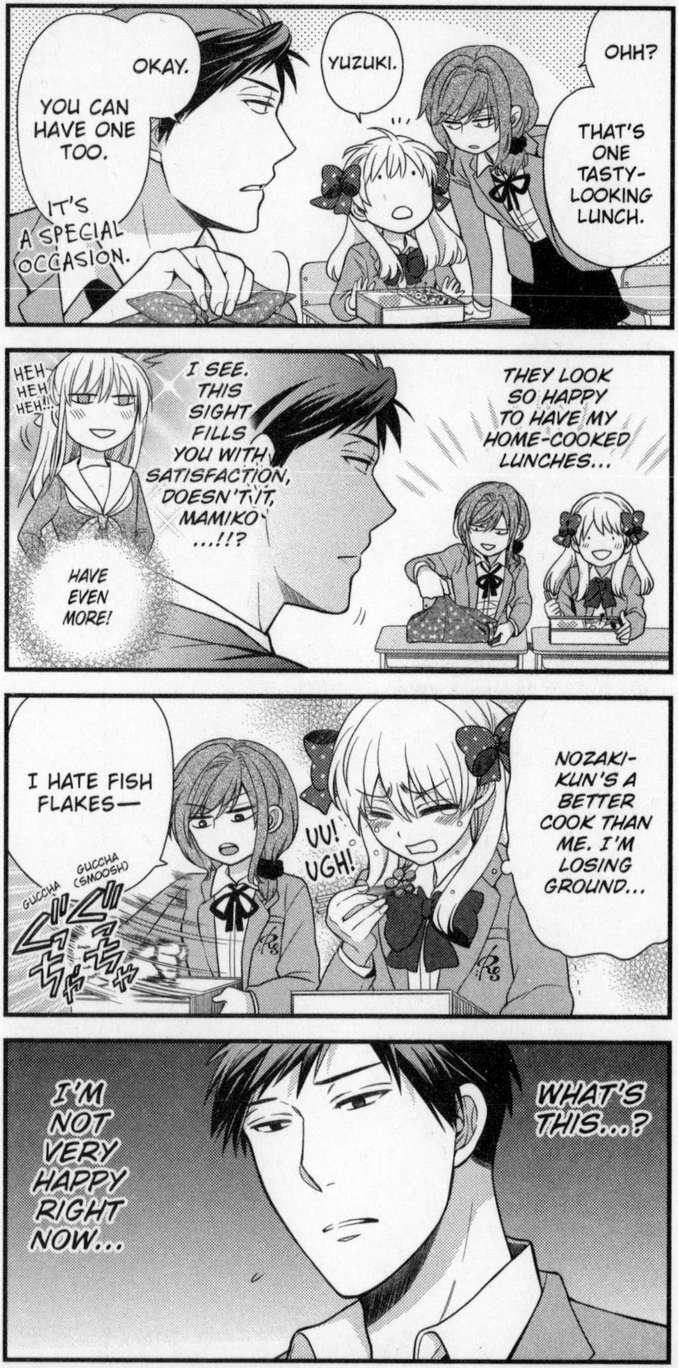
OHH? THAT'S ONE TASTY-LOOKING LUNCH.
YUZUKI.
OKAY. YOU CAN HAVE ONE TOO. IT'S A SPECIAL OCCASION.
THEY LOOK SO HAPPY TO HAVE MY HOME-COOKED LUNCHES...
I SEE. THIS SIGHT FILLS YOU WITH SATISFACTION, DOESN'T IT, MAMIKO...!!?
HEH HEH HEH!!!
HAVE EVEN MORE!
NOZAKI-KUN'S A BETTER COOK THAN ME. I'M LOSING GROUND...
UU! UGH!
I HATE FISH FLAKES—
GUCCHA (SMOOSH)
GUCCHA
WHAT'S THIS...?
I'M NOT VERY HAPPY RIGHT NOW...

THE IDEAL REACTION

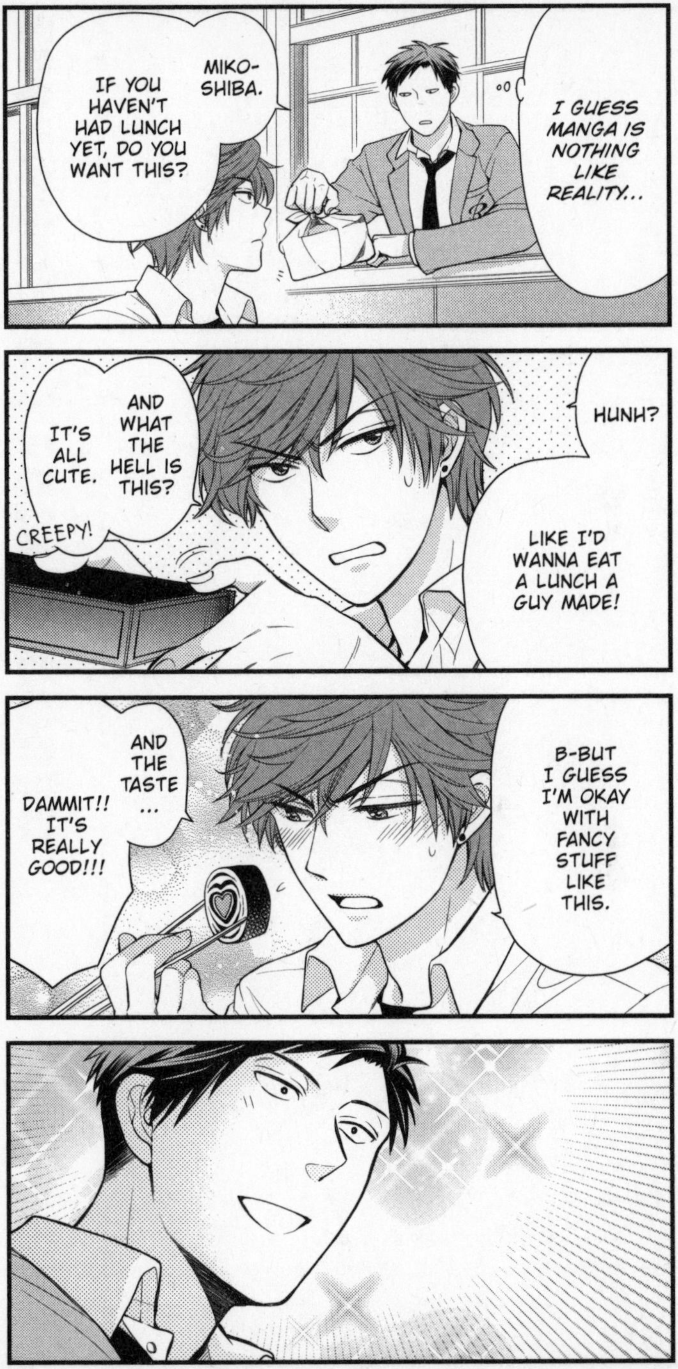
I GUESS MANGA IS NOTHING LIKE REALITY...
MIKO-SHIBA.
IF YOU HAVEN'T HAD LUNCH YET, DO YOU WANT THIS?
HUNH?
LIKE I'D WANNA EAT A LUNCH A GUY MADE!
AND WHAT THE HELL IS THIS?
IT'S ALL CUTE.
CREEPY!
B-BUT I GUESS I'M OKAY WITH FANCY STUFF LIKE THIS.
AND THE TASTE ...
DAMMIT!! IT'S REALLY GOOD!!!

THE HEROINE'S BATTLEGROUND

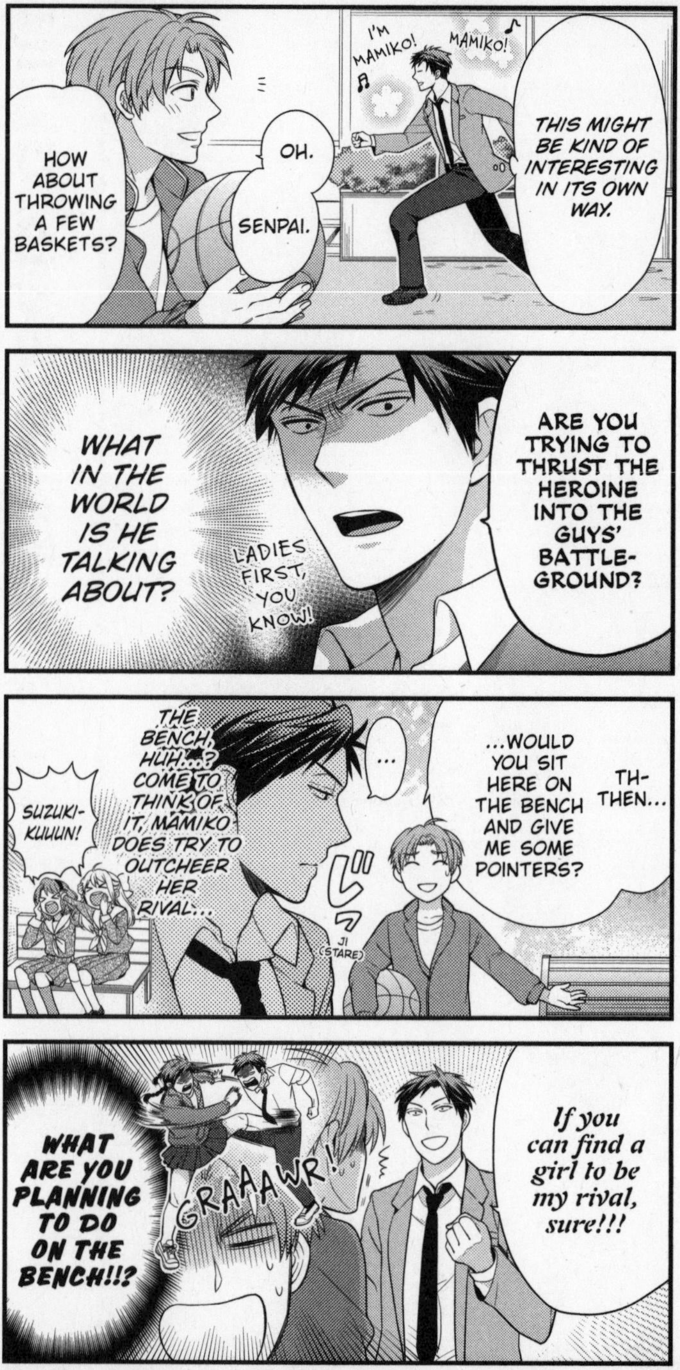
THIS MIGHT BE KIND OF INTERESTING IN ITS OWN WAY.
MAMIKO!
I'M MAMIKO!
OH.
SENPAI.
HOW ABOUT THROWING A FEW BASKETS?
ARE YOU TRYING TO THRUST THE HEROINE INTO THE GUYS' BATTLE-GROUND?
LADIES FIRST, YOU KNOW!
WHAT IN THE WORLD IS HE TALKING ABOUT?
TH-THEN...
...WOULD YOU SIT HERE ON THE BENCH AND GIVE ME SOME POINTERS?
...
JI (STARE)
THE BENCH, HUH...? COME TO THINK OF IT, MAMIKO DOES TRY TO OUTCHEER HER RIVAL...
SUZUKI-KUUUN!
If you can find a girl to be my rival, sure!!!
GRAAAWR!
WHAT ARE YOU PLANNING TO DO ON THE BENCH!!?

ME VS. THE GIRLS

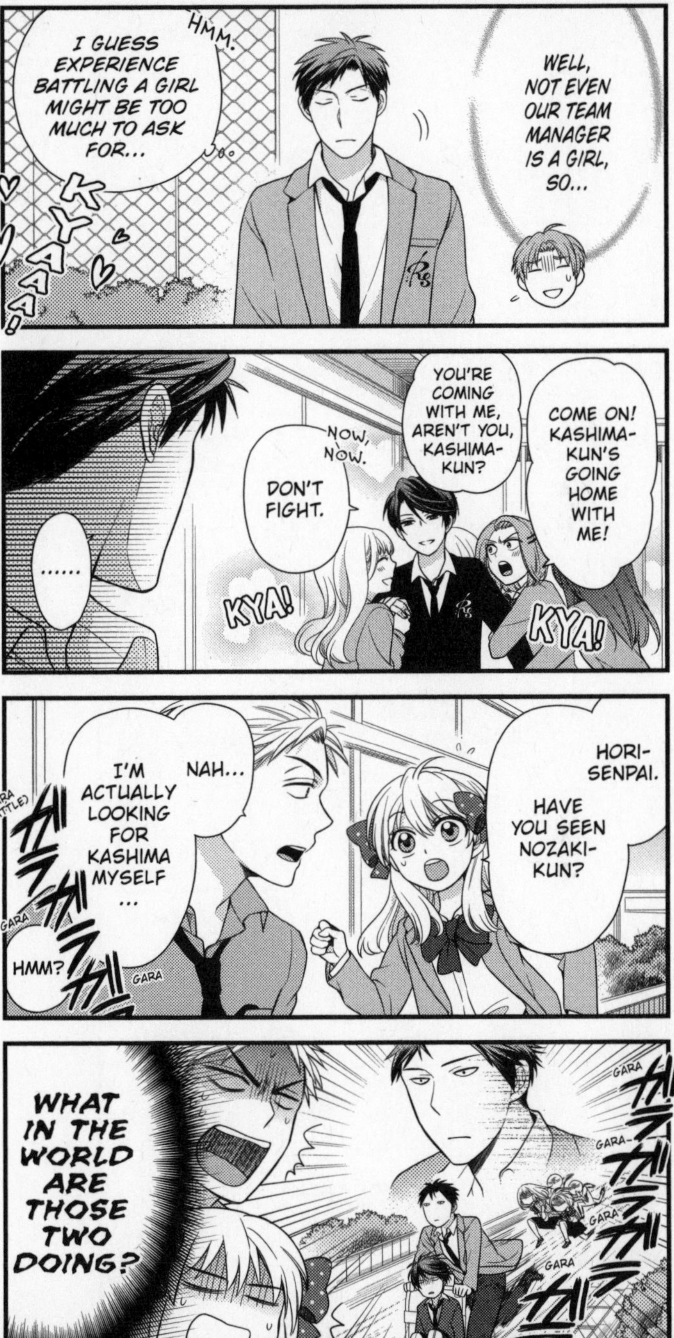
WELL, NOT EVEN OUR TEAM MANAGER IS A GIRL, SO...
HMM.
I GUESS EXPERIENCE BATTLING A GIRL MIGHT BE TOO MUCH TO ASK FOR...
KYAAAA!
COME ON! KASHIMA-KUN'S GOING HOME WITH ME!
YOU'RE COMING WITH ME, AREN'T YOU, KASHIMA-KUN?
KYA!
NOW, NOW.
DON'T FIGHT.
KYA!
......
HORI-SENPAI.
HAVE YOU SEEN NOZAKI-KUN?
NAH...
I'M ACTUALLY LOOKING FOR KASHIMA MYSELF ...
GARA (RATTLE)
GARA
GARA
HMM?
GARA
GARA-
GARA
GARA
WHAT IN THE WORLD ARE THOSE TWO DOING?

WHAT HE LEARNED

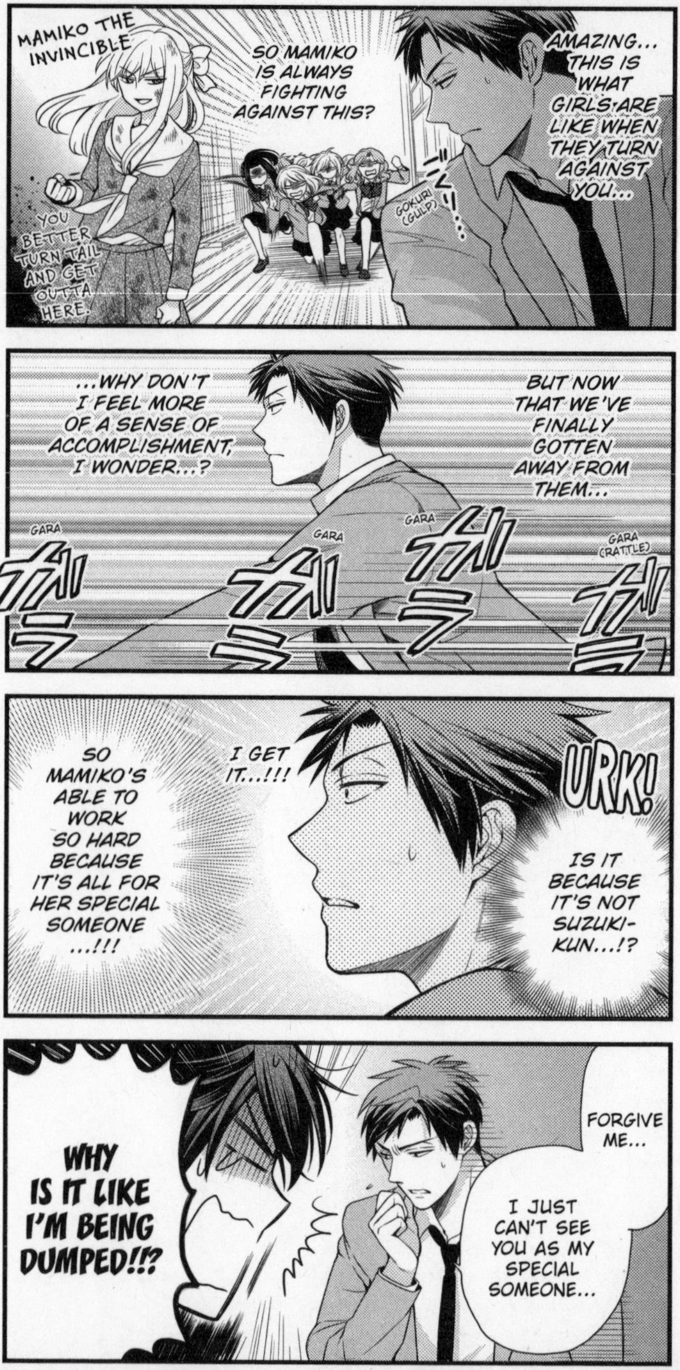
AMAZING... THIS IS WHAT GIRLS ARE LIKE WHEN THEY TURN AGAINST YOU...
GOKURI (GULP)
SO MAMIKO IS ALWAYS FIGHTING AGAINST THIS?
MAMIKO THE INVINCIBLE
YOU BETTER TURN TAIL AND GET OUTTA HERE.
BUT NOW THAT WE'VE FINALLY GOTTEN AWAY FROM THEM...
...WHY DON'T I FEEL MORE OF A SENSE OF ACCOMPLISHMENT, I WONDER...?
GARA (RATTLE)
GARA
GARA
GARA
URK!
IS IT BECAUSE IT'S NOT SUZUKI-KUN...!?
I GET IT...!!!
SO MAMIKO'S ABLE TO WORK SO HARD BECAUSE IT'S ALL FOR HER SPECIAL SOMEONE ...!!!
FORGIVE ME...
I JUST CAN'T SEE YOU AS MY SPECIAL SOMEONE...
WHY IS IT LIKE I'M BEING DUMPED!!?

HER HANG-UP

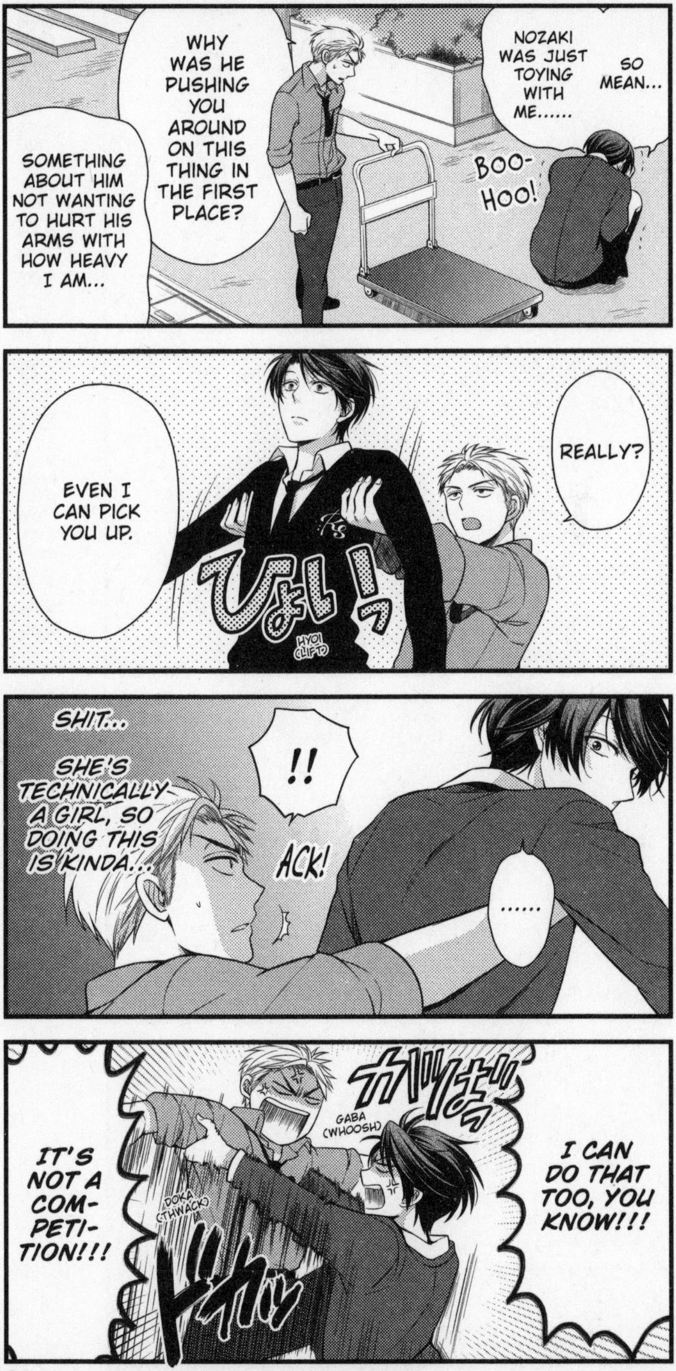
SO MEAN...
NOZAKI WAS JUST TOYING WITH ME......
BOO-HOO!
WHY WAS HE PUSHING YOU AROUND ON THIS THING IN THE FIRST PLACE?
SOMETHING ABOUT HIM NOT WANTING TO HURT HIS ARMS WITH HOW HEAVY I AM...
REALLY?
EVEN I CAN PICK YOU UP.
ひょいっ
HYOI (LIFT)
......
!!
ACK!
SHIT...
SHE'S TECHNICALLY A GIRL, SO DOING THIS IS KINDA...
I CAN DO THAT TOO, YOU KNOW!!!
ガバっ
GABA (WHOOSH)
IT'S NOT A COMPETITION!!!
DOKA (THWACK)
ドカッ

HAPPINESS < WEARINESS

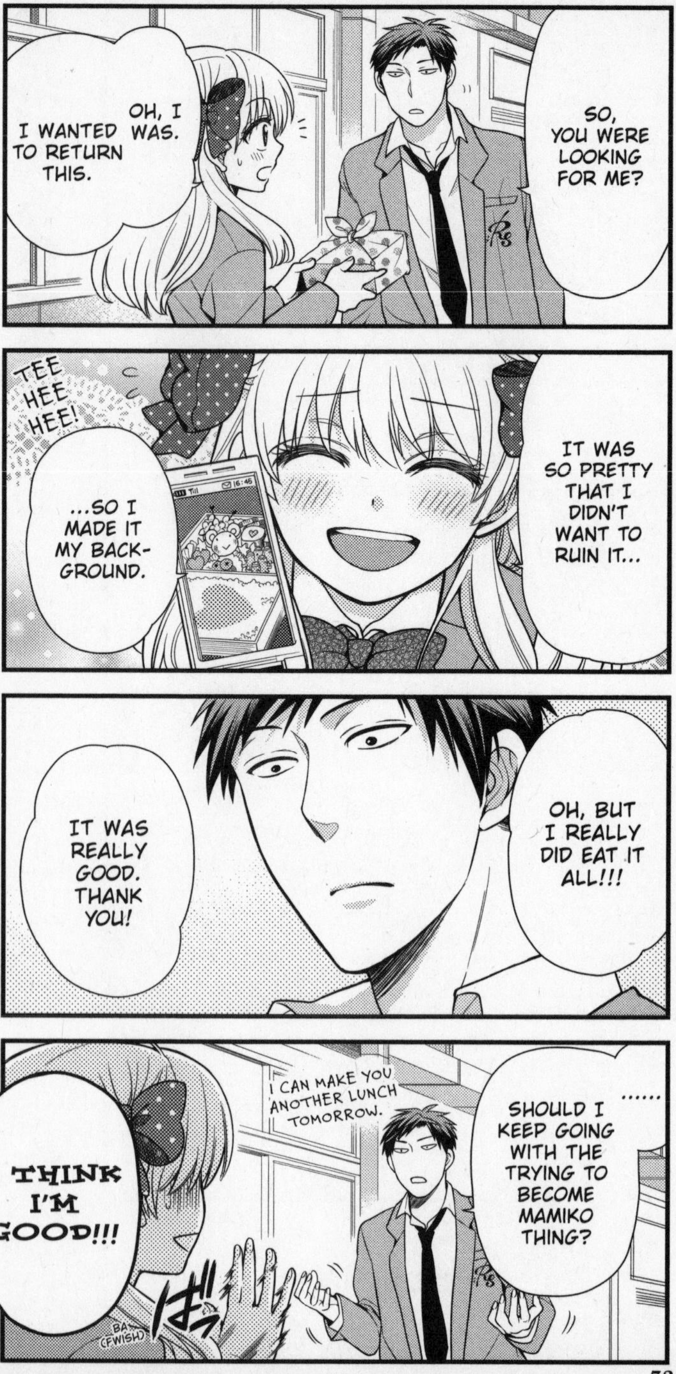

SO, YOU WERE LOOKING FOR ME?
OH, I WAS.
I WANTED TO RETURN THIS.
IT WAS SO PRETTY THAT I DIDN'T WANT TO RUIN IT...
...SO I MADE IT MY BACK-GROUND.
TEE HEE HEE!
OH, BUT I REALLY DID EAT IT ALL!!!
IT WAS REALLY GOOD. THANK YOU!
......
SHOULD I KEEP GOING WITH THE TRYING TO BECOME MAMIKO THING?
I CAN MAKE YOU ANOTHER LUNCH TOMORROW.
I THINK I'M GOOD!!!
BA (FWISH)

WE'VE COME TO AN UNDERSTANDING

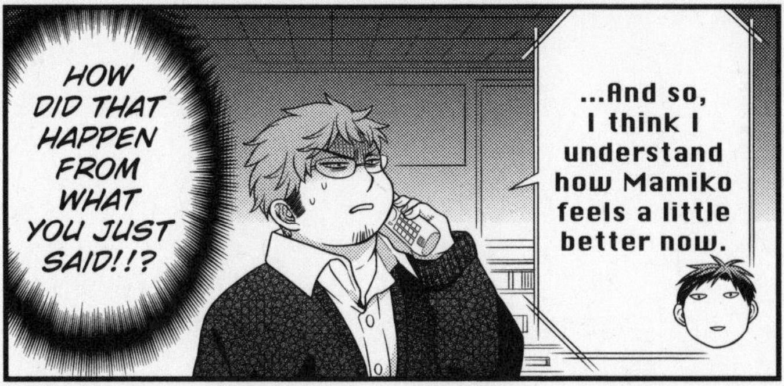
...And so, I think I understand how Mamiko feels a little better now.
HOW DID THAT HAPPEN FROM WHAT YOU JUST SAID!!?

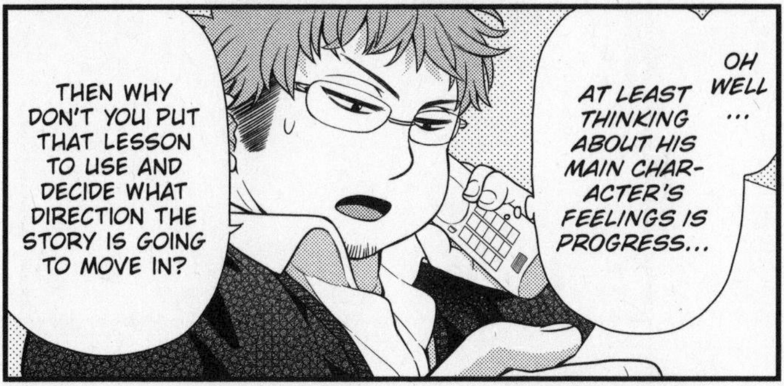
OH WELL ...
AT LEAST THINKING ABOUT HIS MAIN CHARACTER'S FEELINGS IS PROGRESS...
THEN WHY DON'T YOU PUT THAT LESSON TO USE AND DECIDE WHAT DIRECTION THE STORY IS GOING TO MOVE IN?

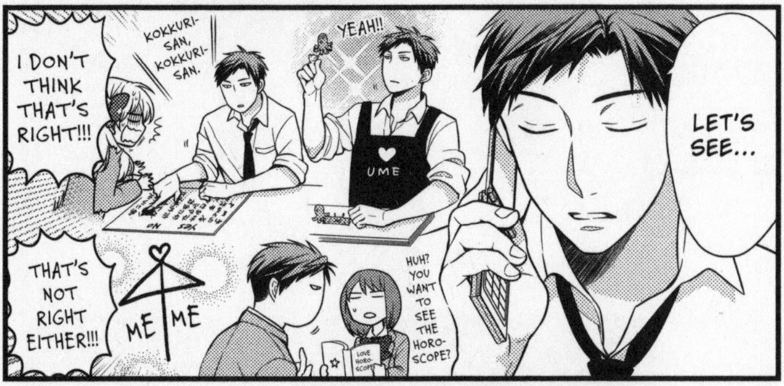
LET'S SEE...
YEAH!!
UME
KOKKURI-SAN, KOKKURI-SAN.
I DON'T THINK THAT'S RIGHT!!!
YES
NO
HUH? YOU WANT TO SEE THE HOROSCOPE?
LOVE HOROSCOPE
ME ME
THAT'S NOT RIGHT EITHER!!!

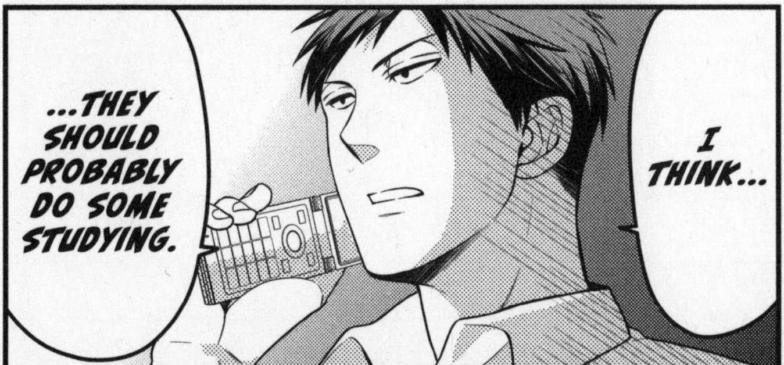
I THINK...
...THEY SHOULD PROBABLY DO SOME STUDYING.

※EVERYTHING NOZAKI IS DOING IN THE THIRD PANEL IS TYPICAL "GIRL IN LOVE" STUFF. THE OCTOPUS-SHAPED SAUSAGES ARE STANDARD FOR HANDMADE LUNCHES. KOKKURI-SAN IS A GAME USED TO ASK ABOUT WHAT THE FUTURE HOLDS, SIMILAR TO A OUIJA BOARD. AND THE DRAWING IS OF A "LOVE-LOVE UMBRELLA" (AI-AIGASA), THE JAPANESE VERSION OF A HEART CARVED INTO A TREE WITH TWO LOVERS' NAMES.

SO, BASICALLY, IT'S LIKE THIS?

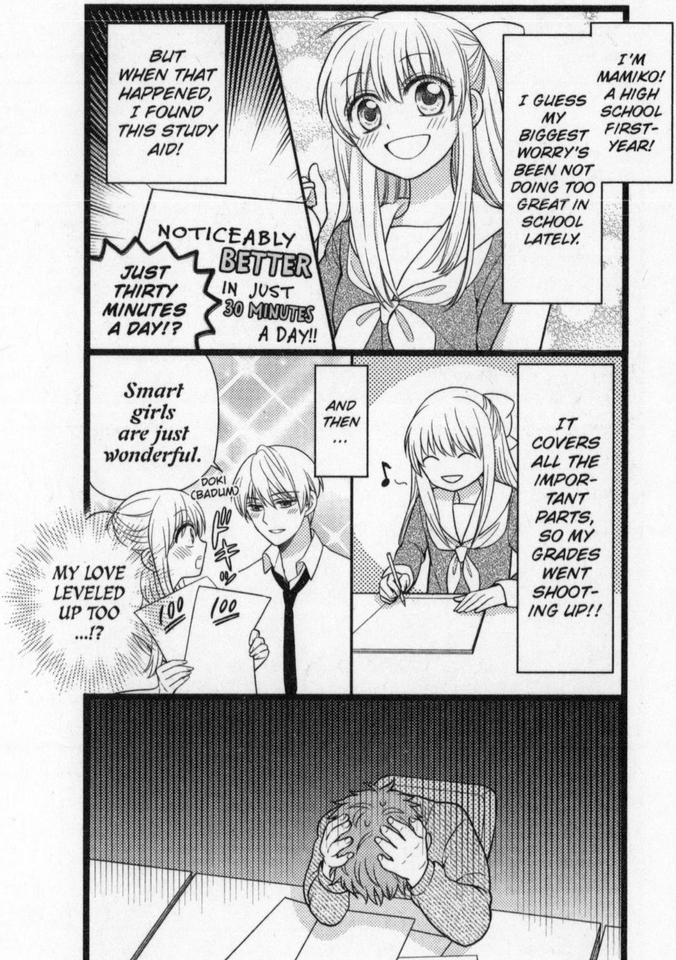
I'M MAMIKO! A HIGH SCHOOL FIRST-YEAR!
I GUESS MY BIGGEST WORRY'S BEEN NOT DOING TOO GREAT IN SCHOOL LATELY.
BUT WHEN THAT HAPPENED, I FOUND THIS STUDY AID!
NOTICEABLY BETTER IN JUST 30 MINUTES A DAY!!
JUST THIRTY MINUTES A DAY!?
IT COVERS ALL THE IMPORTANT PARTS, SO MY GRADES WENT SHOOTING UP!!
AND THEN...
Smart girls are just wonderful.
DOKI (BADUM)
MY LOVE LEVELED UP TOO ...!?
100
100

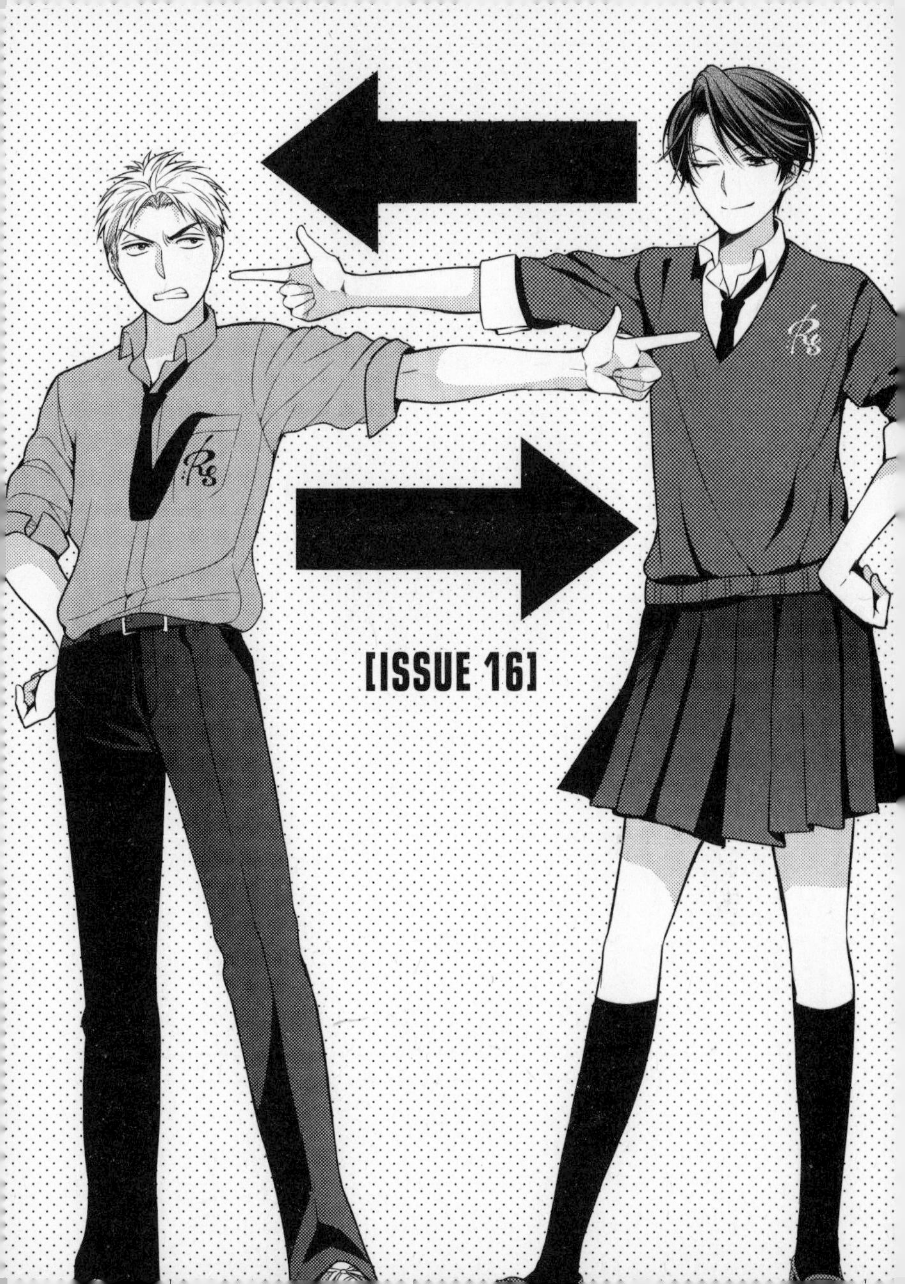
[ISSUE 16]

ADVICE, HANDSOME GUY STYLE

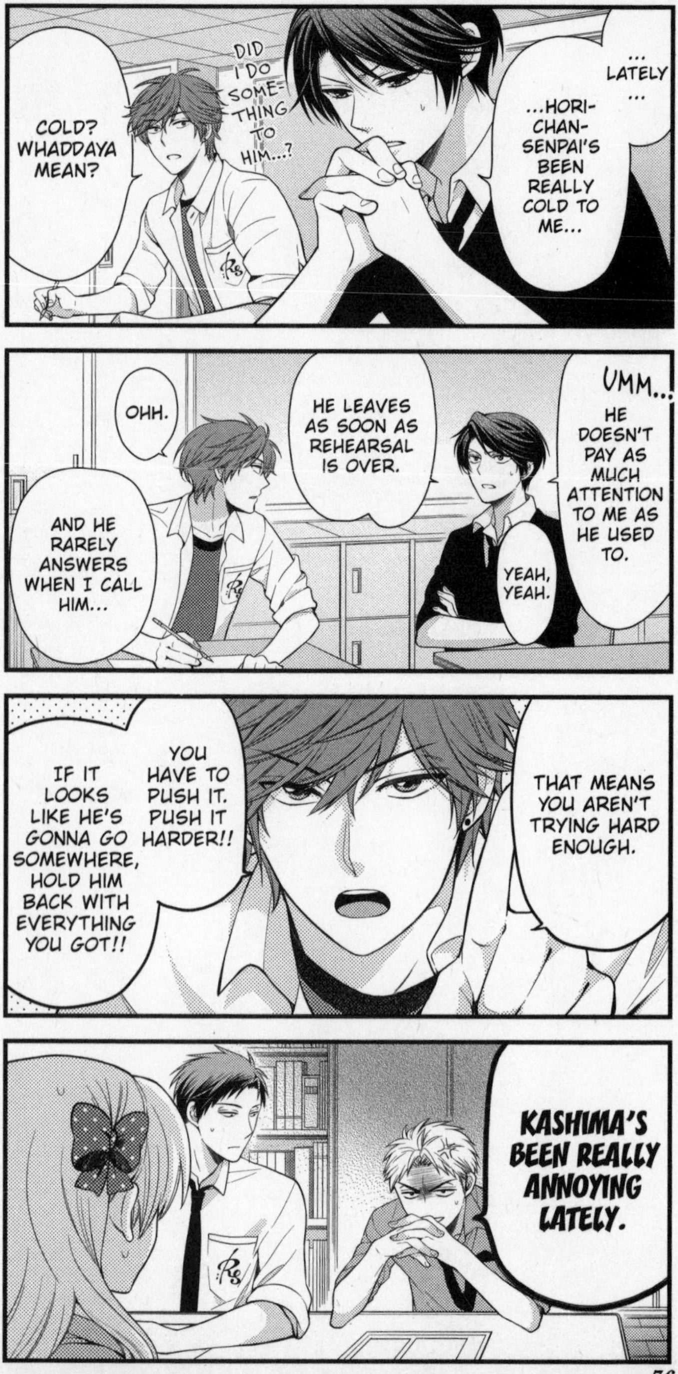
...LATELY...
...HORI-CHAN-SENPAI'S BEEN REALLY COLD TO ME...
DID I DO SOMETHING TO HIM...?
COLD? WHADDAYA MEAN?
UMM... HE DOESN'T PAY AS MUCH ATTENTION TO ME AS HE USED TO.
YEAH, YEAH.
HE LEAVES AS SOON AS REHEARSAL IS OVER.
OHH.
AND HE RARELY ANSWERS WHEN I CALL HIM...
THAT MEANS YOU AREN'T TRYING HARD ENOUGH.
YOU HAVE TO PUSH IT. PUSH IT HARDER!!
IF IT LOOKS LIKE HE'S GONNA GO SOMEWHERE, HOLD HIM BACK WITH EVERYTHING YOU GOT!!
KASHIMA'S BEEN REALLY ANNOYING LATELY.

SOMETHING THAT'S ALWAYS WITH HIM

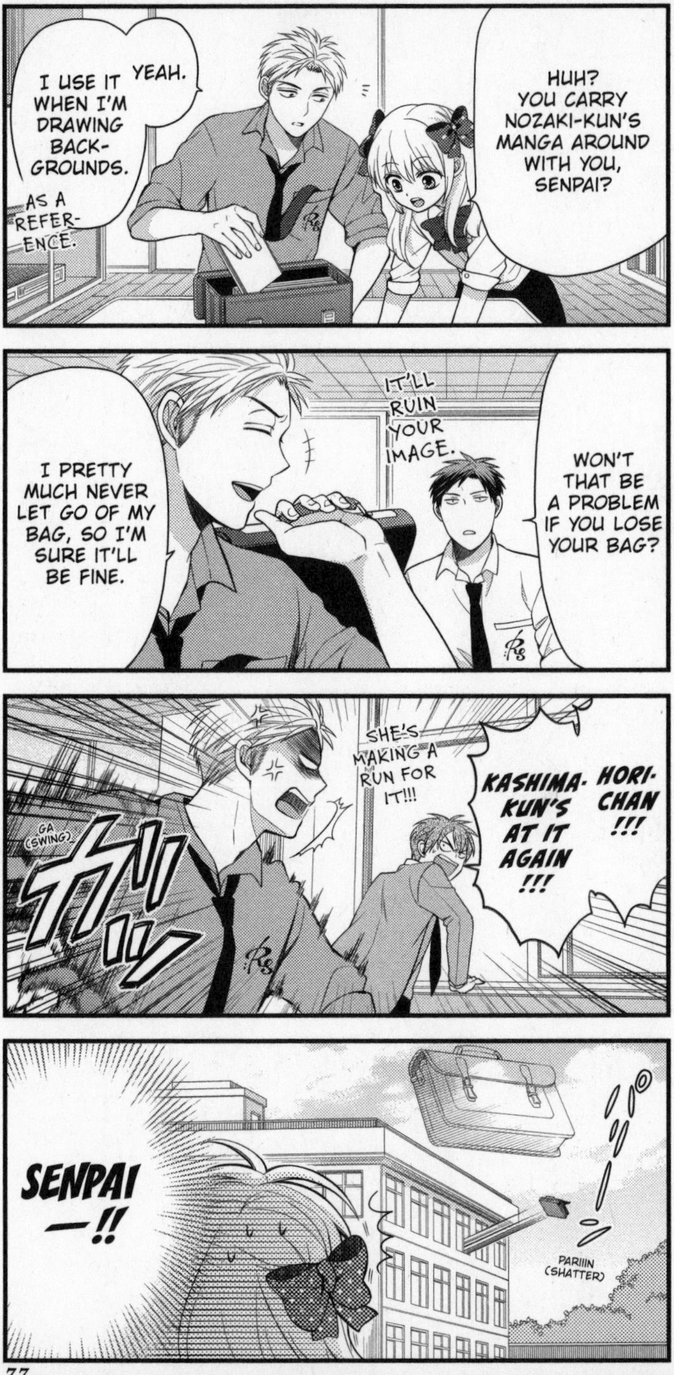
HUH? YOU CARRY NOZAKI-KUN'S MANGA AROUND WITH YOU, SENPAI?
YEAH.
I USE IT WHEN I'M DRAWING BACKGROUNDS.
AS A REFERENCE.
WON'T THAT BE A PROBLEM IF YOU LOSE YOUR BAG?
IT'LL RUIN YOUR IMAGE.
I PRETTY MUCH NEVER LET GO OF MY BAG, SO I'M SURE IT'LL BE FINE.
HORI-CHAN!!!
KASHIMA-KUN'S AT IT AGAIN!!!
SHE'S MAKING A RUN FOR IT!!!
GA (SWING)
PARIIIN (SHATTER)
SENPAI—!!

DESPERATE EXCUSES

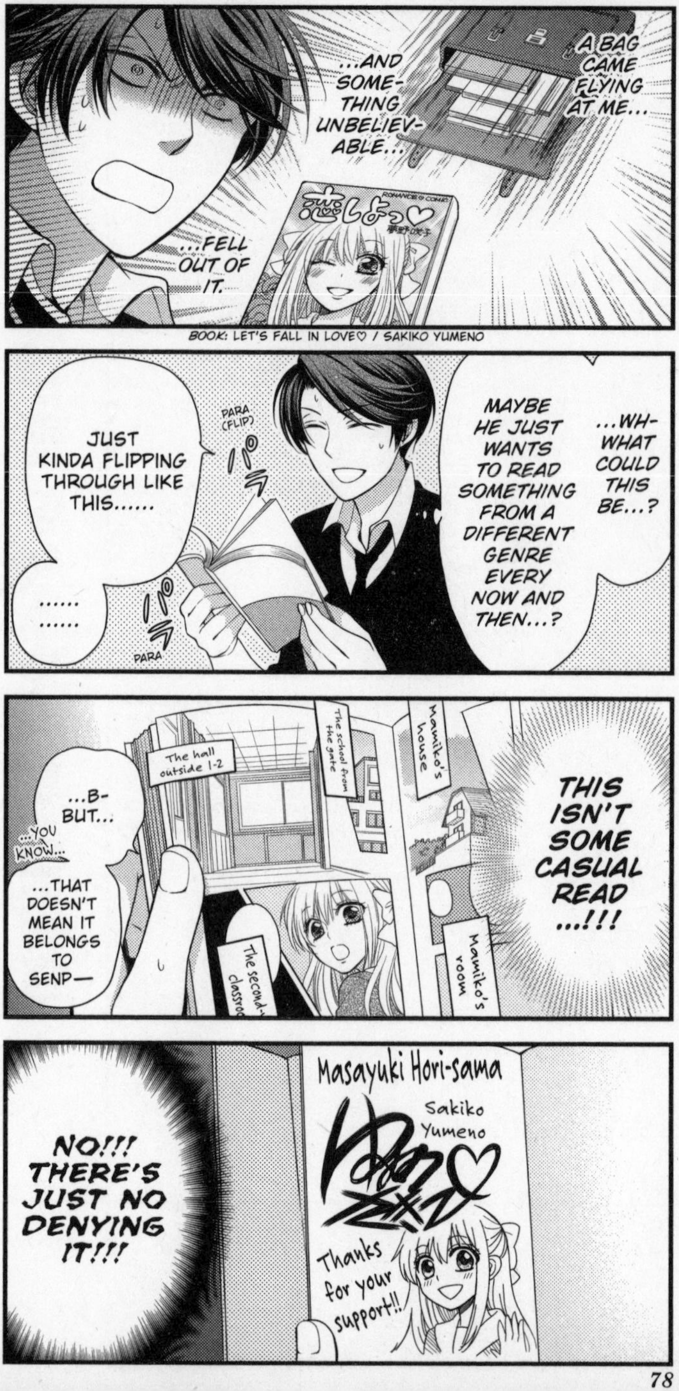
A BAG CAME FLYING AT ME...
...AND SOMETHING UNBELIEVABLE...
...FELL OUT OF IT.
BOOK: LET'S FALL IN LOVE♡ / SAKIKO YUMENO
...WH-WHAT COULD THIS BE...?
MAYBE HE JUST WANTS TO READ SOMETHING FROM A DIFFERENT GENRE EVERY NOW AND THEN...?
PARA (FLIP)
JUST KINDA FLIPPING THROUGH LIKE THIS......
....
PARA
THIS ISN'T SOME CASUAL READ ...!!!
Mamiko's house
The school from the gate
The hall outside 1-2
Mamiko's room
...B-BUT...
...YOU KNOW...
...THAT DOESN'T MEAN IT BELONGS TO SENP—
Masayuki Hori-sama
Sakiko Yumeno
Thanks for your support!!
NO!!! THERE'S JUST NO DENYING IT!!!

A WORLD YOU DON'T KNOW

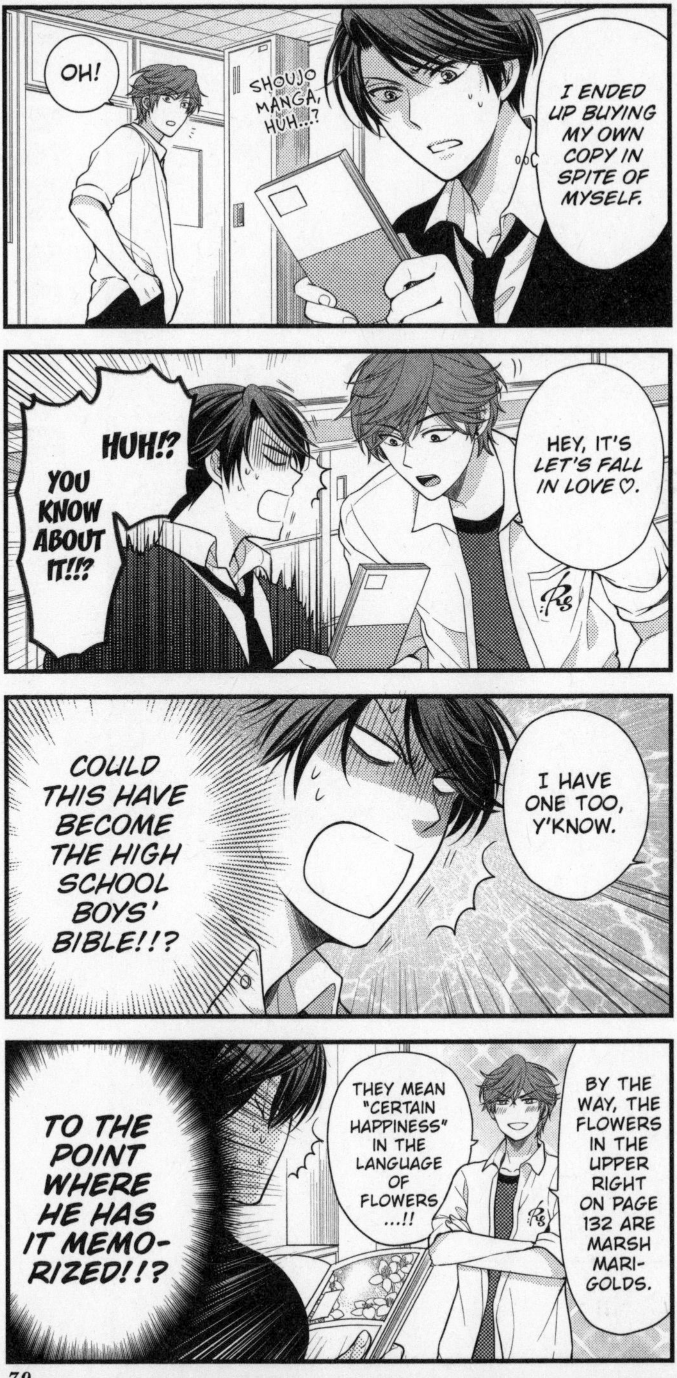
I ENDED UP BUYING MY OWN COPY IN SPITE OF MYSELF.
SHOUJO MANGA, HUH...!?
OH!
HEY, IT'S LET'S FALL IN LOVE♡.
HUH!?
YOU KNOW ABOUT IT!!?
I HAVE ONE TOO, Y'KNOW.
COULD THIS HAVE BECOME THE HIGH SCHOOL BOYS' BIBLE!!?
BY THE WAY, THE FLOWERS IN THE UPPER RIGHT ON PAGE 132 ARE MARSH MARI-GOLDS.
THEY MEAN "CERTAIN HAPPINESS" IN THE LANGUAGE OF FLOWERS ...!!
TO THE POINT WHERE HE HAS IT MEMO-RIZED!!?

DOUBLE ATTACK

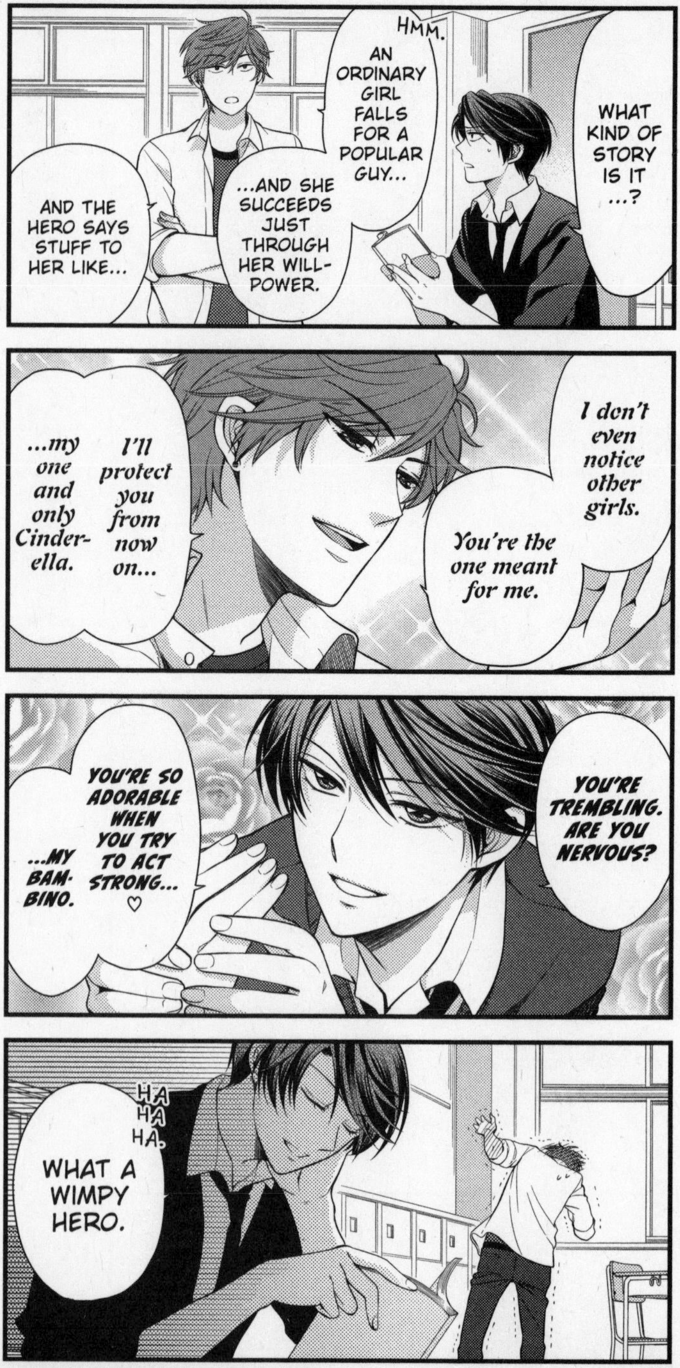
WHAT KIND OF STORY IS IT ...?
HMM.
AN ORDINARY GIRL FALLS FOR A POPULAR GUY...
...AND SHE SUCCEEDS JUST THROUGH HER WILL-POWER.
AND THE HERO SAYS STUFF TO HER LIKE...
I don't even notice other girls.
You're the one meant for me.
I'll protect you from now on...
...my one and only Cinder-ella.
YOU'RE TREMBLING. ARE YOU NERVOUS?
YOU'RE SO ADORABLE WHEN YOU TRY TO ACT STRONG... ♡
...MY BAM-BINO.
HA HA HA.
WHAT A WIMPY HERO.

IRRATIONAL

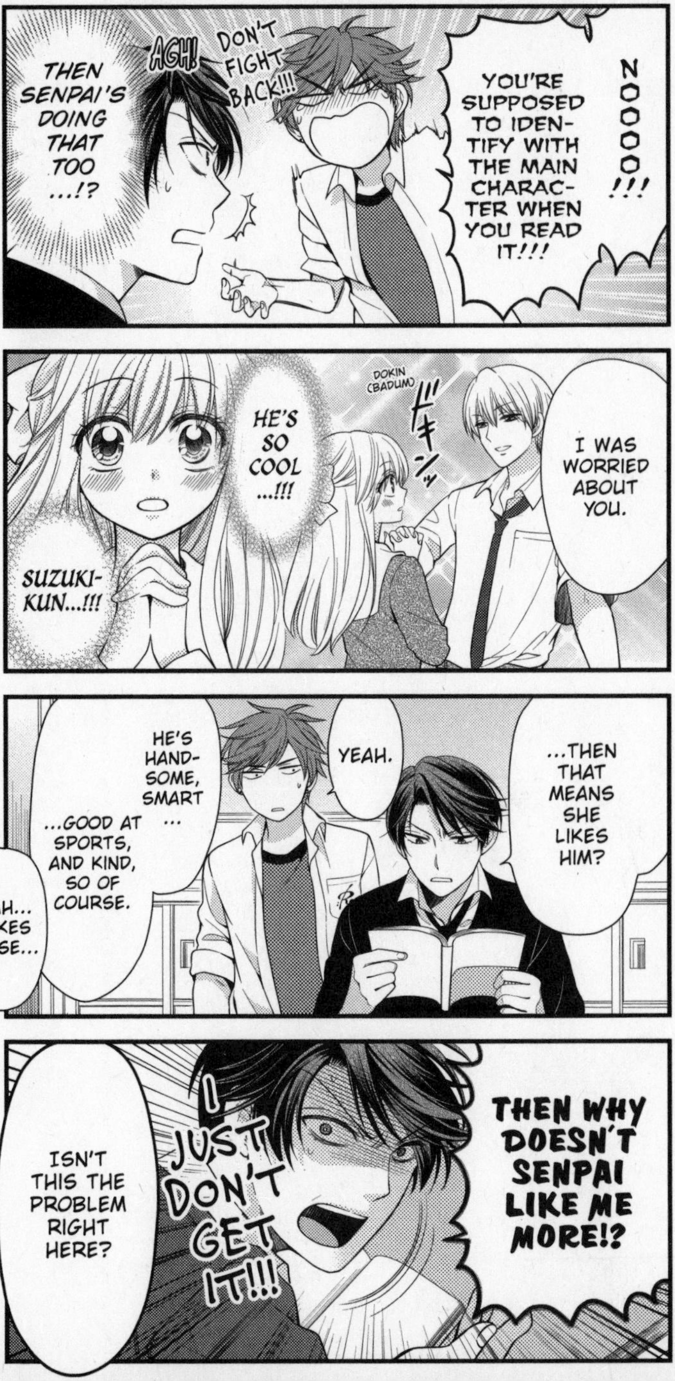
NOOOO!!!
YOU'RE SUPPOSED TO IDENTIFY WITH THE MAIN CHARACTER WHEN YOU READ IT!!!
DON'T FIGHT BACK!!!
AGH!
THEN SENPAI'S DOING THAT TOO...!?
I WAS WORRIED ABOUT YOU.
DOKIN (BADUM)
ドキンッ
HE'S SO COOL...!!!
SUZUKI-KUN...!!!
...THEN THAT MEANS SHE LIKES HIM?
YEAH.
HE'S HANDSOME, SMART...
...GOOD AT SPORTS, AND KIND, SO OF COURSE.
YEAH... MAKES SENSE...
THEN WHY DOESN'T SENPAI LIKE ME MORE!?
I JUST DON'T GET IT!!!
ISN'T THIS THE PROBLEM RIGHT HERE?

EXCITING AND NERVE-RACKING, IN A WAY

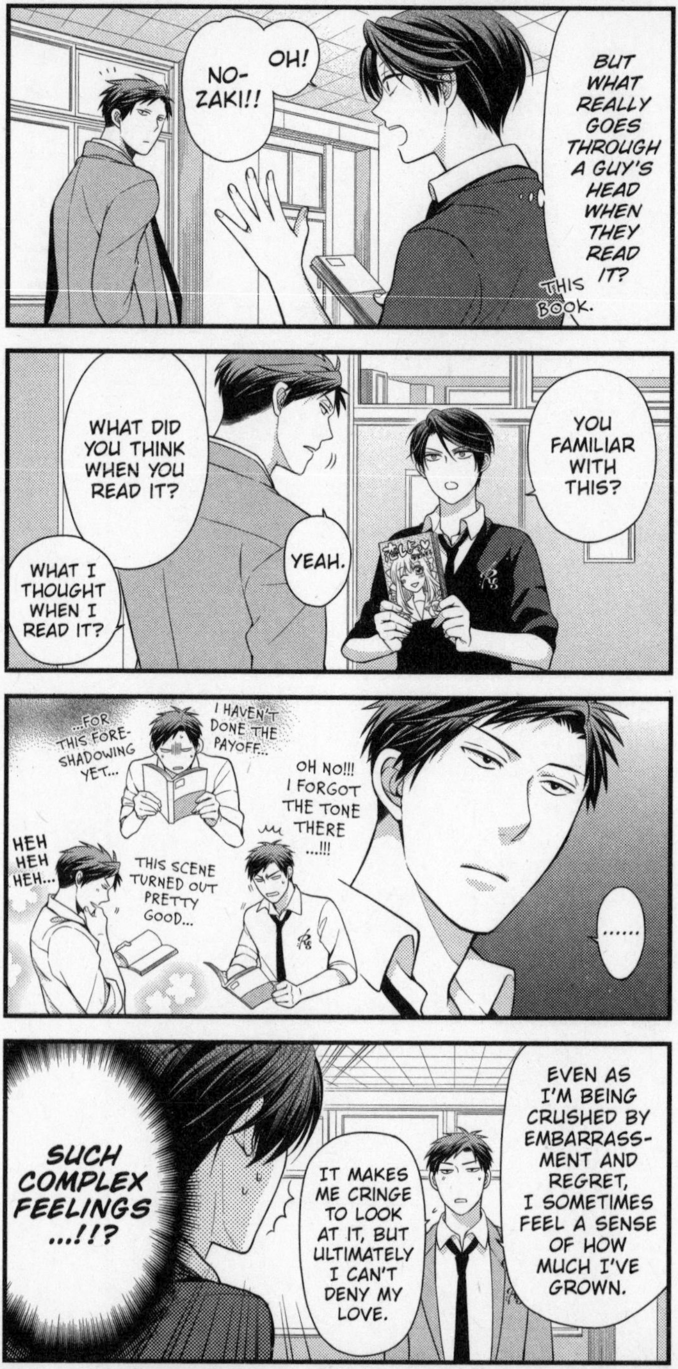
BUT WHAT REALLY GOES THROUGH A GUY'S HEAD WHEN THEY READ IT?
THIS BOOK.
OH!
NO-ZAKI!!
YOU FAMILIAR WITH THIS?
WHAT DID YOU THINK WHEN YOU READ IT?
YEAH.
WHAT I THOUGHT WHEN I READ IT?
......
I HAVEN'T DONE THE PAYOFF...
...FOR THIS FORE-SHADOWING YET...
OH NO!!! I FORGOT THE TONE THERE ...!!!
THIS SCENE TURNED OUT PRETTY GOOD...
HEH HEH HEH...
EVEN AS I'M BEING CRUSHED BY EMBARRASS-MENT AND REGRET, I SOMETIMES FEEL A SENSE OF HOW MUCH I'VE GROWN.
IT MAKES ME CRINGE TO LOOK AT IT, BUT ULTIMATELY I CAN'T DENY MY LOVE.
SUCH COMPLEX FEELINGS ...!!?

THE RESULTS OF KASHIMA-KUN'S INVESTIGATION

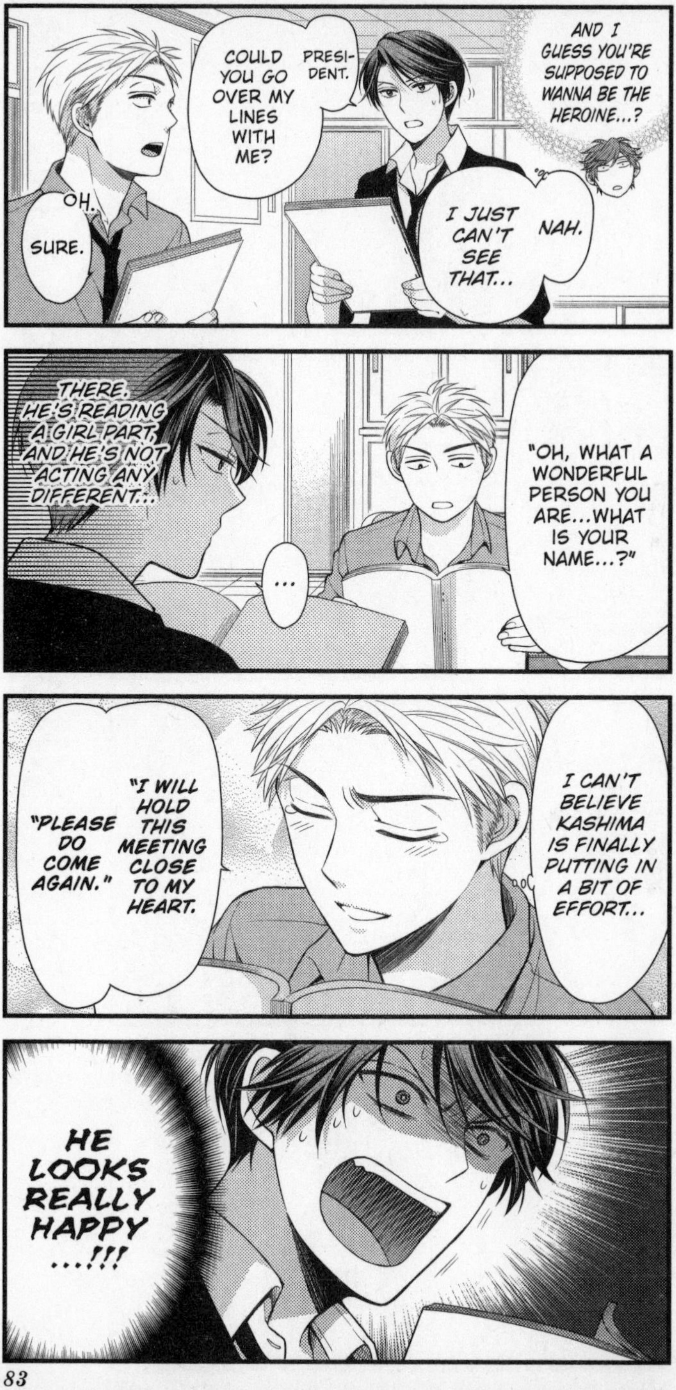
AND I GUESS YOU'RE SUPPOSED TO WANNA BE THE HEROINE...?
PRESI-DENT.
COULD YOU GO OVER MY LINES WITH ME?
NAH.
I JUST CAN'T SEE THAT...
OH.
SURE.
"OH, WHAT A WONDERFUL PERSON YOU ARE...WHAT IS YOUR NAME...?"
...
THERE. HE'S READING A GIRL PART, AND HE'S NOT ACTING ANY DIFFERENT...
I CAN'T BELIEVE KASHIMA IS FINALLY PUTTING IN A BIT OF EFFORT...
"I WILL HOLD THIS MEETING CLOSE TO MY HEART.
"PLEASE DO COME AGAIN."
HE LOOKS REALLY HAPPY ...!!!

WANTING TO BE THE HEROINE

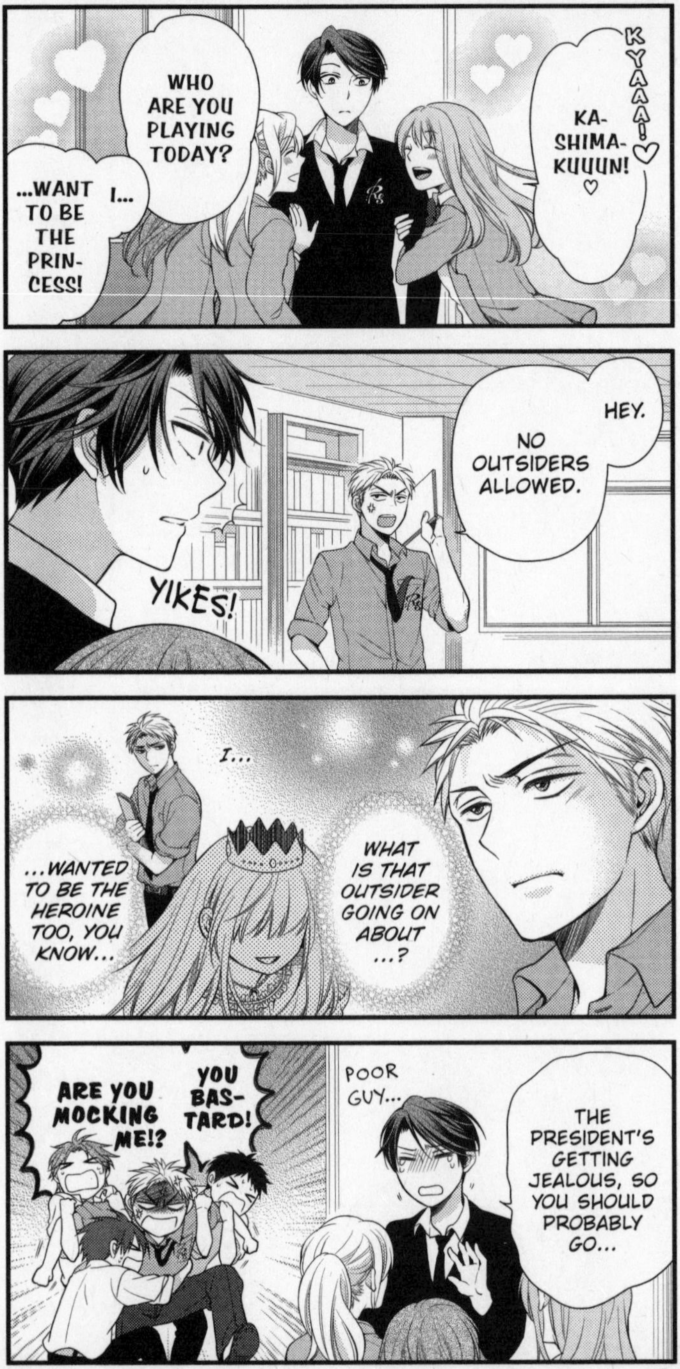
KYAAAA!♥
KA-SHIMA-KUUUN!♥
WHO ARE YOU PLAYING TODAY?
I...
...WANT TO BE THE PRINCESS!
HEY.
NO OUTSIDERS ALLOWED.
YIKES!
I...
WHAT IS THAT OUTSIDER GOING ON ABOUT...?
...WANTED TO BE THE HEROINE TOO, YOU KNOW...
THE PRESIDENT'S GETTING JEALOUS, SO YOU SHOULD PROBABLY GO...
POOR GUY...
YOU BASTARD!
ARE YOU MOCKING ME!?

KASHIMA-KUN'S KINDNESS ①

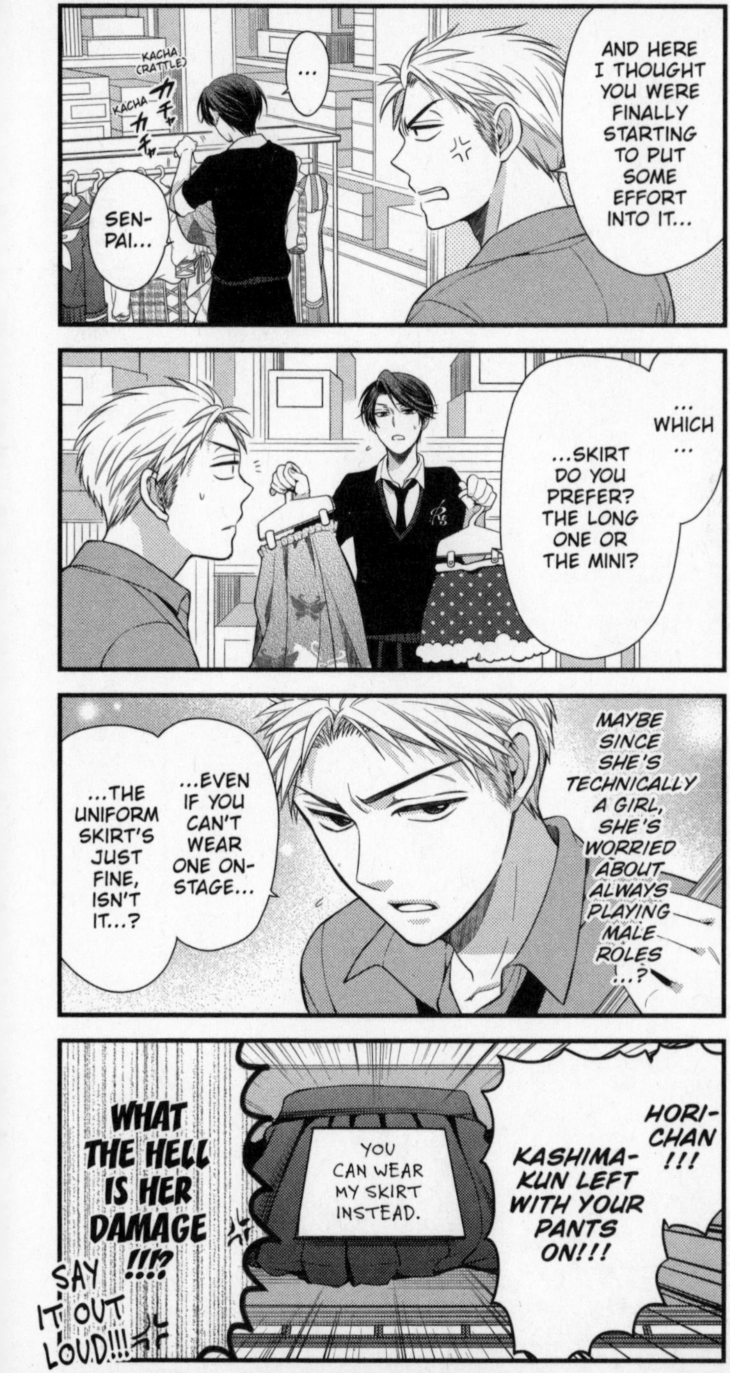
AND HERE I THOUGHT YOU WERE FINALLY STARTING TO PUT SOME EFFORT INTO IT...
...
KACHA (RATTLE)
カチャ
KACHA
カチャ
SEN-PAI...
... WHICH ...
...SKIRT DO YOU PREFER? THE LONG ONE OR THE MINI?
MAYBE SINCE SHE'S TECHNICALLY A GIRL, SHE'S WORRIED ABOUT ALWAYS PLAYING MALE ROLES ...?
...EVEN IF YOU CAN'T WEAR ONE ON-STAGE...
...THE UNIFORM SKIRT'S JUST FINE, ISN'T IT...?
HORI-CHAN!!!
KASHIMA-KUN LEFT WITH YOUR PANTS ON!!!
YOU CAN WEAR MY SKIRT INSTEAD.
WHAT THE HELL IS HER DAMAGE!!!?
SAY IT OUT LOUD!!!

KASHIMA-KUN'S KINDNESS ②

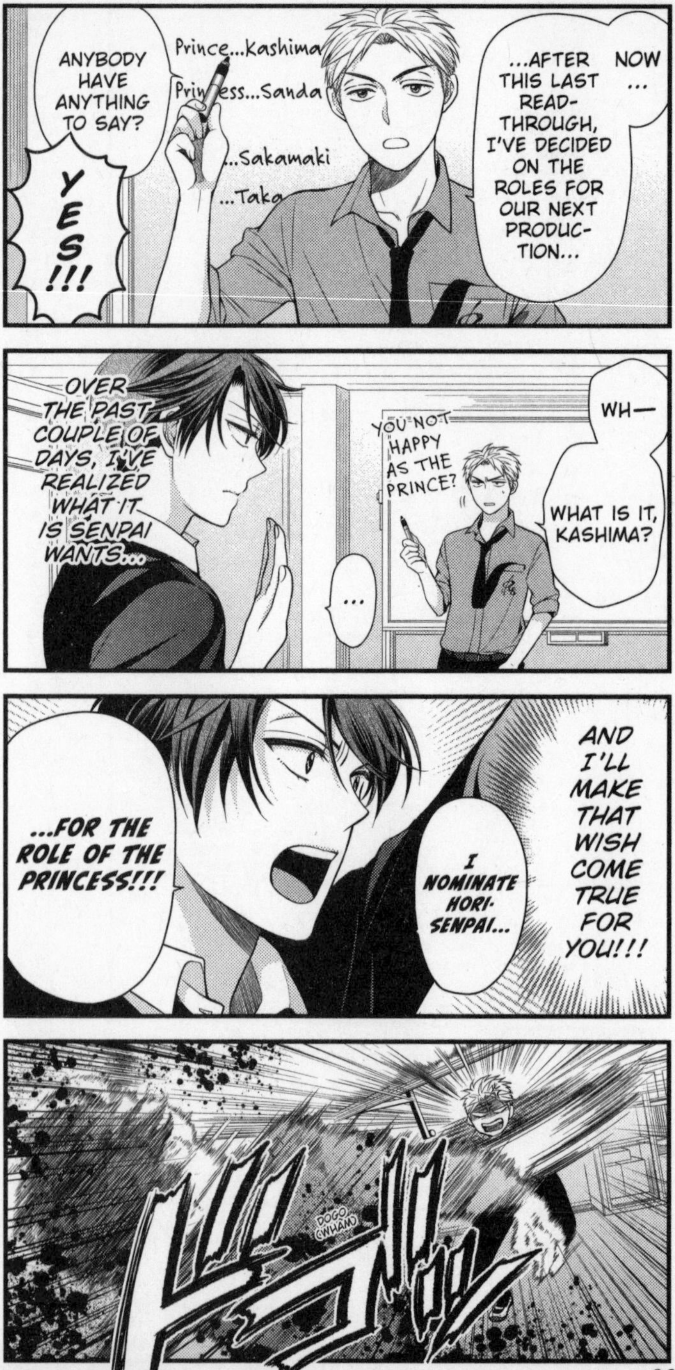
NOW...
...AFTER THIS LAST READ-THROUGH, I'VE DECIDED ON THE ROLES FOR OUR NEXT PRODUCTION...
Prince...Kashima
...Sanda
...Sakamaki
...Taka
ANYBODY HAVE ANYTHING TO SAY?
YES!!!
WH—
WHAT IS IT, KASHIMA?
YOU NOT HAPPY AS THE PRINCE?
...
OVER THE PAST COUPLE OF DAYS, I'VE REALIZED WHAT IT IS SENPAI WANTS...
AND I'LL MAKE THAT WISH COME TRUE FOR YOU!!!
I NOMINATE HORI-SENPAI...
...FOR THE ROLE OF THE PRINCESS!!!
DOGO (WHAM)

THE RESULTS OF HER PLAN TO GAIN FAVOR

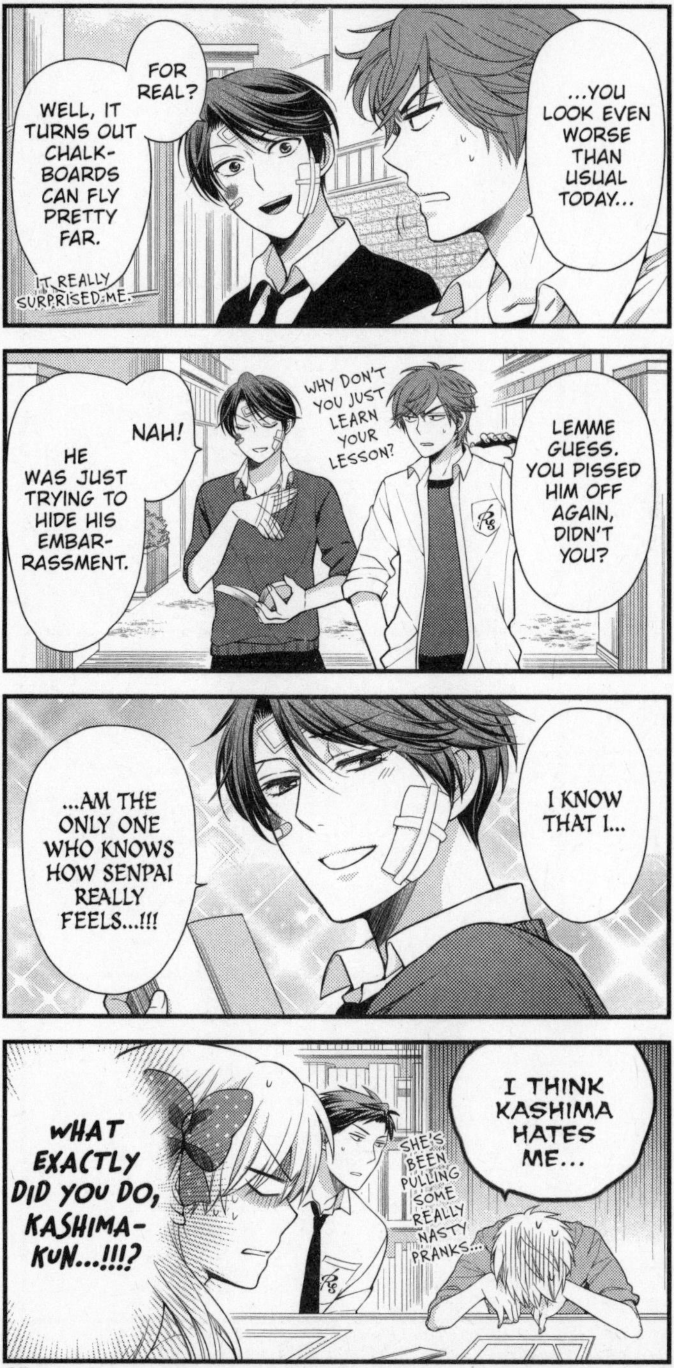

...YOU LOOK EVEN WORSE THAN USUAL TODAY...
FOR REAL?
WELL, IT TURNS OUT CHALKBOARDS CAN FLY PRETTY FAR.
IT REALLY SURPRISED ME.
LEMME GUESS. YOU PISSED HIM OFF AGAIN, DIDN'T YOU?
WHY DON'T YOU JUST LEARN YOUR LESSON?
NAH!
HE WAS JUST TRYING TO HIDE HIS EMBARRASSMENT.
I KNOW THAT I...
...AM THE ONLY ONE WHO KNOWS HOW SENPAI REALLY FEELS...!!!
I THINK KASHIMA HATES ME...
SHE'S BEEN PULLING SOME REALLY NASTY PRANKS...
WHAT EXACTLY DID YOU DO, KASHIMA-KUN...!!!?

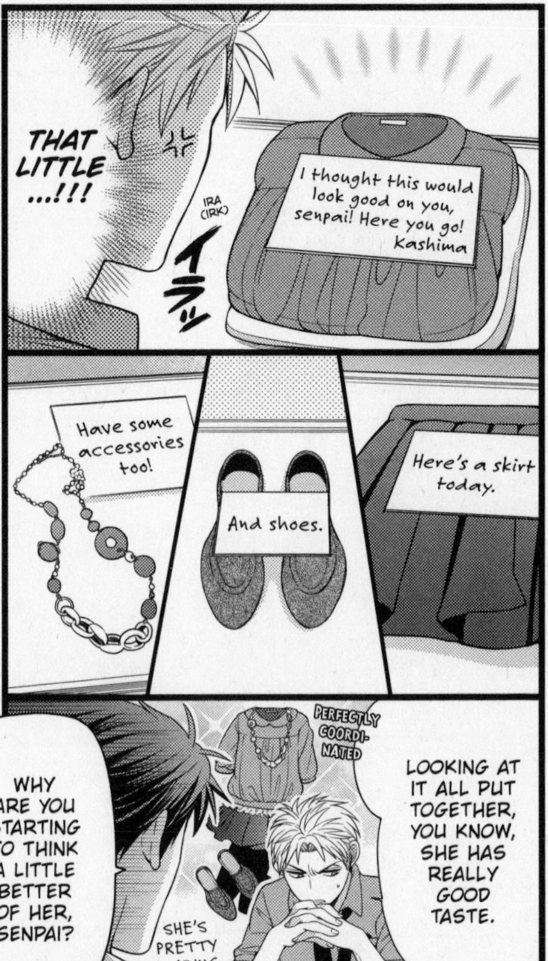
I thought this would look good on you, senpai! Here you go! Kashima
THAT LITTLE ...!!!
IRA (IRK)
Here's a skirt today.
And shoes.
Have some accessories too!
PERFECTLY COORDINATED
LOOKING AT IT ALL PUT TOGETHER, YOU KNOW, SHE HAS REALLY GOOD TASTE.
SHE'S PRETTY AMAZING, ISN'T SHE?
WHY ARE YOU STARTING TO THINK A LITTLE BETTER OF HER, SENPAI?

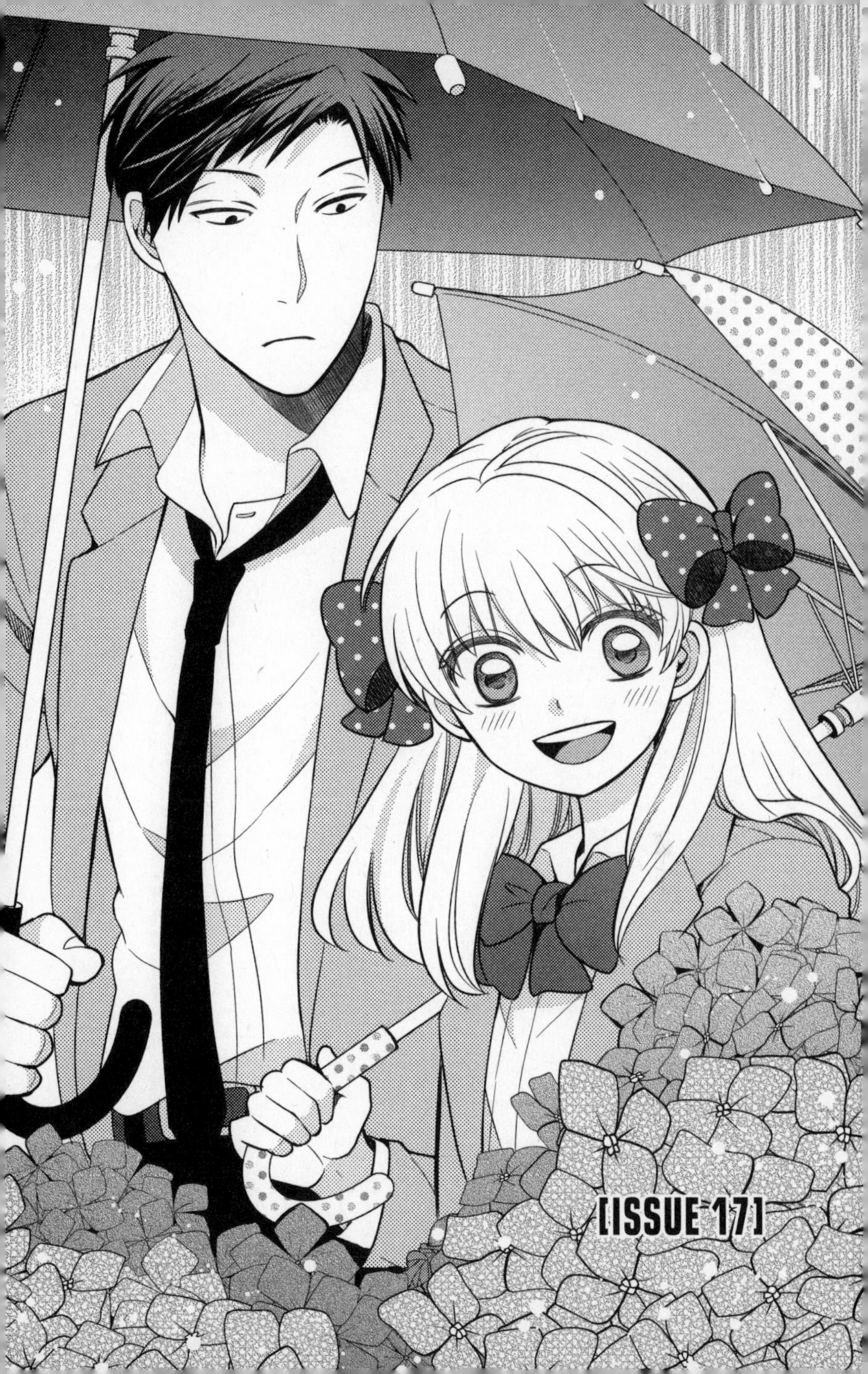
[ISSUE 17]

CARELESS CHIYO

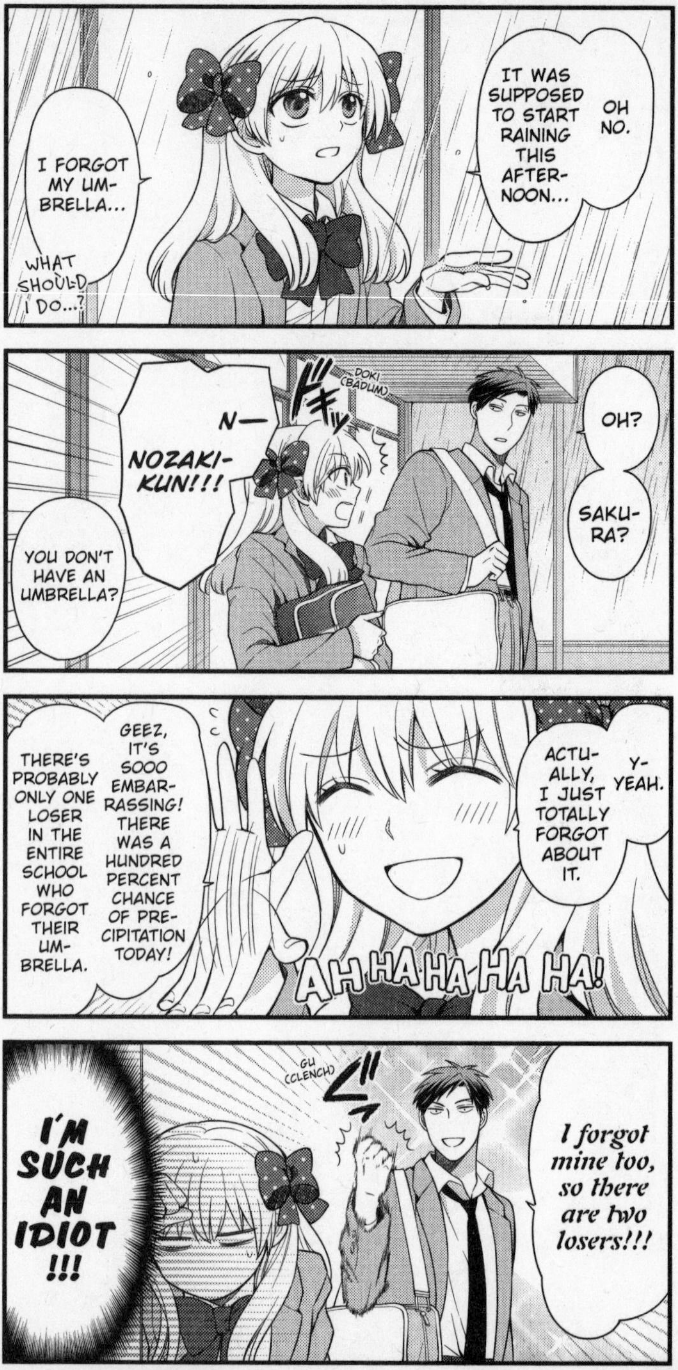
OH NO.
IT WAS SUPPOSED TO START RAINING THIS AFTERNOON...
I FORGOT MY UMBRELLA...
WHAT SHOULD I DO...?
OH?
SAKURA?
DOKI (BADUM)
N— NOZAKI-KUN!!!
YOU DON'T HAVE AN UMBRELLA?
Y-YEAH.
ACTUALLY, I JUST TOTALLY FORGOT ABOUT IT.
AH HA HA HA HA!
GEEZ, IT'S SOOO EMBARRASSING! THERE WAS A HUNDRED PERCENT CHANCE OF PRECIPITATION TODAY!
THERE'S PROBABLY ONLY ONE LOSER IN THE ENTIRE SCHOOL WHO FORGOT THEIR UMBRELLA.
I forgot mine too, so there are two losers!!!
GU (CLENCH)
I'M SUCH AN IDIOT!!!

STRESSING FUNCTIONALITY

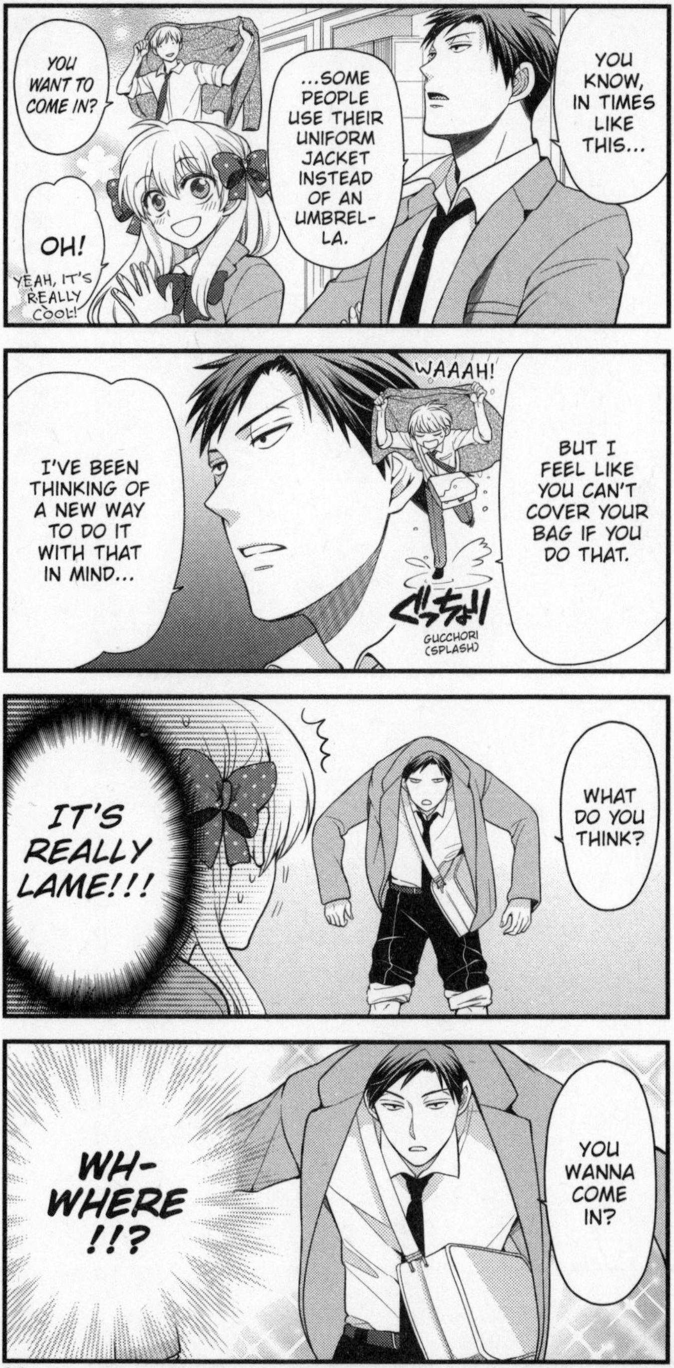

YOU KNOW, IN TIMES LIKE THIS...
...SOME PEOPLE USE THEIR UNIFORM JACKET INSTEAD OF AN UMBREL-LA.
YOU WANT TO COME IN?
OH!
YEAH, IT'S REALLY COOL!
BUT I FEEL LIKE YOU CAN'T COVER YOUR BAG IF YOU DO THAT.
WAAAH!
ぐっちょり
GUCCHORI (SPLASH)
I'VE BEEN THINKING OF A NEW WAY TO DO IT WITH THAT IN MIND...
WHAT DO YOU THINK?
IT'S REALLY LAME!!!
YOU WANNA COME IN?
WH-WHERE!!?

SHE TRIED GOING IN

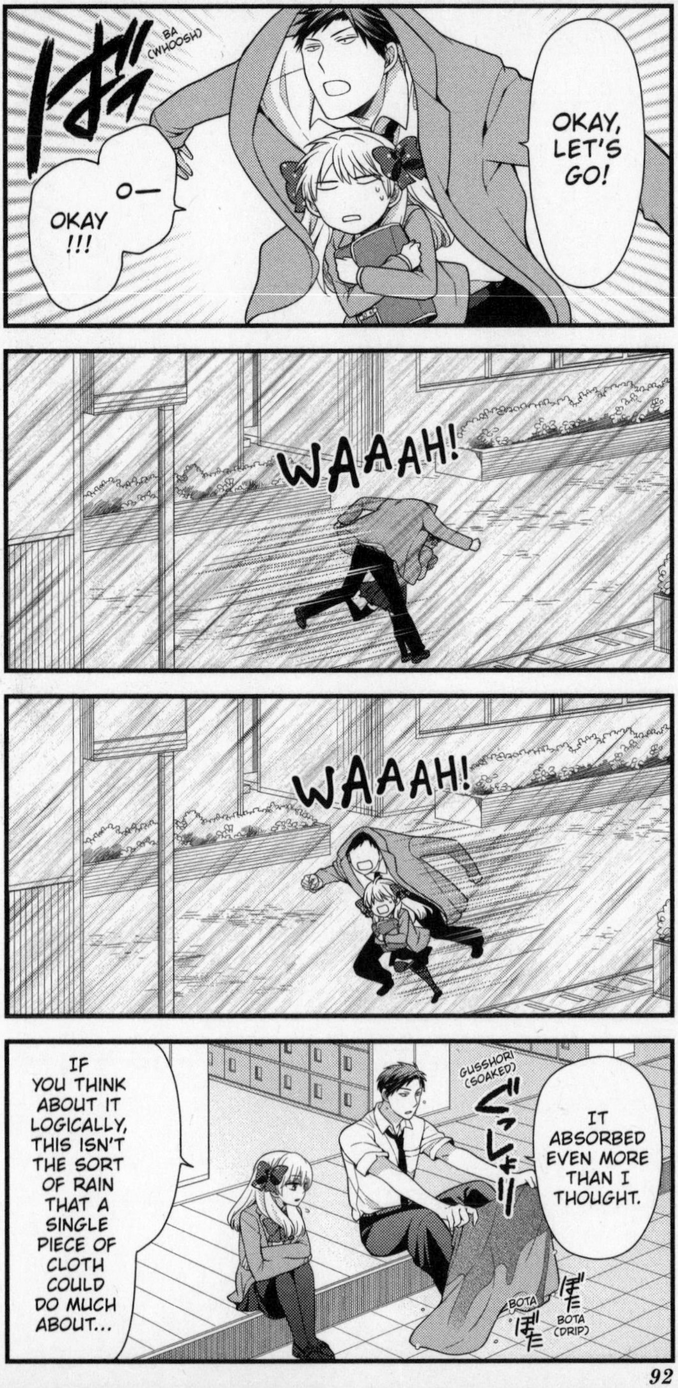

OKAY, LET'S GO!
BA (WHOOSH)
O— OKAY!!!
WAAAH!
WAAAH!
GUSSHORI (SOAKED)
IT ABSORBED EVEN MORE THAN I THOUGHT.
BOTA BOTA (DRIP)
IF YOU THINK ABOUT IT LOGICALLY, THIS ISN'T THE SORT OF RAIN THAT A SINGLE PIECE OF CLOTH COULD DO MUCH ABOUT...

A HEART-POUNDING☆RAINY DAY SITUATION

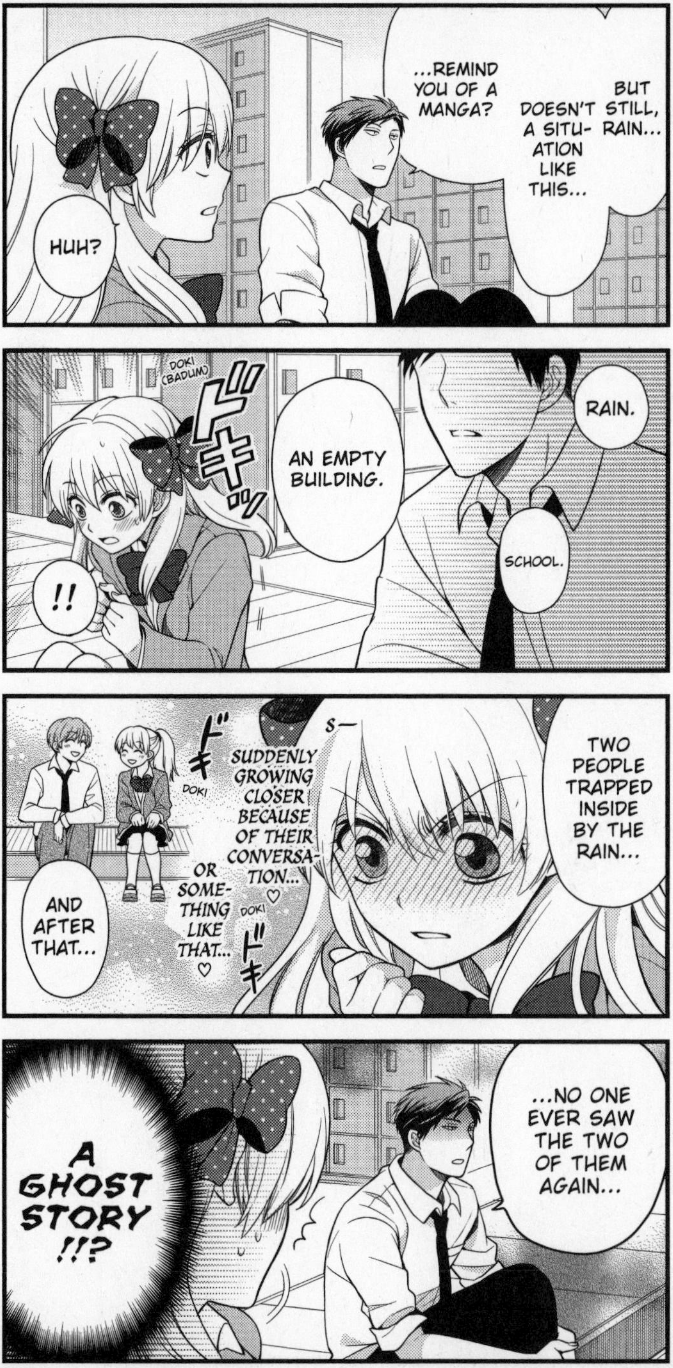
BUT STILL, RAIN...
DOESN'T A SITUATION LIKE THIS...
...REMIND YOU OF A MANGA?
HUH?
RAIN.
SCHOOL.
AN EMPTY BUILDING.
ドキッ
DOKI (BADUM)
!!
TWO PEOPLE TRAPPED INSIDE BY THE RAIN...
S—
SUDDENLY GROWING CLOSER BECAUSE OF THEIR CONVERSATION... ♡
ドキ
DOKI
OR SOMETHING LIKE THAT... ♡
ドキ
DOKI
AND AFTER THAT...
...NO ONE EVER SAW THE TWO OF THEM AGAIN...
A GHOST STORY!!?

FOR EXAMPLE

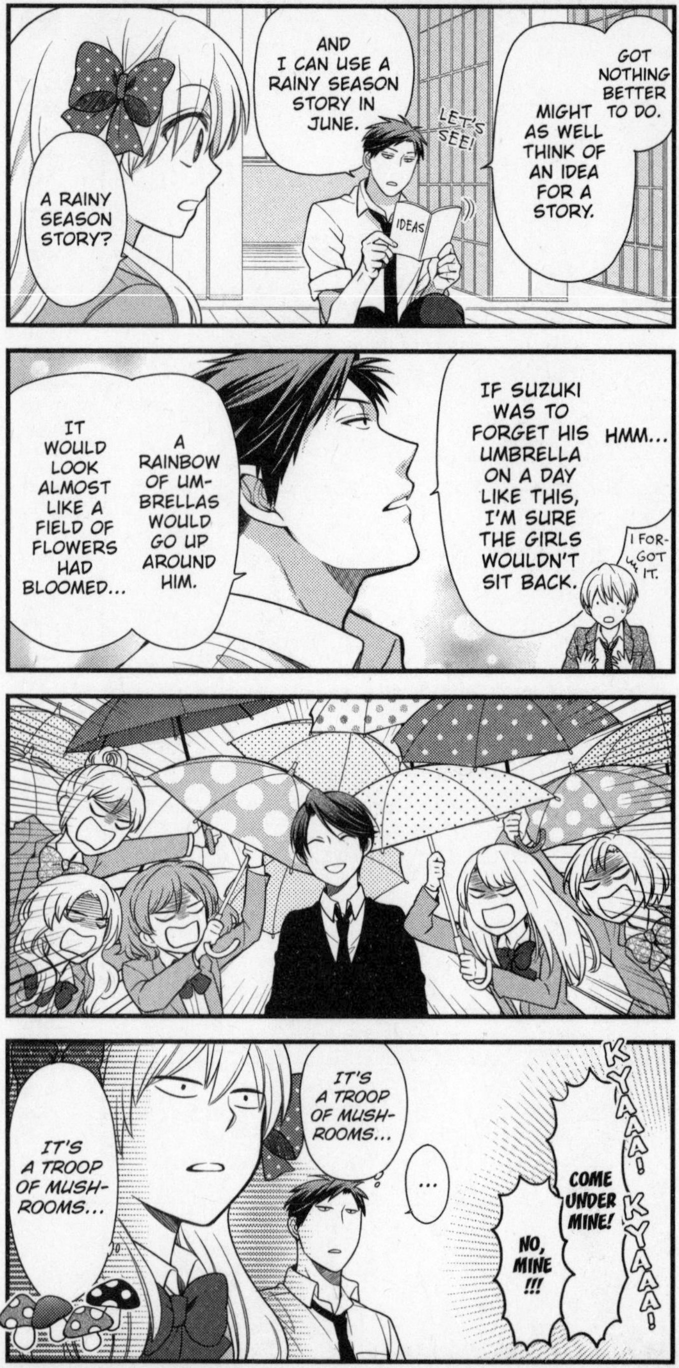

GOT NOTHING BETTER TO DO.
MIGHT AS WELL THINK OF AN IDEA FOR A STORY.
LET'S SEE!
IDEAS
AND I CAN USE A RAINY SEASON STORY IN JUNE.
A RAINY SEASON STORY?
HMM...
IF SUZUKI WAS TO FORGET HIS UMBRELLA ON A DAY LIKE THIS, I'M SURE THE GIRLS WOULDN'T SIT BACK.
I FOR-GOT IT.
A RAINBOW OF UM-BRELLAS WOULD GO UP AROUND HIM.
IT WOULD LOOK ALMOST LIKE A FIELD OF FLOWERS HAD BLOOMED...
KYAAA! KYAAA!
COME UNDER MINE!
NO, MINE!!!
...
IT'S A TROOP OF MUSH-ROOMS...
IT'S A TROOP OF MUSH-ROOMS...

A WILD WAY TO OFFER IT

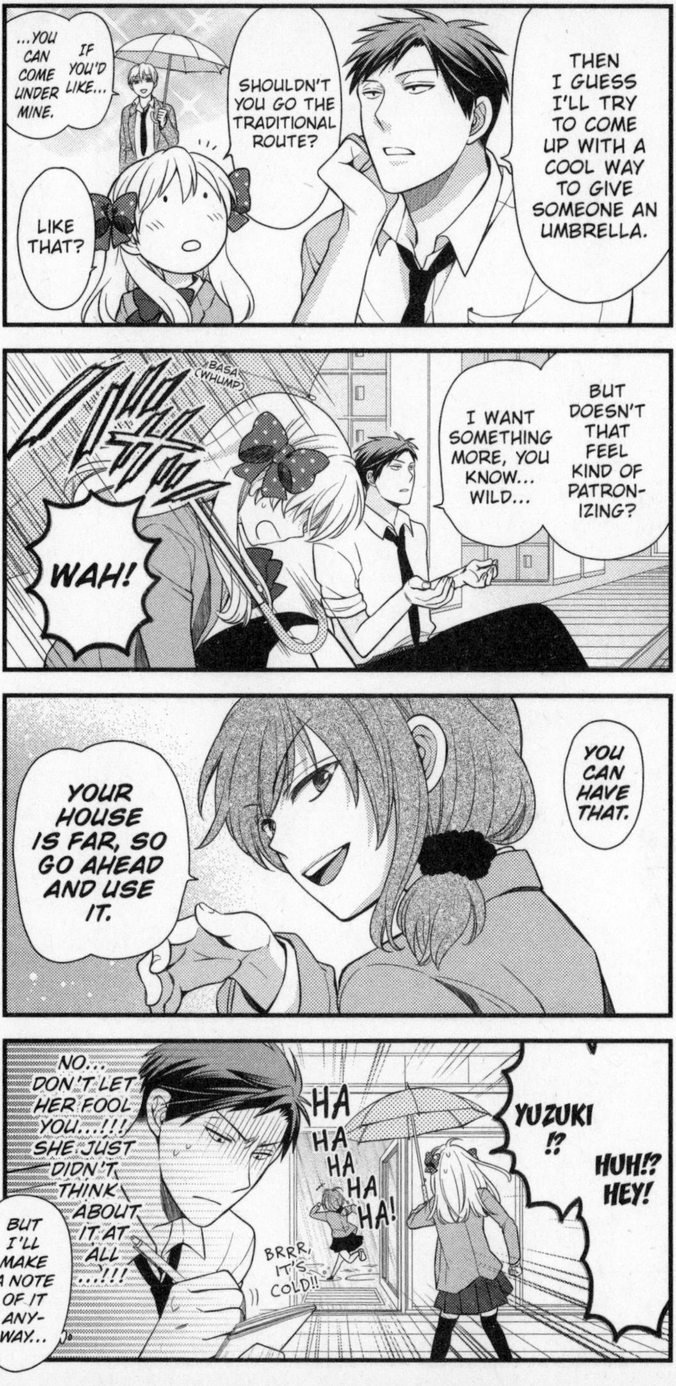
THEN I GUESS I'LL TRY TO COME UP WITH A COOL WAY TO GIVE SOMEONE AN UMBRELLA.
SHOULDN'T YOU GO THE TRADITIONAL ROUTE?
IF YOU'D LIKE...
...YOU CAN COME UNDER MINE.
LIKE THAT?
BUT DOESN'T THAT FEEL KIND OF PATRON-IZING?
I WANT SOMETHING MORE, YOU KNOW... WILD...
BASA (WHUMP)
WAH!
YOU CAN HAVE THAT.
YOUR HOUSE IS FAR, SO GO AHEAD AND USE IT.
YUZUKI!?
HUH!? HEY!
HA HA HA HA HA!
BRRR, IT'S COLD!!
NO... DON'T LET HER FOOL YOU...!!! SHE JUST DIDN'T THINK ABOUT IT AT ALL...!!!
BUT I'LL MAKE A NOTE OF IT ANYWAY...

A PROBLEM OF HEIGHT DIFFERENTIAL

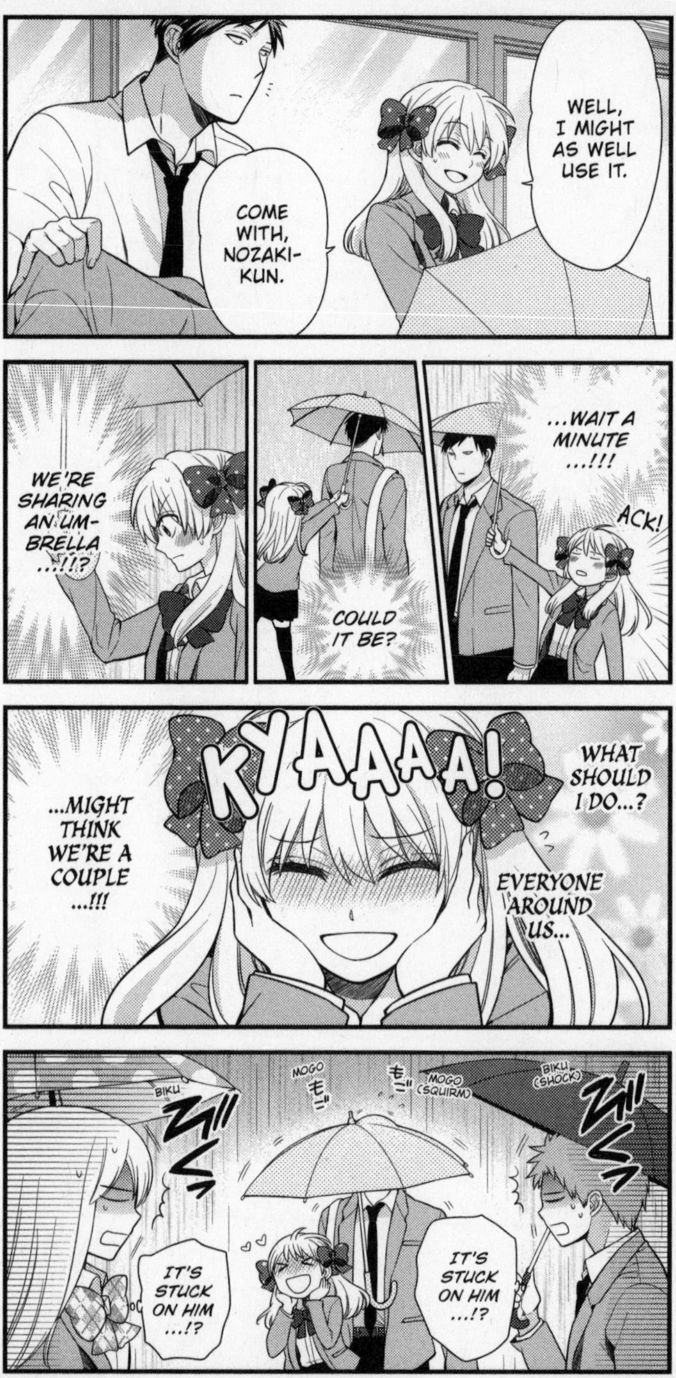
WELL, I MIGHT AS WELL USE IT.
COME WITH, NOZAKI-KUN.
...WAIT A MINUTE ...!!!
ACK!
COULD IT BE?
WE'RE SHARING AN UM-BRELLA ...!!?
WHAT SHOULD I DO...?
KYAAAA!
EVERYONE AROUND US...
...MIGHT THINK WE'RE A COUPLE ...!!!
BIKU (SHOCK)
MOGO (SQUIRM)
もご
MOGO
もご
BIKU
IT'S STUCK ON HIM ...!?
IT'S STUCK ON HIM ...!?

A PROBLEM OF HEIGHT DIFFERENTIAL AND ANGLE

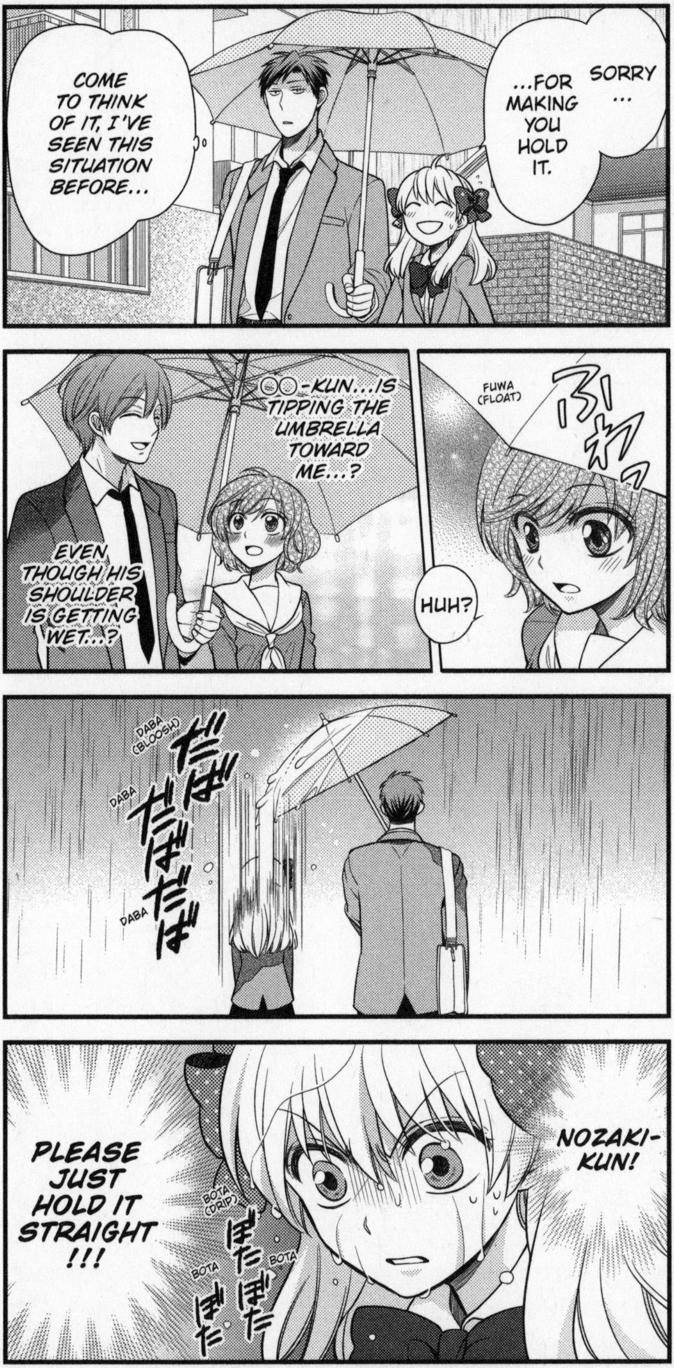
SORRY ...
...FOR MAKING YOU HOLD IT.
COME TO THINK OF IT, I'VE SEEN THIS SITUATION BEFORE...
FUWA (FLOAT)
ふわっ
HUH?
○○-KUN...IS TIPPING THE UMBRELLA TOWARD ME...?
EVEN THOUGH HIS SHOULDER IS GETTING WET...?
DABA (BLOOSH)
だば
DABA
だば
DABA
だば
NOZAKI-KUN!
PLEASE JUST HOLD IT STRAIGHT!!!
BOTA (DRIP)
ぼた
BOTA
ぼた
BOTA
ぼた

I'LL DO EVERYTHING IN MY POWER TO PROTECT YOU

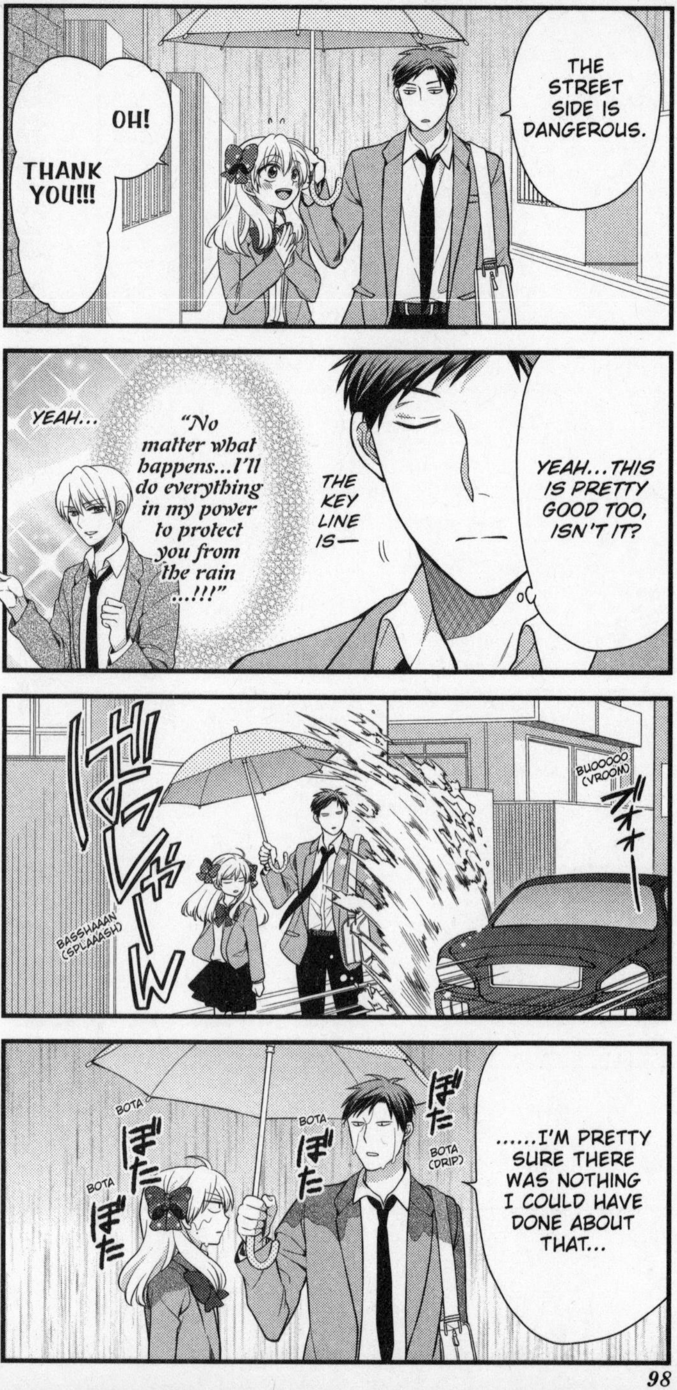
THE STREET SIDE IS DANGEROUS.
OH!
THANK YOU!!!
YEAH...THIS IS PRETTY GOOD TOO, ISN'T IT?
THE KEY LINE IS—
"No matter what happens...I'll do everything in my power to protect you from the rain ...!!!"
YEAH...
ブォォー
BUOOOOO (VROOM)
ばっしゃーん
BASSHAAAN (SPLAAASH)
......I'M PRETTY SURE THERE WAS NOTHING I COULD HAVE DONE ABOUT THAT...
ぼた
BOTA (DRIP)
ぼた
BOTA
ぼた
BOTA
ぼた
BOTA

IT GETS SADDER THE CLOSER WE GET

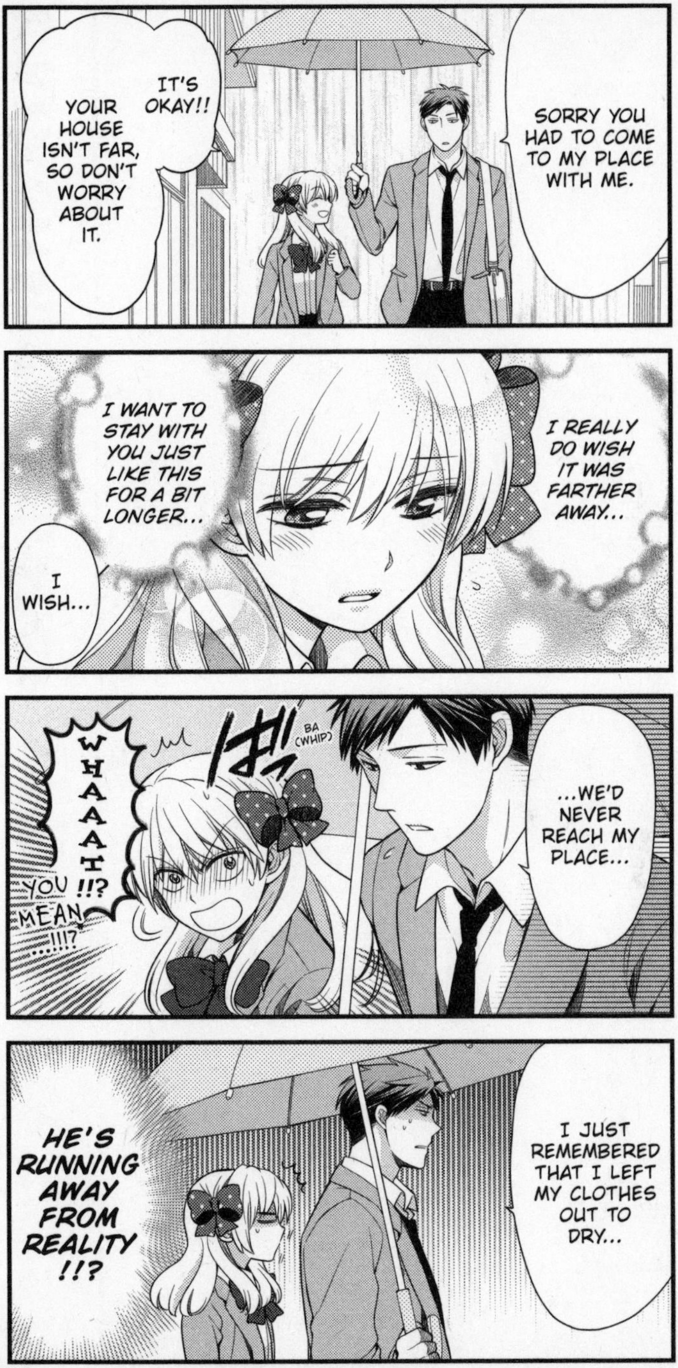
SORRY YOU HAD TO COME TO MY PLACE WITH ME.
IT'S OKAY!!
YOUR HOUSE ISN'T FAR, SO DON'T WORRY ABOUT IT.
I REALLY DO WISH IT WAS FARTHER AWAY...
I WANT TO STAY WITH YOU JUST LIKE THIS FOR A BIT LONGER...
I WISH...
...WE'D NEVER REACH MY PLACE...
BA (WHIP)
WHAAAAT!!?
YOU MEAN......!!!?
I JUST REMEMBERED THAT I LEFT MY CLOTHES OUT TO DRY...
HE'S RUNNING AWAY FROM REALITY!!?

WHEN GIVEN THE CHANCE

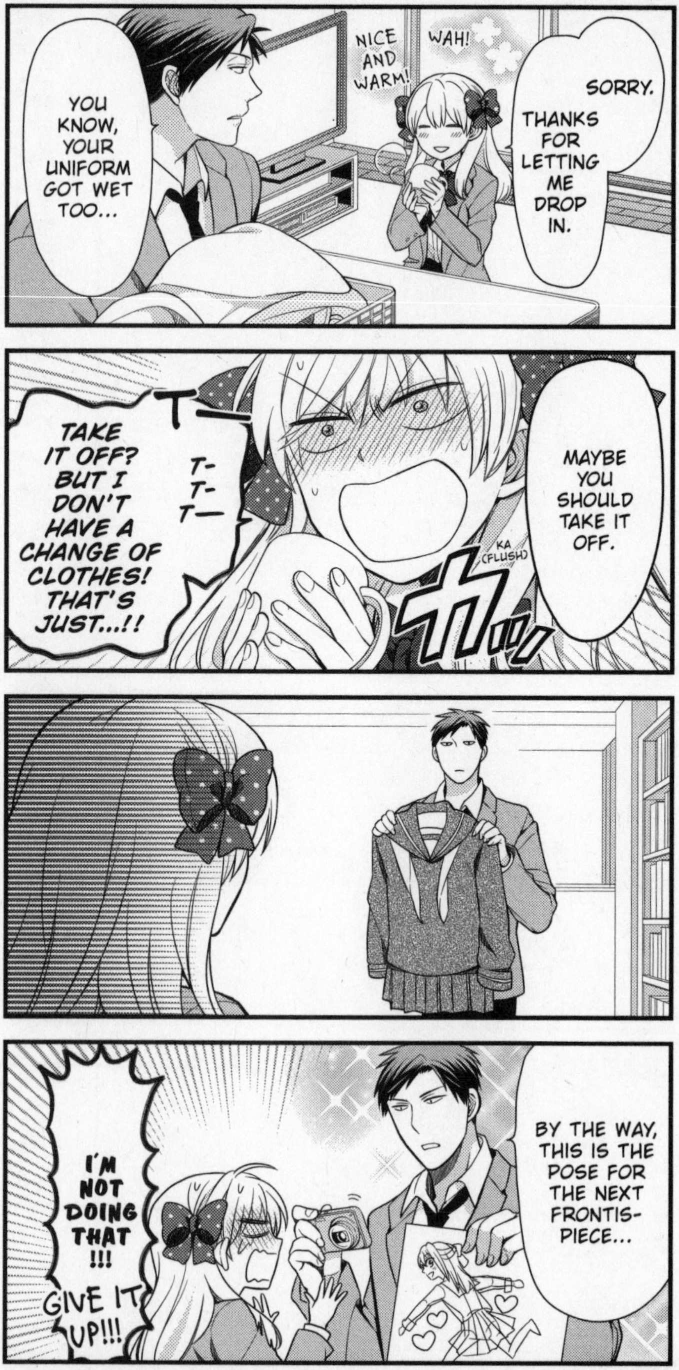
SORRY.
THANKS FOR LETTING ME DROP IN.
WAH!
NICE AND WARM!
YOU KNOW, YOUR UNIFORM GOT WET TOO...
MAYBE YOU SHOULD TAKE IT OFF.
KA (FLUSH)
T- T- T—
TAKE IT OFF? BUT I DON'T HAVE A CHANGE OF CLOTHES! THAT'S JUST...!!
BY THE WAY, THIS IS THE POSE FOR THE NEXT FRONTIS-PIECE...
I'M NOT DOING THAT !!!
GIVE IT UP!!!

THE MOMENT THAT STOLE HIS HEART

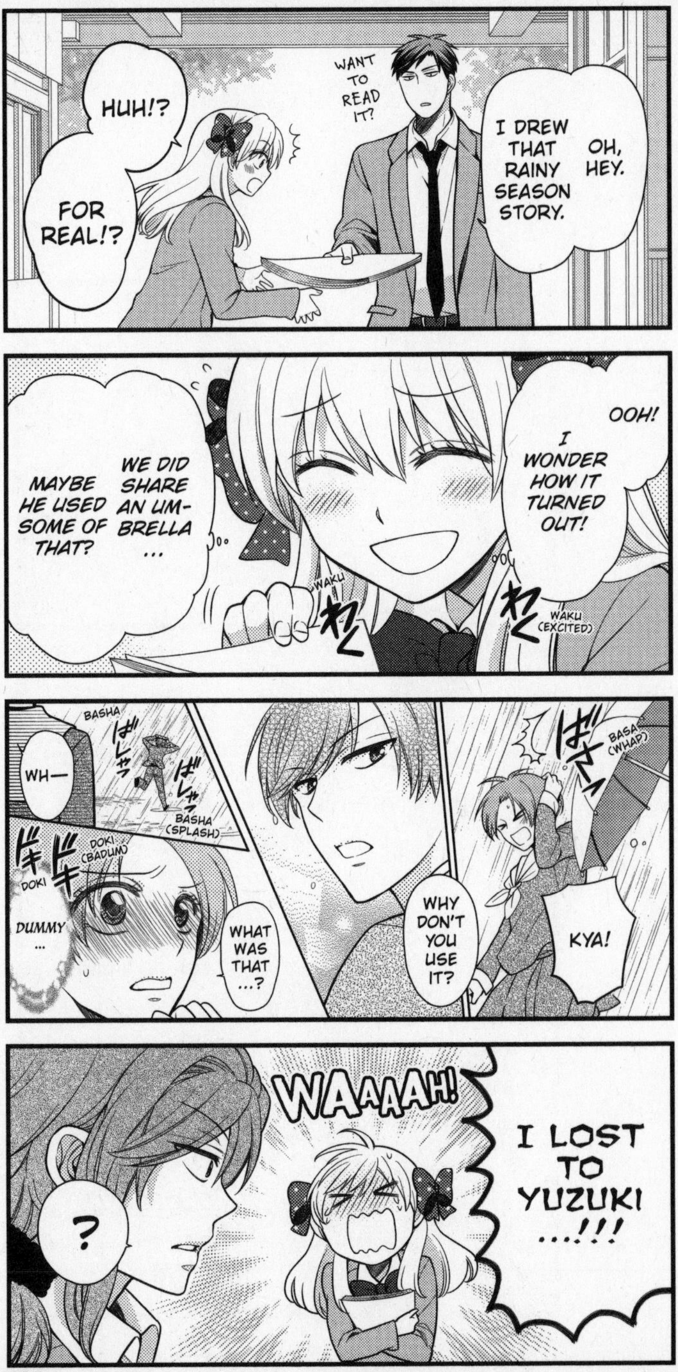

OH, HEY.
I DREW THAT RAINY SEASON STORY.
WANT TO READ IT?
HUH!?
FOR REAL!?
OOH!
I WONDER HOW IT TURNED OUT!
WAKU (EXCITED)
WAKU
WE DID SHARE AN UM-BRELLA ...
MAYBE HE USED SOME OF THAT?
BASA (WHAP)
KYA!
WHY DON'T YOU USE IT?
WHAT WAS THAT ...?
WH—
BASHA
BASHA (SPLASH)
DOKI (BADUM)
DOKI
DUMMY ...
I LOST TO YUZUKI ...!!!
WAAAAH!
?

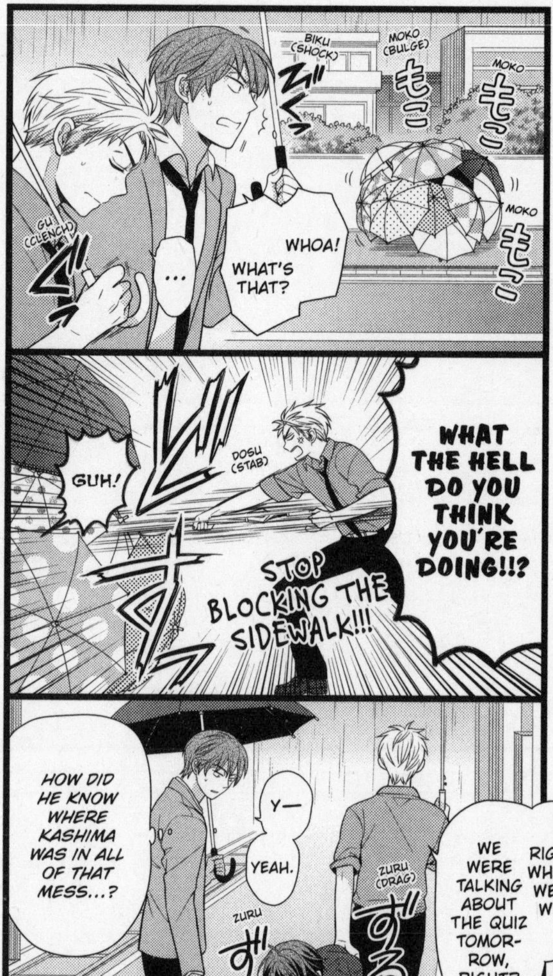
MOKO
もこ
MOKO (BULGE)
もこ
BIKU (SHOCK)
WHOA! WHAT'S THAT?
MOKO
もこ
...
GU (CLENCH)
WHAT THE HELL DO YOU THINK YOU'RE DOING!!?
STOP BLOCKING THE SIDEWALK!!!
DOSU (STAB)
GUH!
RIGHT. WHERE WERE WE?
WE WERE TALKING ABOUT THE QUIZ TOMORROW, RIGHT?
ZURU (DRAG)
ずる
ZURU
ずる
Y—
YEAH.
HOW DID HE KNOW WHERE KASHIMA WAS IN ALL OF THAT MESS...?

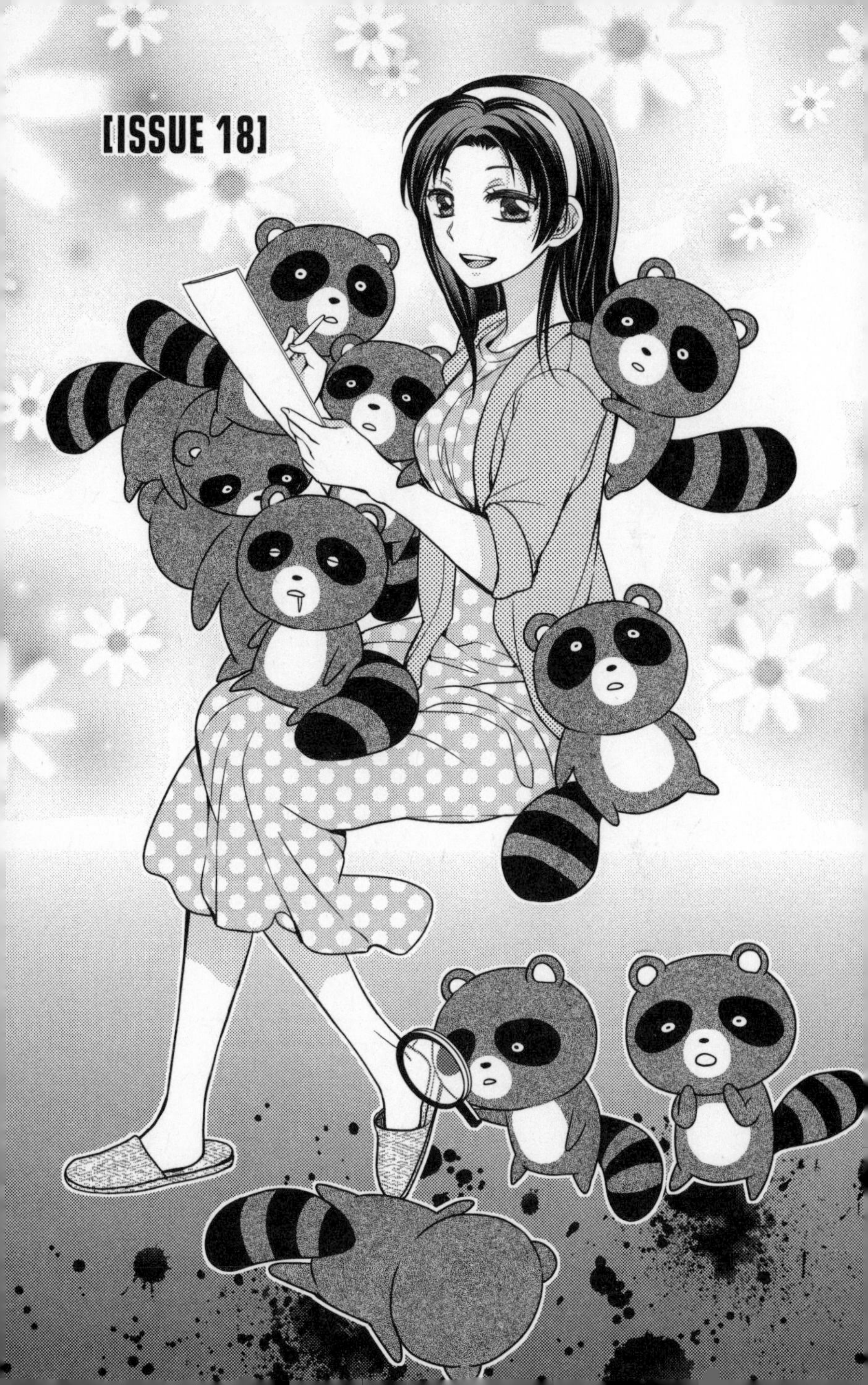
[ISSUE 18]

REAFFIRMING HAPPINESS

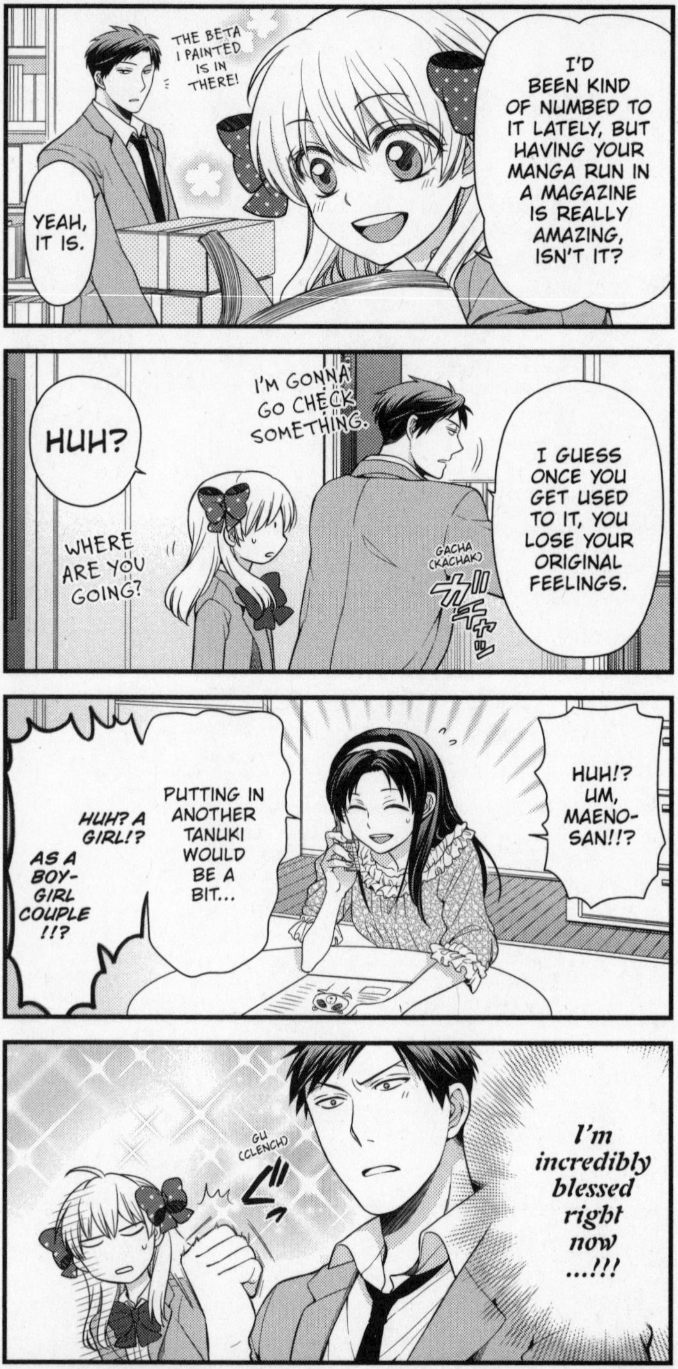
I'D BEEN KIND OF NUMBED TO IT LATELY, BUT HAVING YOUR MANGA RUN IN A MAGAZINE IS REALLY AMAZING, ISN'T IT?
THE BETA I PAINTED IS IN THERE!
YEAH, IT IS.
I GUESS ONCE YOU GET USED TO IT, YOU LOSE YOUR ORIGINAL FEELINGS.
GACHA (KACHAK)
I'M GONNA GO CHECK SOMETHING.
HUH?
WHERE ARE YOU GOING?
HUH!? UM, MAENO-SAN!!?
PUTTING IN ANOTHER TANUKI WOULD BE A BIT...
HUH? A GIRL!?
AS A BOY-GIRL COUPLE!!?
I'm incredibly blessed right now ...!!!
GU (CLENCH)

THAT SPECIAL PERSON

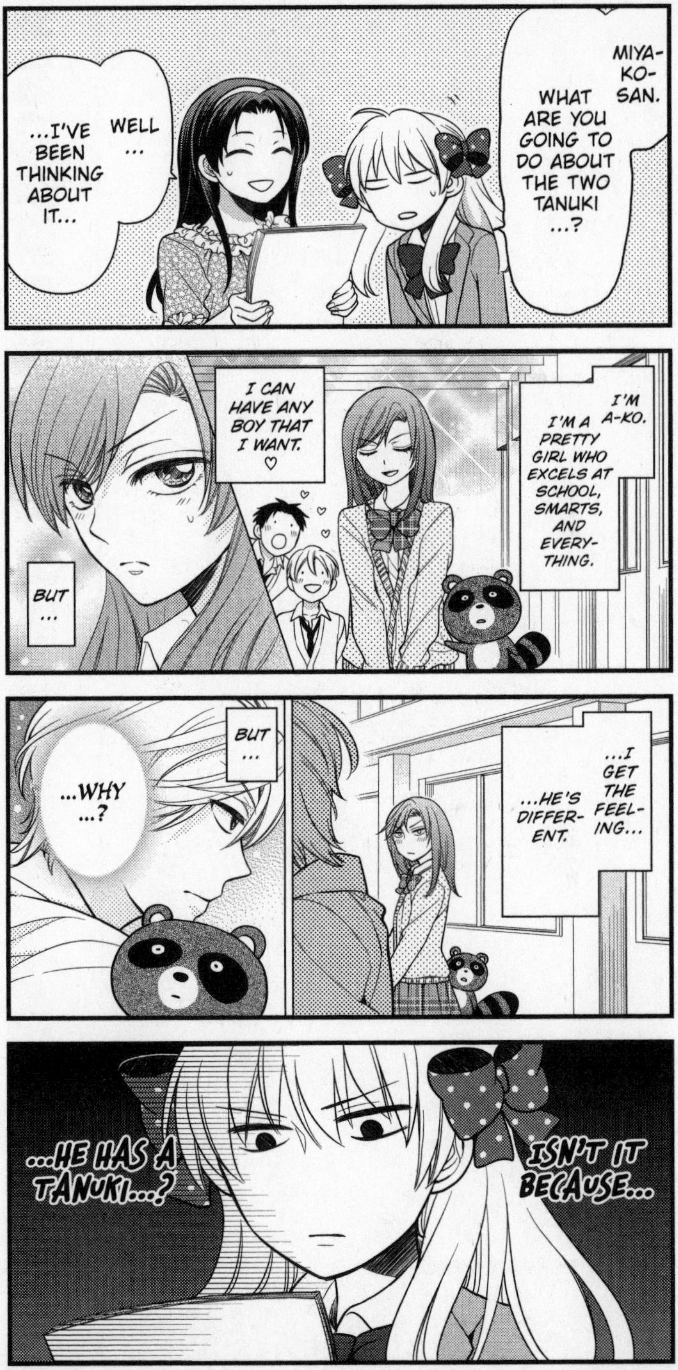
MIYA-KO-SAN. WHAT ARE YOU GOING TO DO ABOUT THE TWO TANUKI ...?
WELL ... ...I'VE BEEN THINKING ABOUT IT...
I'M A-KO. I'M A PRETTY GIRL WHO EXCELS AT SCHOOL, SMARTS, AND EVERYTHING.
I CAN HAVE ANY BOY THAT I WANT. ♡
BUT ...
...I GET THE FEELING... ...HE'S DIFFERENT.
BUT ...
...WHY ...?
ISN'T IT BECAUSE...
...HE HAS A TANUKI...?

A WORLD OF ABSOLUTES

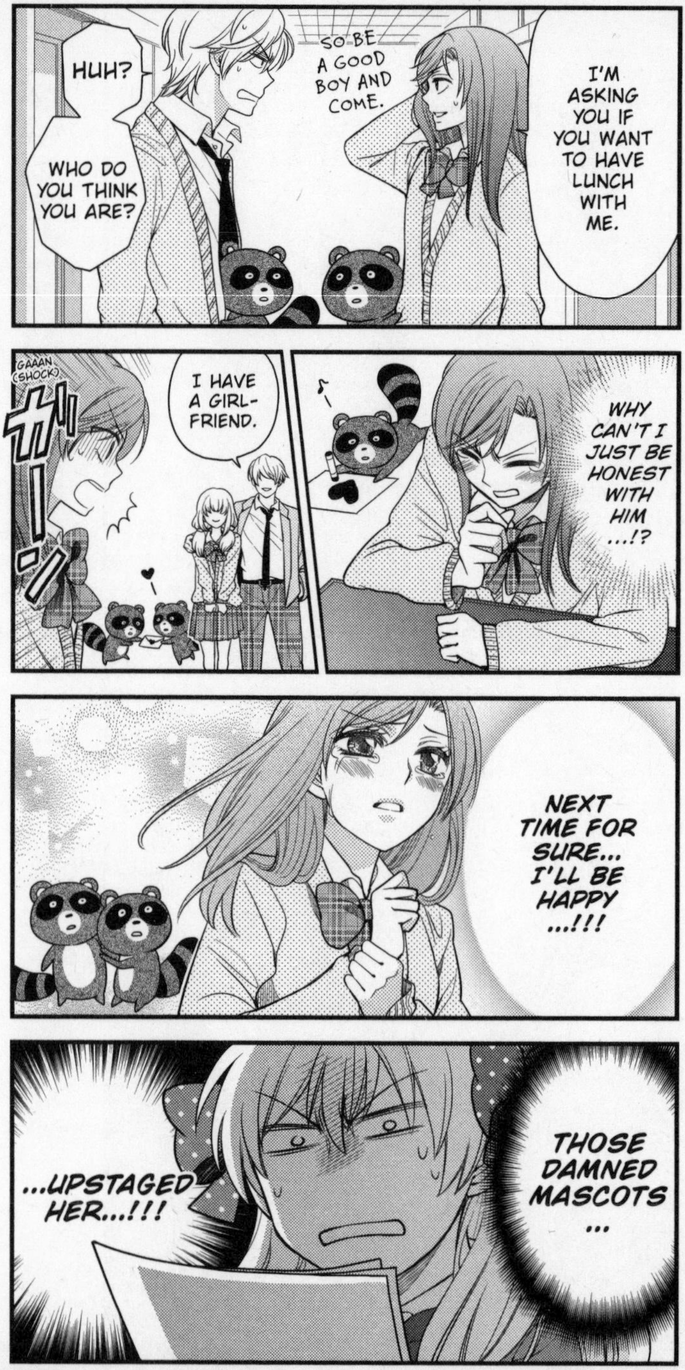
I'M ASKING YOU IF YOU WANT TO HAVE LUNCH WITH ME.
SO BE A GOOD BOY AND COME.
HUH?
WHO DO YOU THINK YOU ARE?
WHY CAN'T I JUST BE HONEST WITH HIM ...!?
I HAVE A GIRL-FRIEND.
GAAAN (SHOCK)
NEXT TIME FOR SURE... I'LL BE HAPPY ...!!!
THOSE DAMNED MASCOTS ...
...UPSTAGED HER...!!!

A DOUBLE ACCIDENT

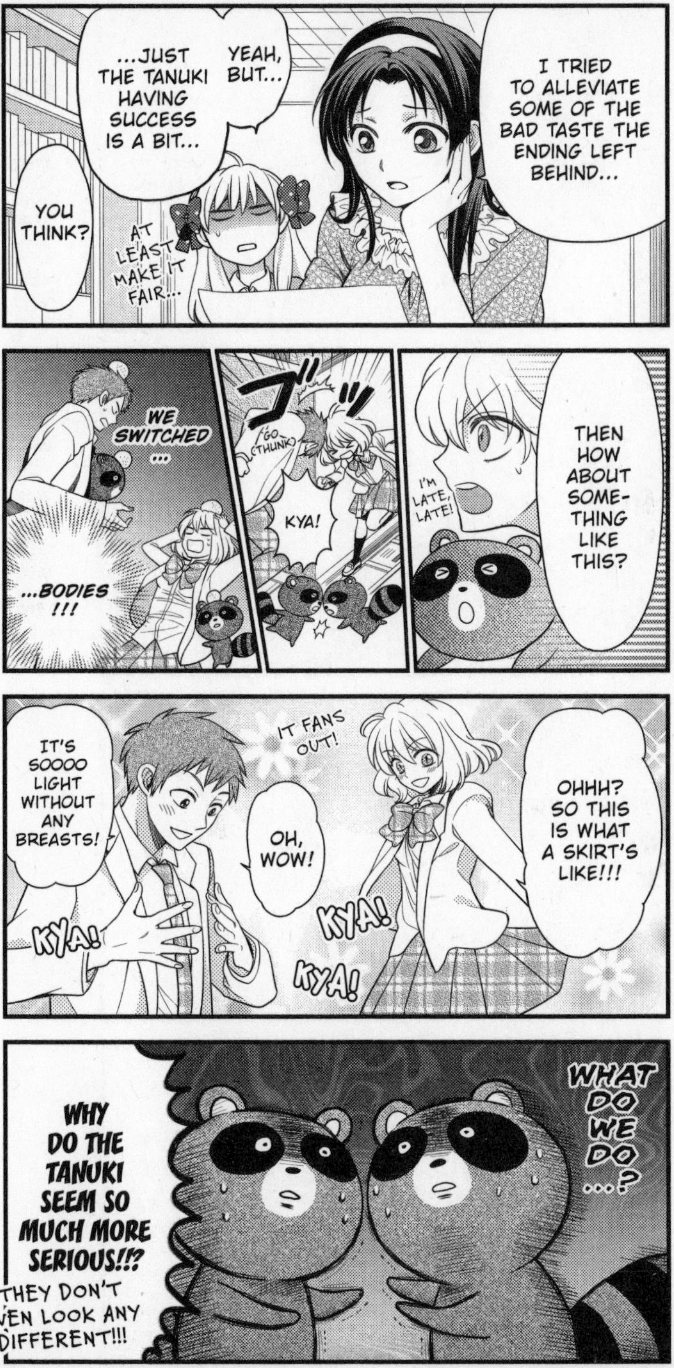
I TRIED TO ALLEVIATE SOME OF THE BAD TASTE THE ENDING LEFT BEHIND...
YEAH, BUT...
...JUST THE TANUKI HAVING SUCCESS IS A BIT...
YOU THINK?
AT LEAST MAKE IT FAIR...
THEN HOW ABOUT SOME-THING LIKE THIS?
I'M LATE, LATE!
ゴッ
(GO-THUNK)
KYA!
WE SWITCHED...
...BODIES!!!
OHHH? SO THIS IS WHAT A SKIRT'S LIKE!!!
IT FANS OUT!
OH, WOW!
IT'S SOOOO LIGHT WITHOUT ANY BREASTS!
KYA!
KYA!
KYA!
WHAT DO WE DO...?
WHY DO THE TANUKI SEEM SO MUCH MORE SERIOUS!!?
THEY DON'T EVEN LOOK ANY DIFFERENT!!!

SHE FOUGHT AND WON

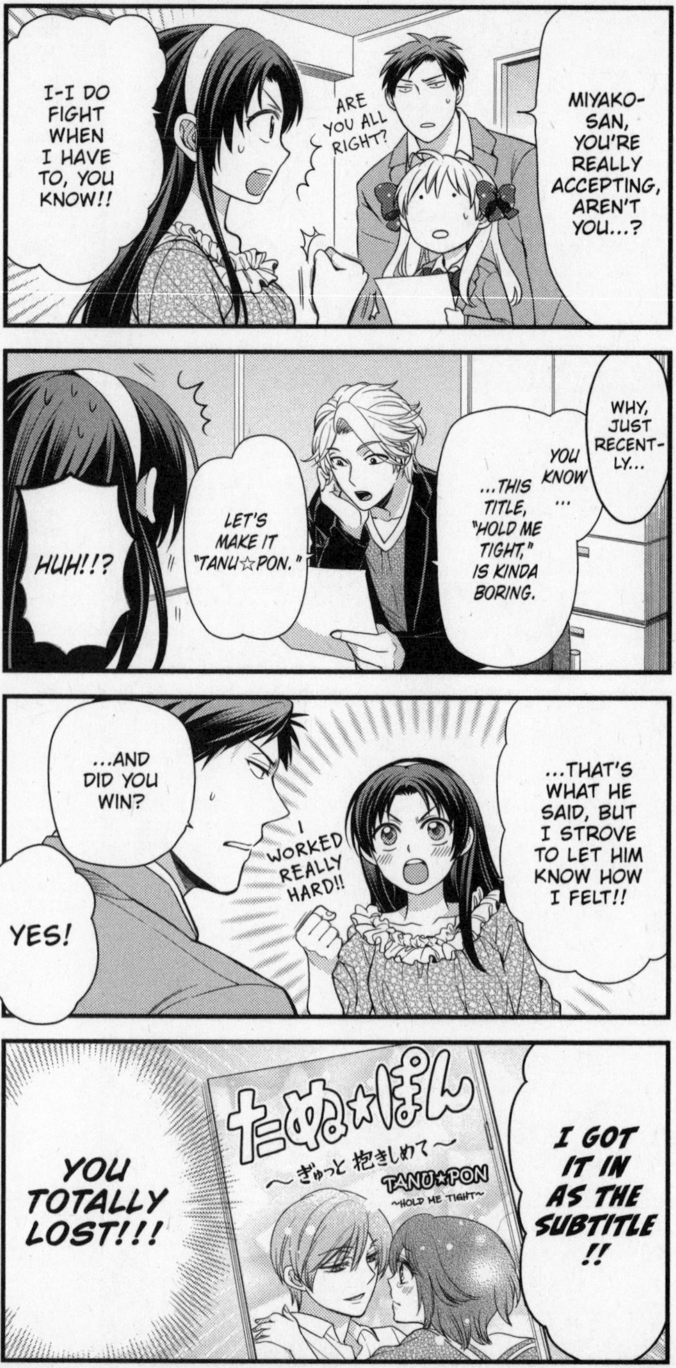
MIYAKO-SAN, YOU'RE REALLY ACCEPTING, AREN'T YOU...?
ARE YOU ALL RIGHT?
I-I DO FIGHT WHEN I HAVE TO, YOU KNOW!!
WHY, JUST RECENTLY...
YOU KNOW...
...THIS TITLE, "HOLD ME TIGHT," IS KINDA BORING.
LET'S MAKE IT "TANU☆PON."
HUH!!?
...THAT'S WHAT HE SAID, BUT I STROVE TO LET HIM KNOW HOW I FELT!!
I WORKED REALLY HARD!!
...AND DID YOU WIN?
YES!
I GOT IT IN AS THE SUBTITLE!!
たぬ★ぽん
〜ぎゅっと 抱きしめて〜
TANU★PON
~HOLD ME TIGHT~
YOU TOTALLY LOST!!!

TI☆TLE

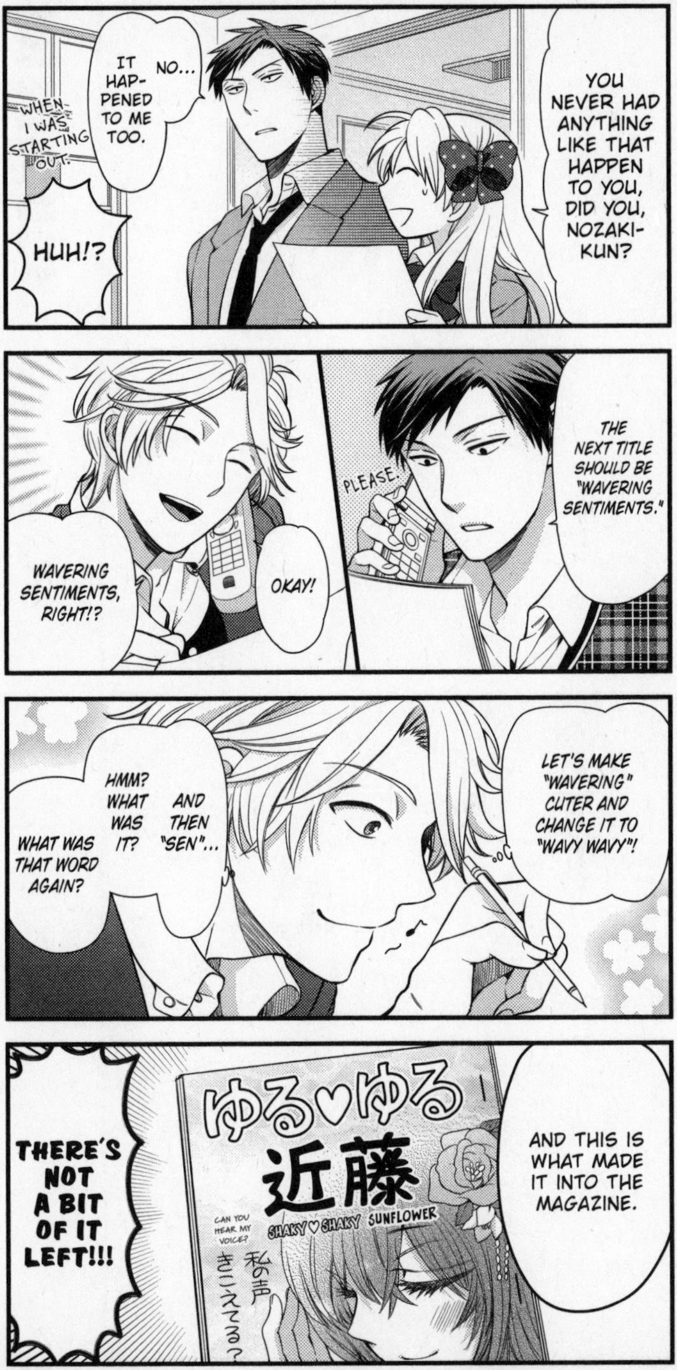

YOU NEVER HAD ANYTHING LIKE THAT HAPPEN TO YOU, DID YOU, NOZAKI-KUN?
NO...
IT HAPPENED TO ME TOO.
WHEN I WAS STARTING OUT.
HUH!?
THE NEXT TITLE SHOULD BE "WAVERING SENTIMENTS."
PLEASE.
OKAY!
WAVERING SENTIMENTS, RIGHT!?
LET'S MAKE "WAVERING" CUTER AND CHANGE IT TO "WAVY WAVY"!
AND THEN "SEN"...
HMM? WHAT WAS IT?
WHAT WAS THAT WORD AGAIN?
AND THIS IS WHAT MADE IT INTO THE MAGAZINE.
ゆる♡ゆる
近藤
SHAKY♡SHAKY SUNFLOWER
CAN YOU HEAR MY VOICE?
私の声きこえてる?
THERE'S NOT A BIT OF IT LEFT!!!

MISPRINTS

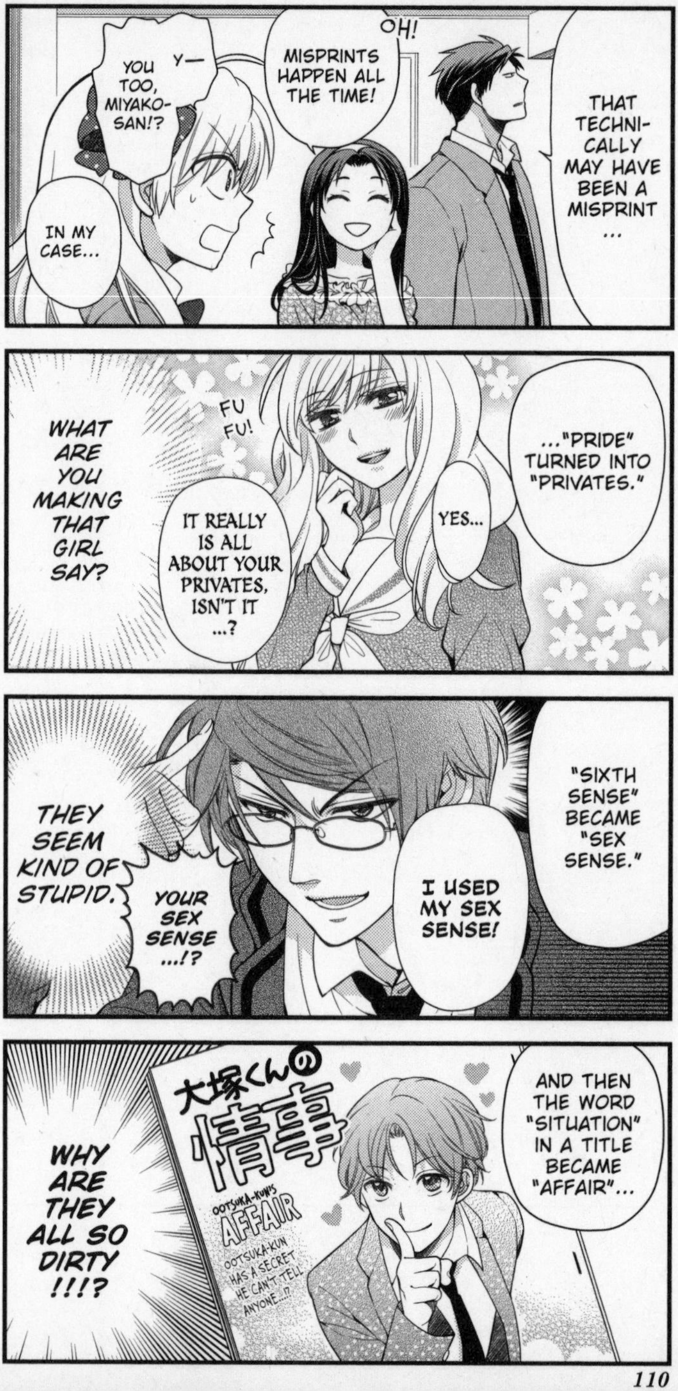
THAT TECHNICALLY MAY HAVE BEEN A MISPRINT ...
OH!
MISPRINTS HAPPEN ALL THE TIME!
Y—
YOU TOO, MIYAKO-SAN!?
IN MY CASE...
..."PRIDE" TURNED INTO "PRIVATES."
YES...
FU FU!
IT REALLY IS ALL ABOUT YOUR PRIVATES, ISN'T IT ...?
WHAT ARE YOU MAKING THAT GIRL SAY?
"SIXTH SENSE" BECAME "SEX SENSE."
I USED MY SEX SENSE!
YOUR SEX SENSE ...!?
THEY SEEM KIND OF STUPID.
AND THEN THE WORD "SITUATION" IN A TITLE BECAME "AFFAIR"...
大塚くんの情事
OOTSUKA-KUN'S AFFAIR
OOTSUKA-KUN HAS A SECRET HE CAN'T TELL ANYONE...!?
WHY ARE THEY ALL SO DIRTY!!!?

I WON'T MAKE ANY EXCUSES

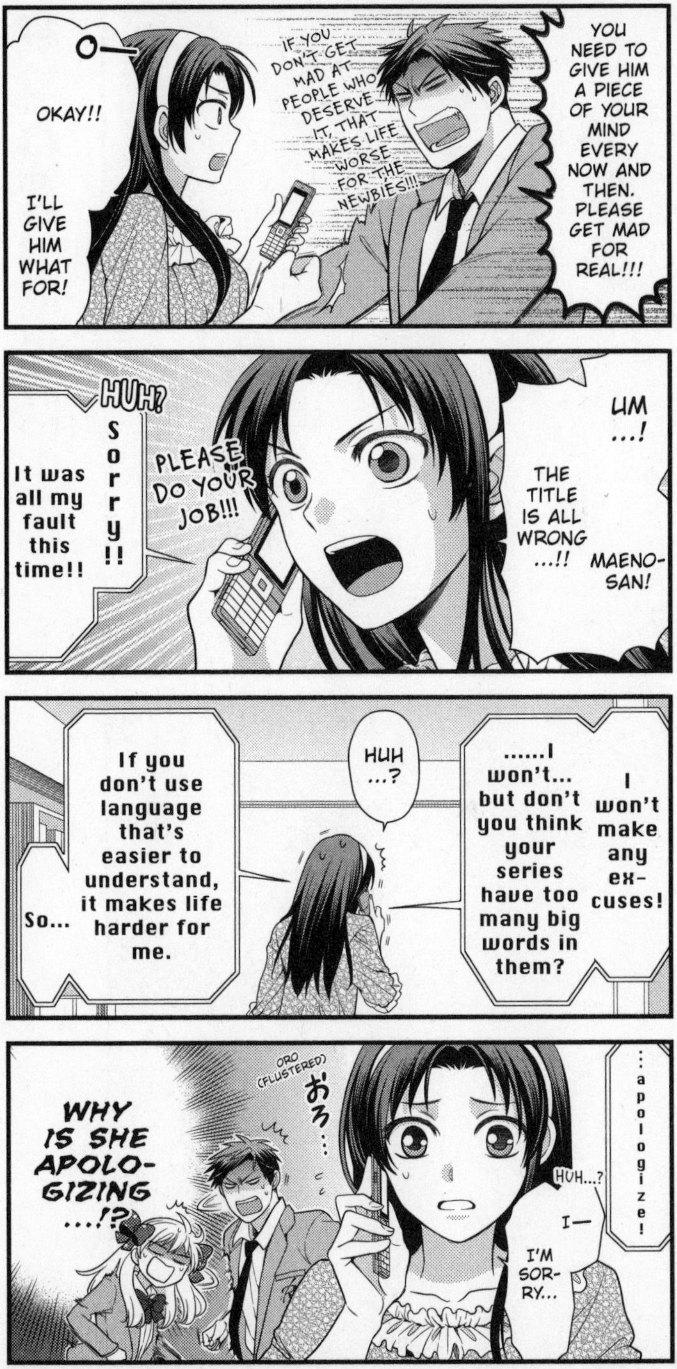
YOU NEED TO GIVE HIM A PIECE OF YOUR MIND EVERY NOW AND THEN. PLEASE GET MAD FOR REAL!!!
IF YOU DON'T GET MAD AT PEOPLE WHO DESERVE IT, THAT MAKES LIFE WORSE FOR THE NEWBIES!!!
O—
OKAY!!
I'LL GIVE HIM WHAT FOR!
UM ...!
MAENO-SAN!
THE TITLE IS ALL WRONG ...!!
PLEASE DO YOUR JOB!!!
HUH?
Sorry!!
It was all my fault this time!!
I won't make any ex-cuses!
......I won't... but don't you think your series have too many big words in them?
HUH ...?
If you don't use language that's easier to understand, it makes life harder for me.
So...
...apologize!
HUH...?
I—
I'M SOR-RY...
ORO (FLUSTERED)
おろ…
WHY IS SHE APOLOGIZING ...!?

※IN THE ORIGINAL, MAENO IS ASKING MIYAKO FOR BOTH EASIER WORDS AND FURIGANA, WHICH ARE OFTEN FOUND IN MANGA NEXT TO KANJI TO HELP MAKE THE PRONUNCIATION AND READING OF THE WORDS EASIER TO UNDERSTAND. THIS IS WHY MAENO MISUNDERSTOOD "SITUATION" AS "AFFAIR" EARLIER.

A SECRET MESSAGE

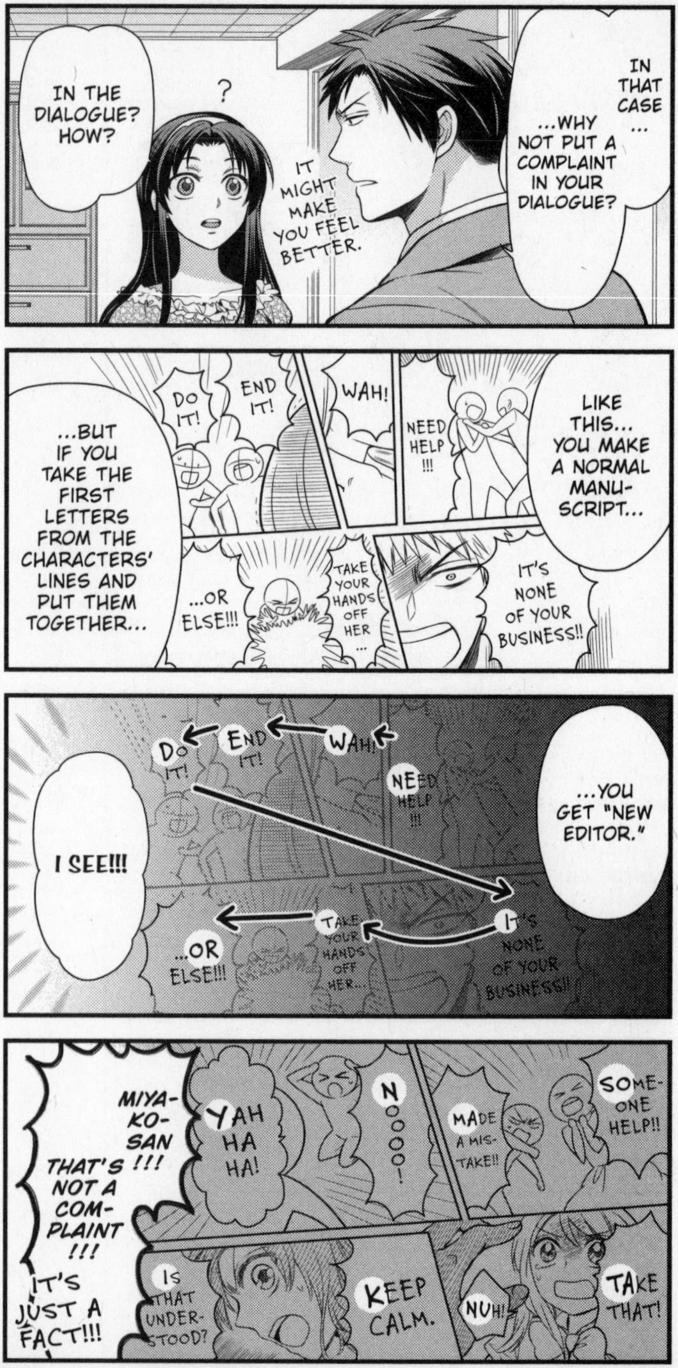

IN THAT CASE ...
...WHY NOT PUT A COMPLAINT IN YOUR DIALOGUE?
IT MIGHT MAKE YOU FEEL BETTER.
?
IN THE DIALOGUE? HOW?
LIKE THIS... YOU MAKE A NORMAL MANU-SCRIPT...
NEED HELP !!!
WAH!
END IT!
DO IT!
IT'S NONE OF YOUR BUSINESS!!
TAKE YOUR HANDS OFF HER ...
...OR ELSE!!!
...BUT IF YOU TAKE THE FIRST LETTERS FROM THE CHARACTERS' LINES AND PUT THEM TOGETHER...
...YOU GET "NEW EDITOR."
WAH!
END IT!
DO IT!
NEED HELP !!!
IT'S NONE OF YOUR BUSINESS!!
TAKE YOUR HANDS OFF HER...
...OR ELSE!!!
I SEE!!!
SOME-ONE HELP!!
MADE A MIS-TAKE!!
NOOOO!
YAH HA HA!
TAKE THAT!
NUH!
KEEP CALM.
IS THAT UNDER-STOOD?
MIYA-KO-SAN !!!
THAT'S NOT A COM-PLAINT !!!
IT'S JUST A FACT!!!

LET'S BE REALISTIC!!

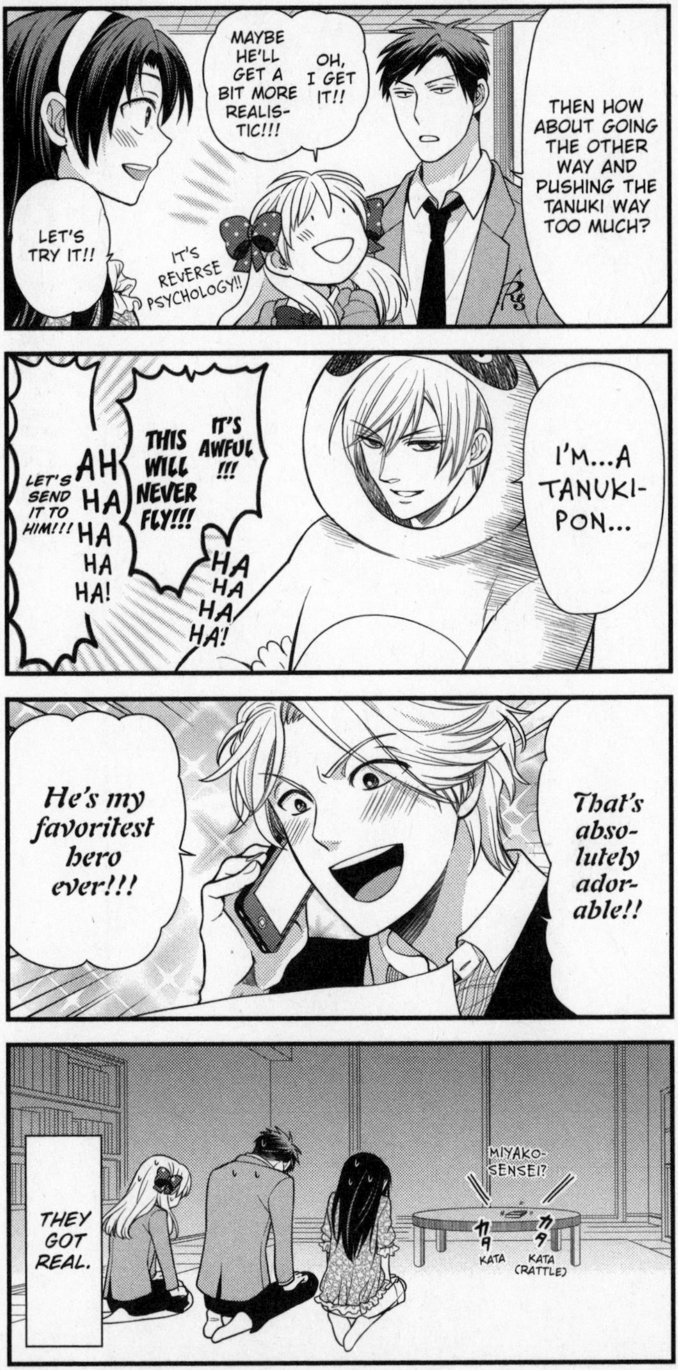
THEN HOW ABOUT GOING THE OTHER WAY AND PUSHING THE TANUKI WAY TOO MUCH?
OH, I GET IT!!
MAYBE HE'LL GET A BIT MORE REALIS-TIC!!!
IT'S REVERSE PSYCHOLOGY!!
LET'S TRY IT!!
I'M...A TANUKI-PON...
HA HA HA HA HA!
IT'S AWFUL!!!
THIS WILL NEVER FLY!!!
AH HA HA HA HA!
LET'S SEND IT TO HIM!!!
That's abso-lutely ador-able!!
He's my favoritest hero ever!!!
MIYAKO-SENSEI?
カタ KATA (RATTLE)
カタ KATA
THEY GOT REAL.

A WONDERFUL HERO

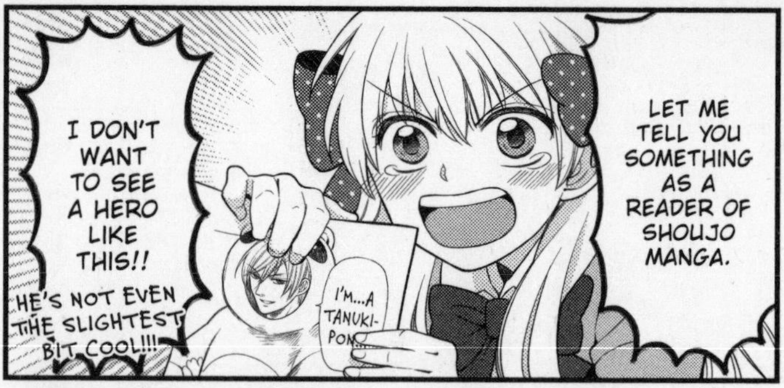
LET ME TELL YOU SOMETHING AS A READER OF SHOUJO MANGA.
I'M...A TANUKI-PON...
I DON'T WANT TO SEE A HERO LIKE THIS!!
HE'S NOT EVEN THE SLIGHTEST BIT COOL!!!

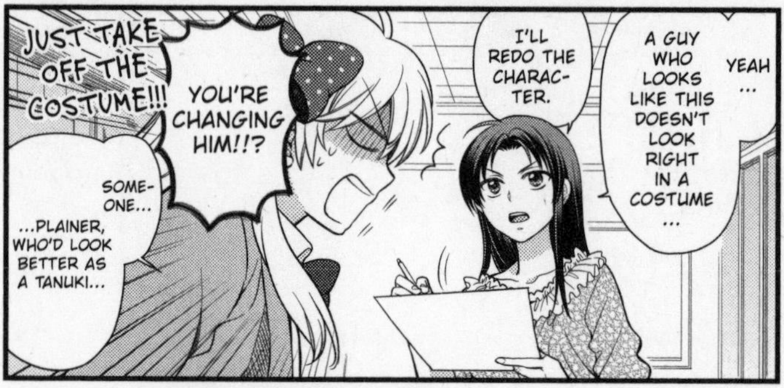
YEAH ...
A GUY WHO LOOKS LIKE THIS DOESN'T LOOK RIGHT IN A COSTUME ...
I'LL REDO THE CHARACTER.
YOU'RE CHANGING HIM!!?
JUST TAKE OFF THE COSTUME!!!
SOME-ONE...
...PLAINER, WHO'D LOOK BETTER AS A TANUKI...

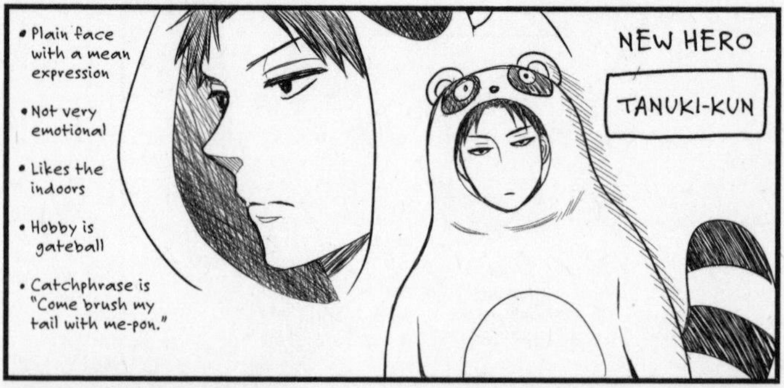
NEW HERO
TANUKI-KUN
• Plain face with a mean expression
• Not very emotional
• Likes the indoors
• Hobby is gateball
• Catchphrase is "Come brush my tail with me-pon."

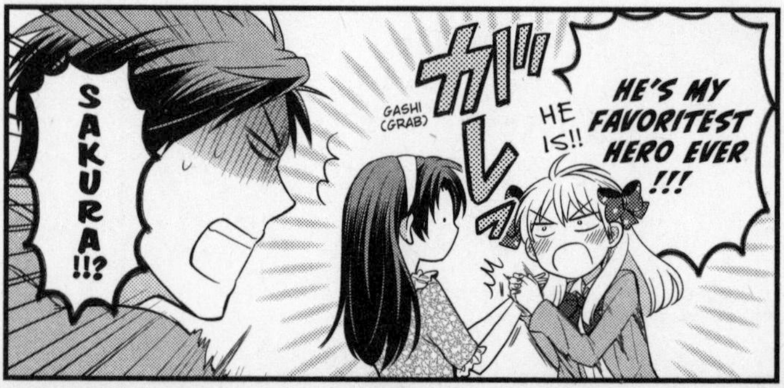
HE'S MY FAVORITEST HERO EVER !!!
HE IS!!
GASHI (GRAB)
SAKURA!!?

※GATEBALL IS A JAPANESE SPORT THAT IS SIMILAR TO CROQUET.

ARE YOU HAPPY?

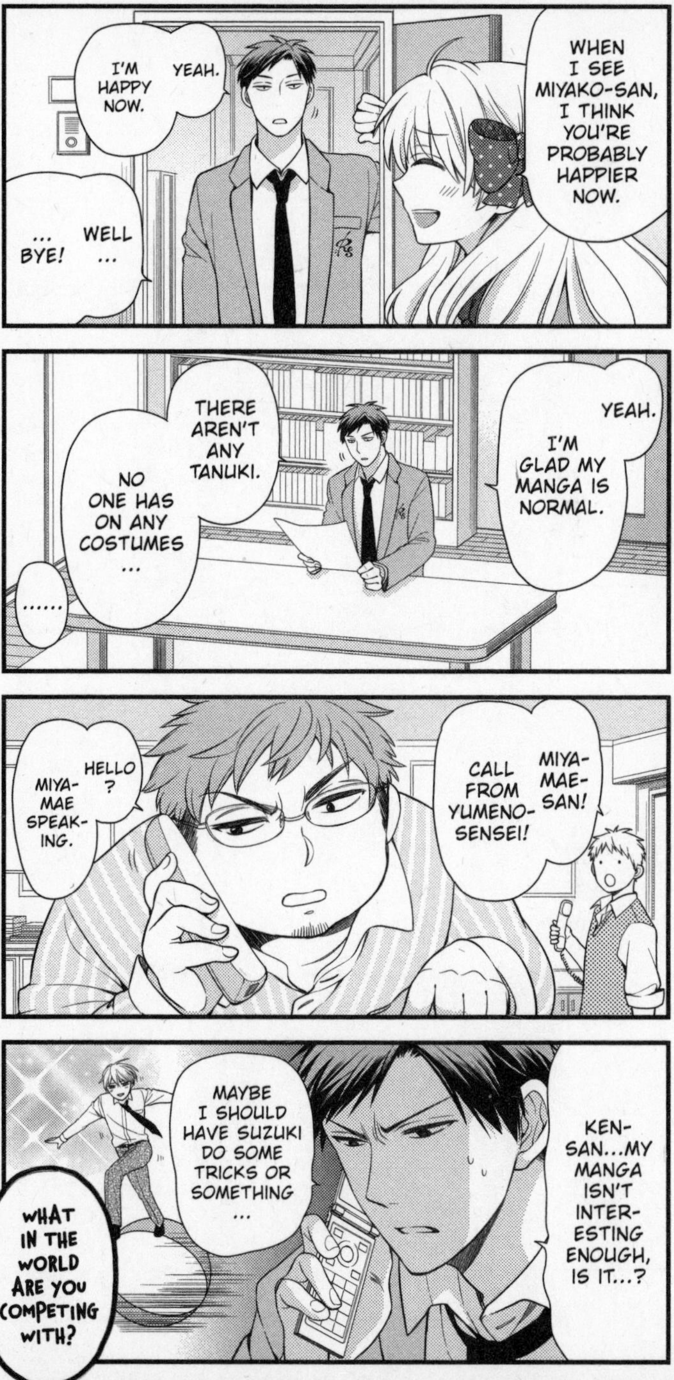

WHEN I SEE MIYAKO-SAN, I THINK YOU'RE PROBABLY HAPPIER NOW.
YEAH.
I'M HAPPY NOW.
WELL ...
... BYE!
YEAH.
I'M GLAD MY MANGA IS NORMAL.
THERE AREN'T ANY TANUKI.
NO ONE HAS ON ANY COSTUMES ...
......
MIYA-MAE-SAN!
CALL FROM YUMENO-SENSEI!
HELLO?
MIYA-MAE SPEAKING.
KEN-SAN...MY MANGA ISN'T INTERESTING ENOUGH, IS IT...?
MAYBE I SHOULD HAVE SUZUKI DO SOME TRICKS OR SOMETHING ...
WHAT IN THE WORLD ARE YOU COMPETING WITH?

SAKIKO YUMENO'S PRIDE

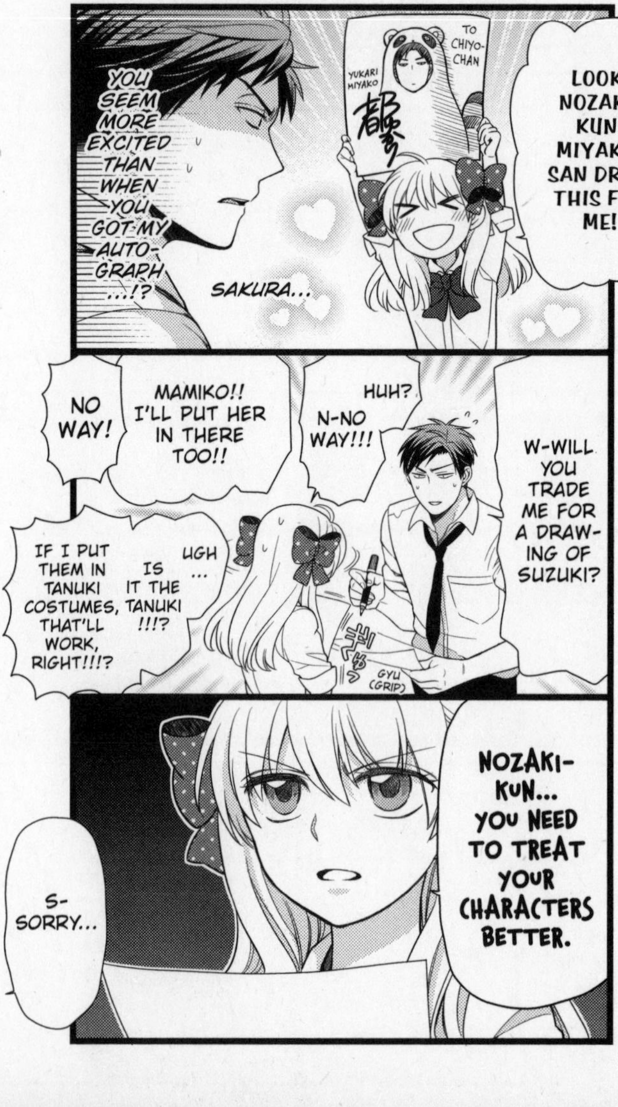

LOOK, NOZAKI-KUN! MIYAKO-SAN DREW THIS FOR ME!
TO CHIYO-CHAN
YUKARI MIYAKO
SAKURA...
YOU SEEM MORE EXCITED THAN WHEN YOU GOT MY AUTO-GRAPH...!?
W-WILL YOU TRADE ME FOR A DRAWING OF SUZUKI?
HUH?
N-NO WAY!!!
MAMIKO!! I'LL PUT HER IN THERE TOO!!
NO WAY!
UGH ...
IS IT THE TANUKI !!!?
IF I PUT THEM IN TANUKI COSTUMES, THAT'LL WORK, RIGHT!!!?
GYU (GRIP)
NOZAKI-KUN... YOU NEED TO TREAT YOUR CHARACTERS BETTER.
S-SORRY...

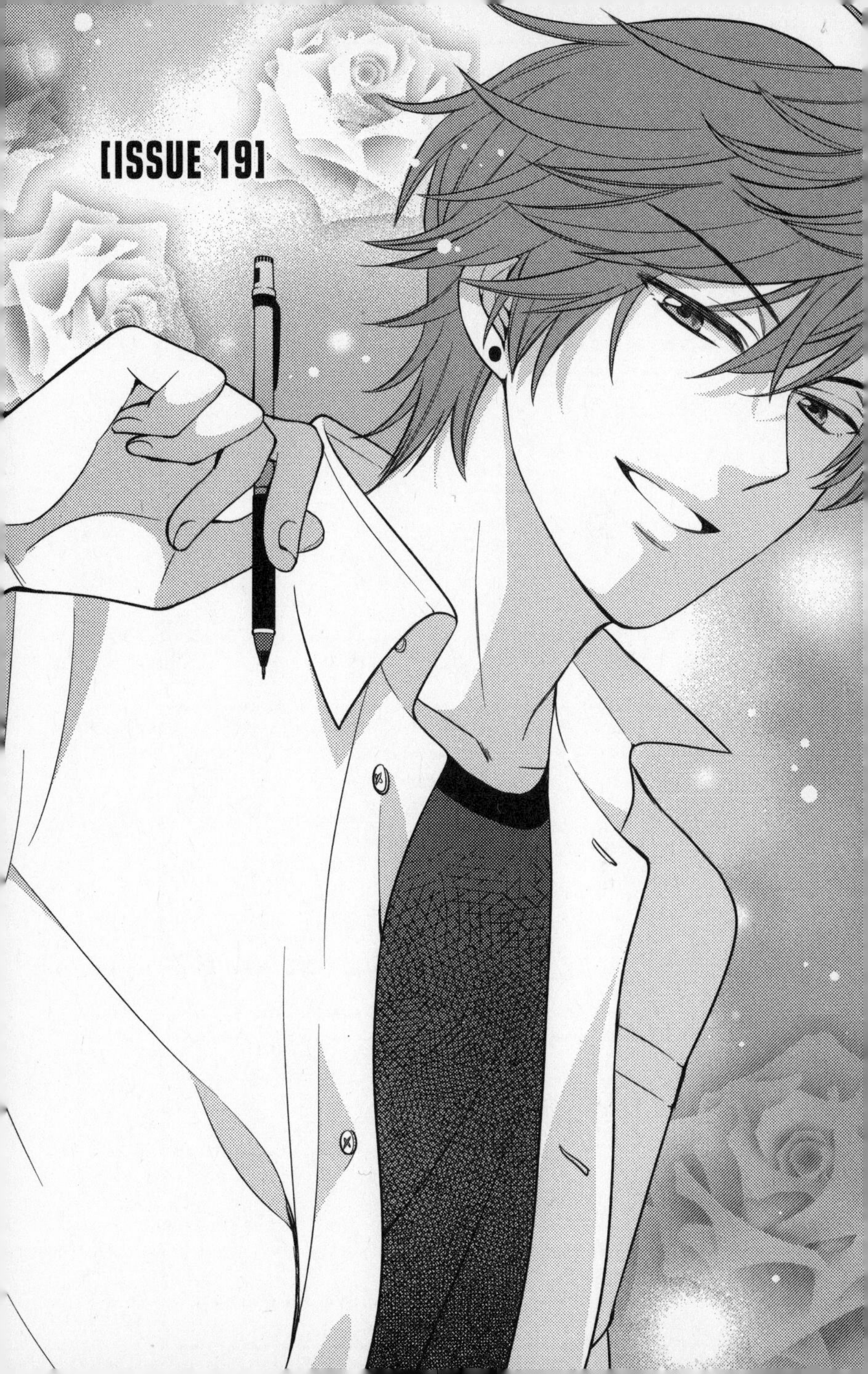
[ISSUE 19]

AS A FRIEND

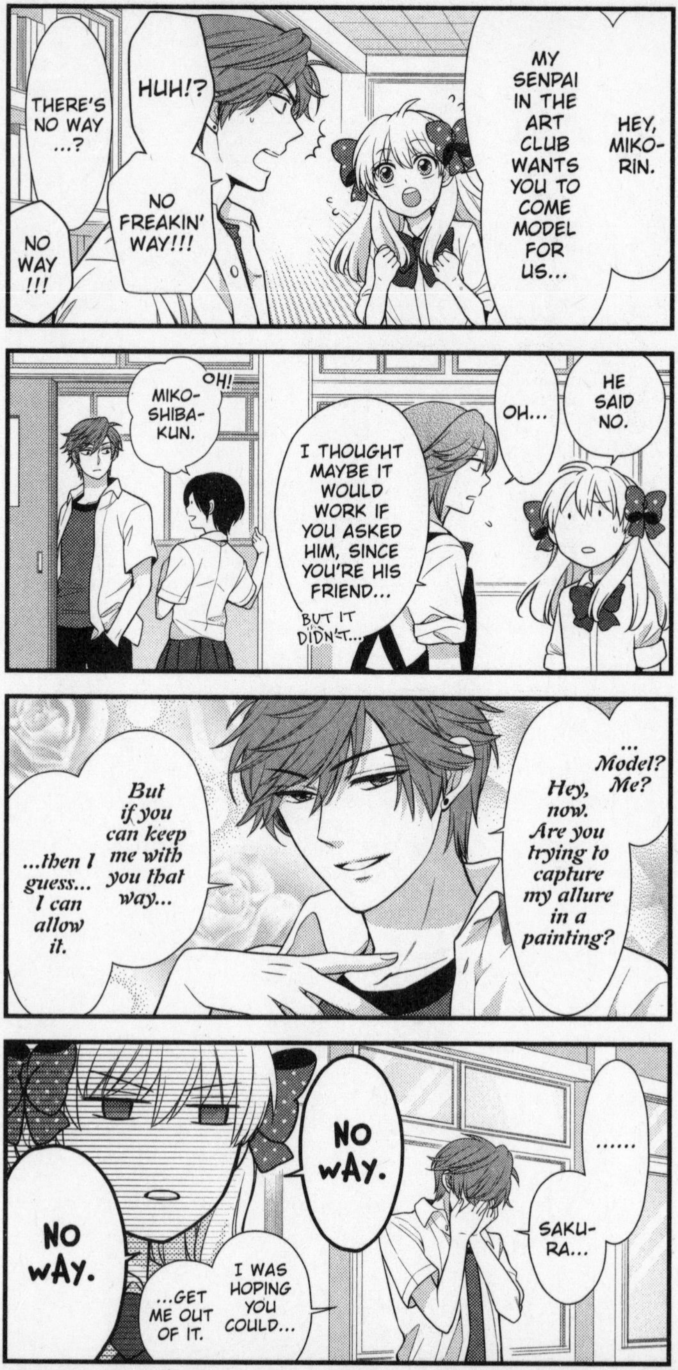
HEY, MIKO-RIN.
MY SENPAI IN THE ART CLUB WANTS YOU TO COME MODEL FOR US...
HUH!?
NO FREAKIN' WAY!!!
THERE'S NO WAY ...?
NO WAY !!!
HE SAID NO.
OH...
I THOUGHT MAYBE IT WOULD WORK IF YOU ASKED HIM, SINCE YOU'RE HIS FRIEND...
BUT IT DIDN'T...
OH!
MIKO-SHIBA-KUN.
...Model? Me?
Hey, now. Are you trying to capture my allure in a painting?
But if you can keep me with you that way...
...then I guess... I can allow it.
......
SAKU-RA...
I WAS HOPING YOU COULD...
...GET ME OUT OF IT.
NO WAY.
NO WAY.

PRACTICING POSES

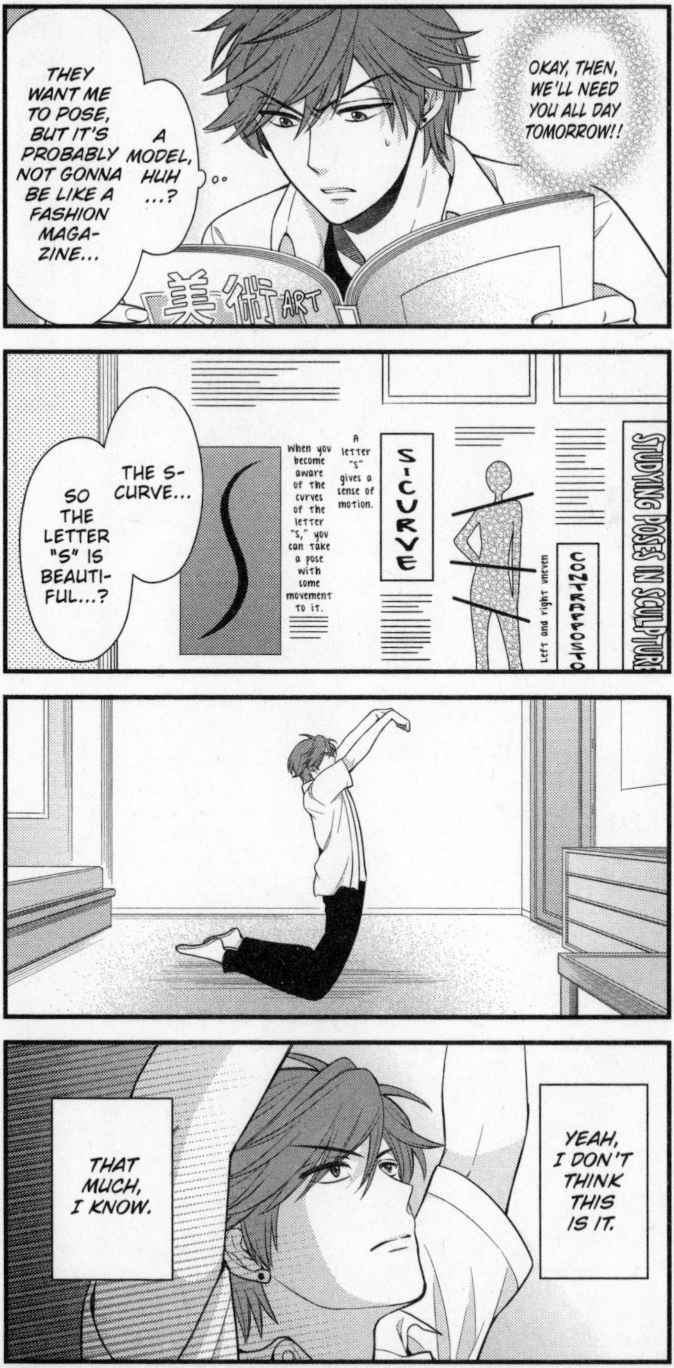
OKAY, THEN, WE'LL NEED YOU ALL DAY TOMORROW!!
A MODEL, HUH ...?
THEY WANT ME TO POSE, BUT IT'S PROBABLY NOT GONNA BE LIKE A FASHION MAGA-ZINE...
美術 ART
STUDYING POSES IN SCULPTURE
CONTRAPPOSTO
Left and right uneven
S-CURVE
A letter "S" gives a sense of motion.
When you become aware of the curves of the letter "S," you can take a pose with some movement to it.
THE S-CURVE...
SO THE LETTER "S" IS BEAUTIFUL...?
YEAH, I DON'T THINK THIS IS IT.
THAT MUCH, I KNOW.

EXAMPLE POSES

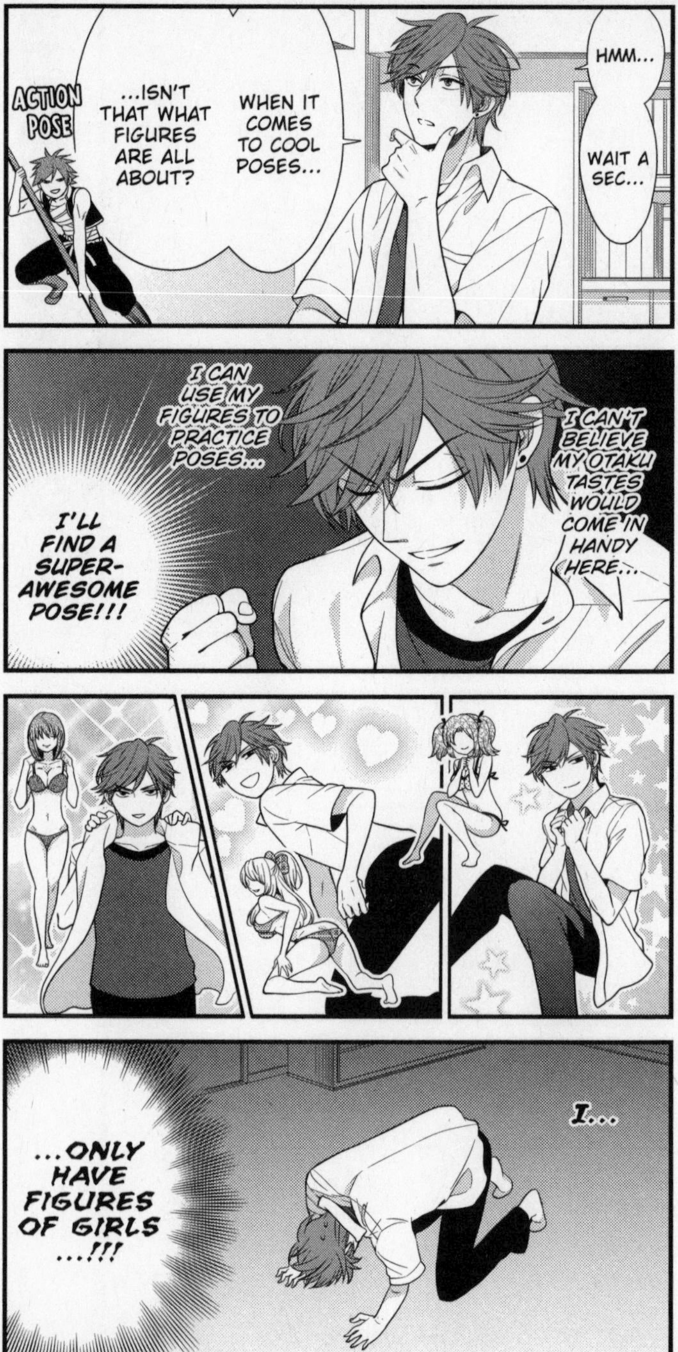
HMM...
WAIT A SEC...
WHEN IT COMES TO COOL POSES...
...ISN'T THAT WHAT FIGURES ARE ALL ABOUT?
ACTION POSE
I CAN'T BELIEVE MY OTAKU TASTES WOULD COME IN HANDY HERE...
I CAN USE MY FIGURES TO PRACTICE POSES...
I'LL FIND A SUPER-AWESOME POSE!!!
I...
...ONLY HAVE FIGURES OF GIRLS ...!!!

POSE INSTRUCTIONS

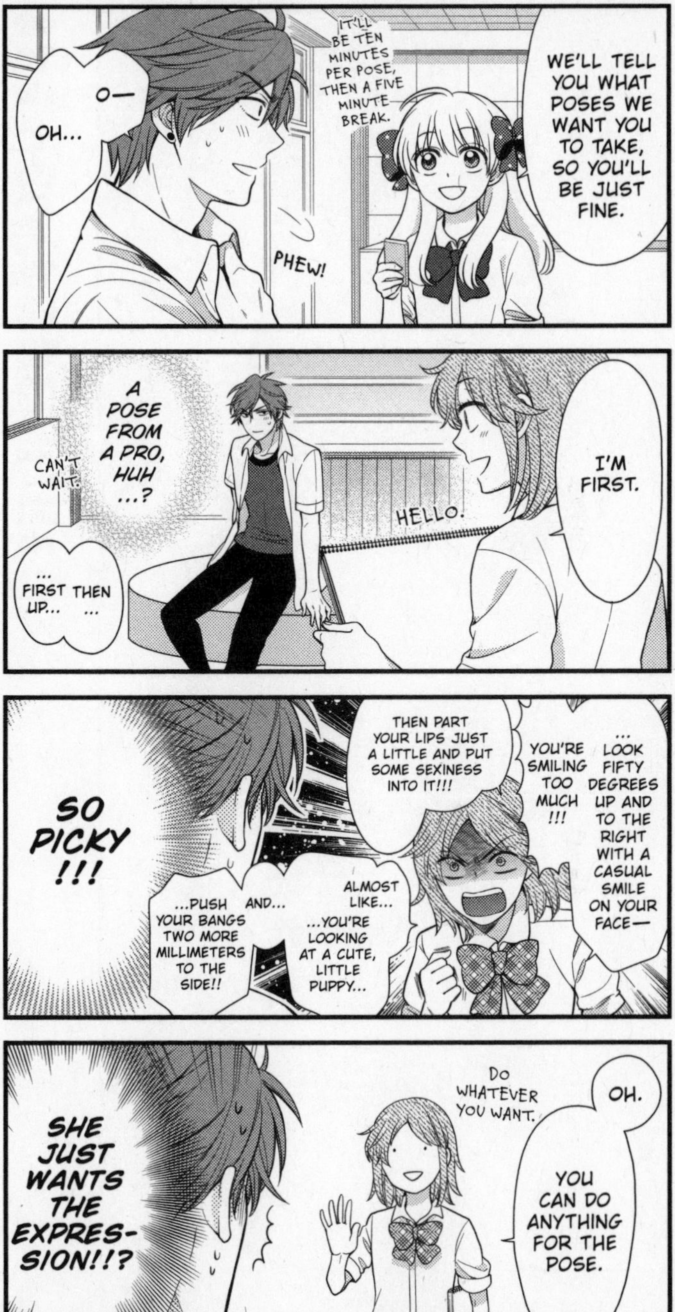

WE'LL TELL YOU WHAT POSES WE WANT YOU TO TAKE, SO YOU'LL BE JUST FINE.
IT'LL BE TEN MINUTES PER POSE, THEN A FIVE MINUTE BREAK.
PHEW!
O— OH...
I'M FIRST.
HELLO.
A POSE FROM A PRO, HUH ...?
CAN'T WAIT.
... FIRST UP... THEN ...
... LOOK FIFTY DEGREES UP AND TO THE RIGHT WITH A CASUAL SMILE ON YOUR FACE—
YOU'RE SMILING TOO MUCH !!!
THEN PART YOUR LIPS JUST A LITTLE AND PUT SOME SEXINESS INTO IT!!!
ALMOST LIKE... ...YOU'RE LOOKING AT A CUTE, LITTLE PUPPY...
AND... ...PUSH YOUR BANGS TWO MORE MILLIMETERS TO THE SIDE!!
SO PICKY !!!
OH. YOU CAN DO ANYTHING FOR THE POSE.
DO WHATEVER YOU WANT.
SHE JUST WANTS THE EXPRESSION!!?

THE POSES THEY LIKE

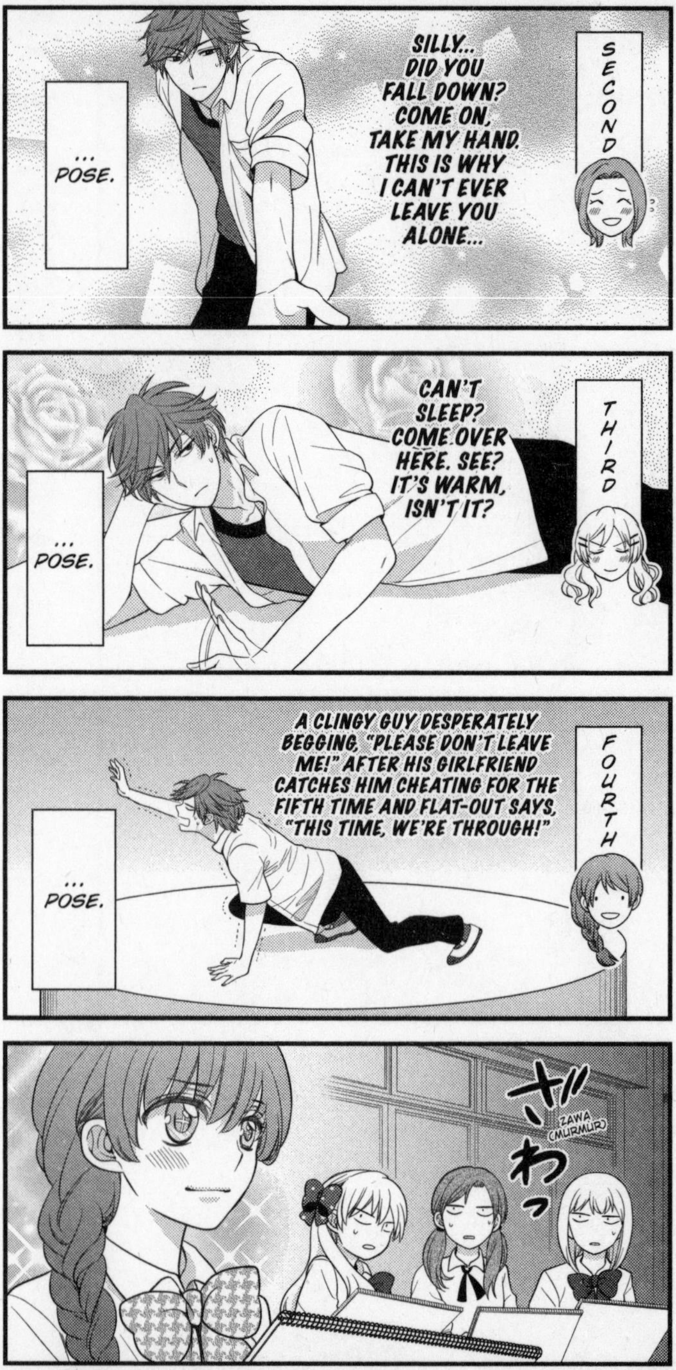
SECOND
SILLY... DID YOU FALL DOWN? COME ON, TAKE MY HAND. THIS IS WHY I CAN'T EVER LEAVE YOU ALONE...
... POSE.
THIRD
CAN'T SLEEP? COME OVER HERE. SEE? IT'S WARM, ISN'T IT?
... POSE.
FOURTH
A CLINGY GUY DESPERATELY BEGGING, "PLEASE DON'T LEAVE ME!" AFTER HIS GIRLFRIEND CATCHES HIM CHEATING FOR THE FIFTH TIME AND FLAT-OUT SAYS, "THIS TIME, WE'RE THROUGH!"
... POSE.
ZAWA (MURMUR)

I CAN ONLY ASK THIS OF YOU

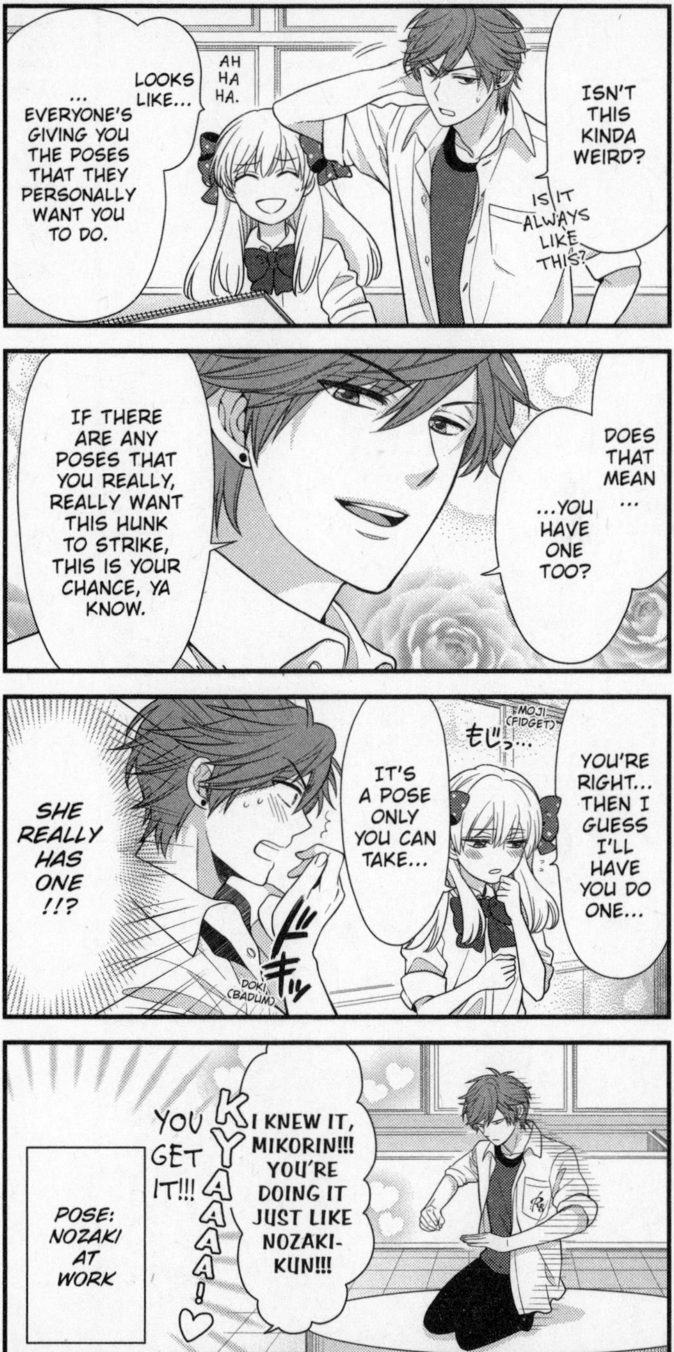
ISN'T THIS KINDA WEIRD?
IS IT ALWAYS LIKE THIS?
AH HA HA.
LOOKS LIKE...
...EVERYONE'S GIVING YOU THE POSES THAT THEY PERSONALLY WANT YOU TO DO.
DOES THAT MEAN ...
...YOU HAVE ONE TOO?
IF THERE ARE ANY POSES THAT YOU REALLY, REALLY WANT THIS HUNK TO STRIKE, THIS IS YOUR CHANCE, YA KNOW.
MOJI (FIDGET)
もじっ…
YOU'RE RIGHT... THEN I GUESS I'LL HAVE YOU DO ONE...
IT'S A POSE ONLY YOU CAN TAKE...
DOKI (BADUM)
ドキッ
SHE REALLY HAS ONE !!?
I KNEW IT, MIKORIN!!! YOU'RE DOING IT JUST LIKE NOZAKI-KUN!!!
KYAAAAAA!♥
YOU GET IT!!!
POSE: NOZAKI AT WORK

HE'S ALWAYS A BOTHER

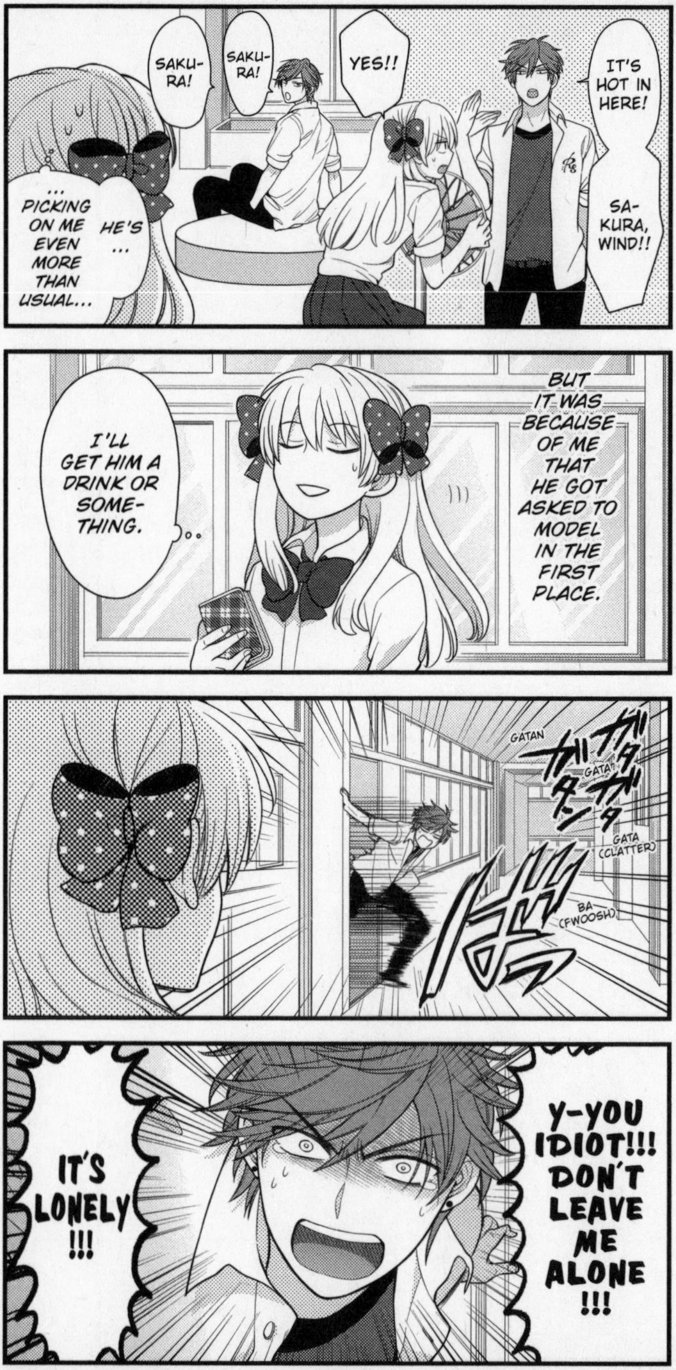
IT'S HOT IN HERE!
SA-KURA, WIND!!
YES!!
SAKU-RA!
SAKU-RA!
HE'S ...
... PICKING ON ME EVEN MORE THAN USUAL...
BUT IT WAS BECAUSE OF ME THAT HE GOT ASKED TO MODEL IN THE FIRST PLACE.
I'LL GET HIM A DRINK OR SOME-THING.
GATAN
GATA
GATA (CLATTER)
BA (FWOOSH)
Y-YOU IDIOT!!! DON'T LEAVE ME ALONE !!!
IT'S LONELY !!!

NOZAKI'S SPECIALTY

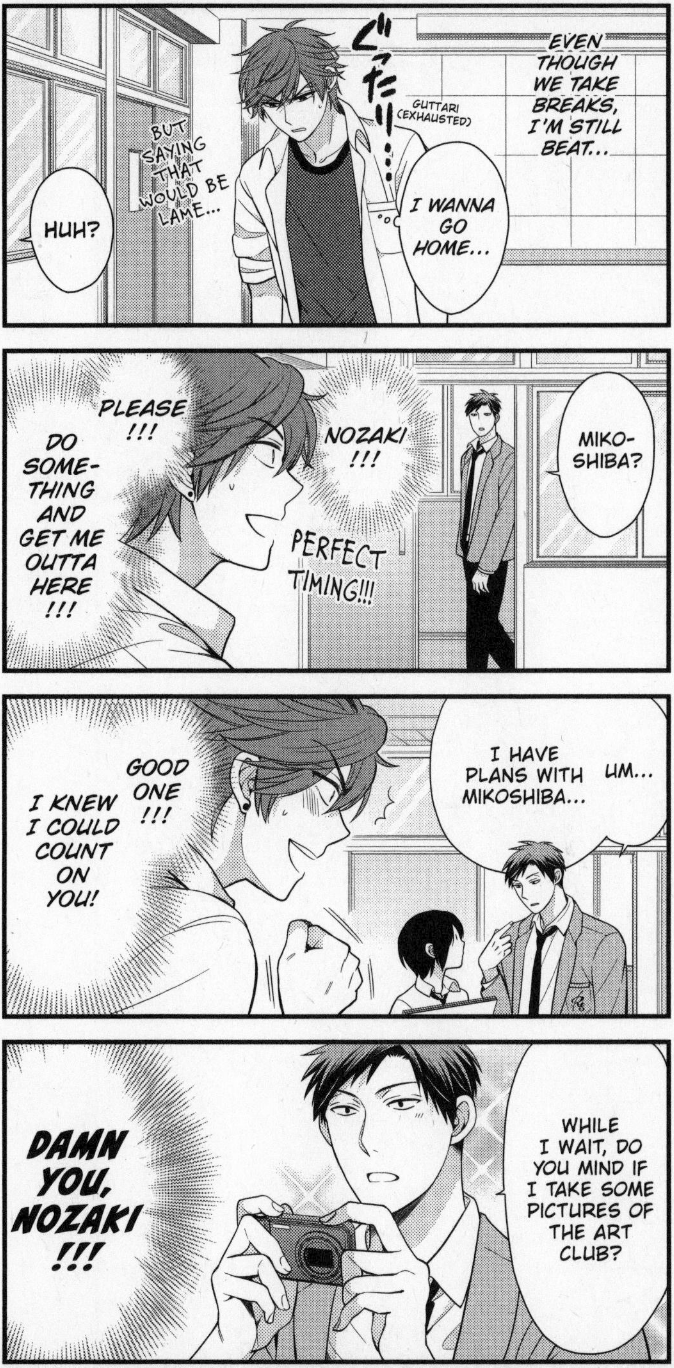

EVEN THOUGH WE TAKE BREAKS, I'M STILL BEAT...
ぐったり
GUTTARI (EXHAUSTED)
I WANNA GO HOME...
BUT SAYING THAT WOULD BE LAME...
HUH?
MIKO-SHIBA?
NOZAKI!!!
PERFECT TIMING!!!
PLEASE!!!
DO SOMETHING AND GET ME OUTTA HERE!!!
UM...
I HAVE PLANS WITH MIKOSHIBA...
GOOD ONE!!!
I KNEW I COULD COUNT ON YOU!
WHILE I WAIT, DO YOU MIND IF I TAKE SOME PICTURES OF THE ART CLUB?
DAMN YOU, NOZAKI!!!

AN ALLURING POSE

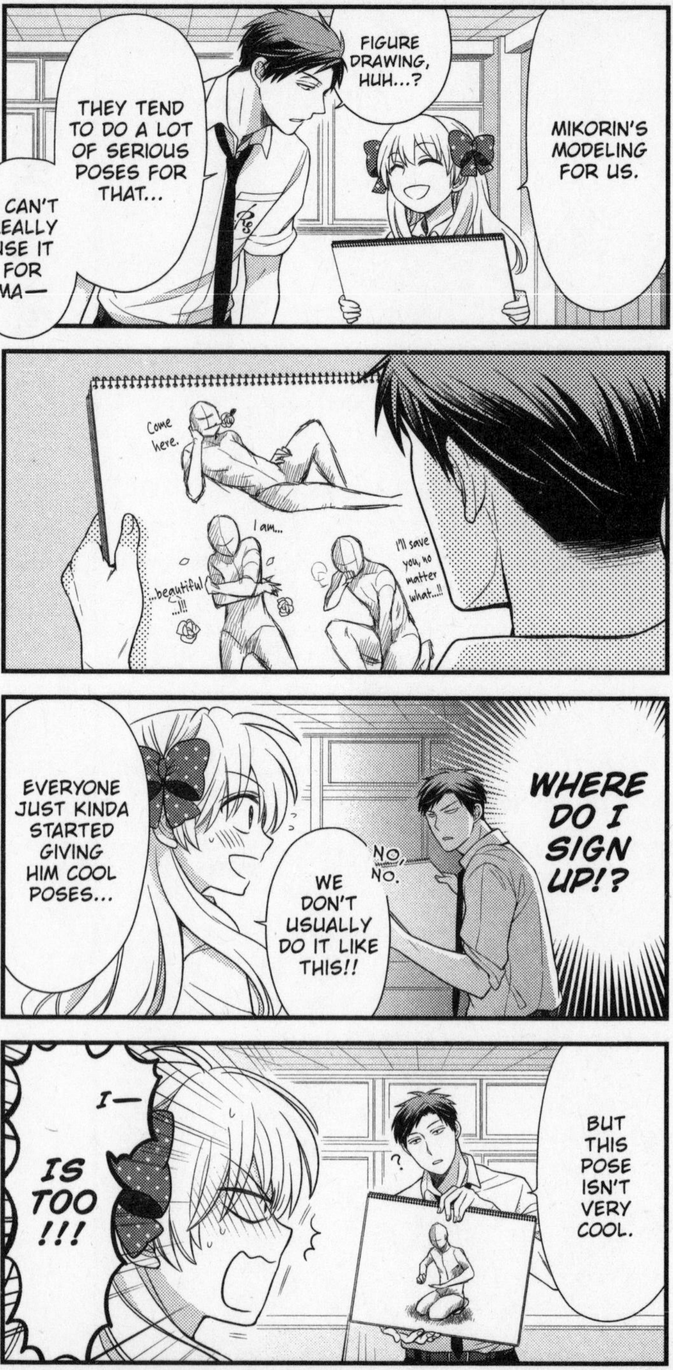

MIKORIN'S MODELING FOR US.
FIGURE DRAWING, HUH...?
THEY TEND TO DO A LOT OF SERIOUS POSES FOR THAT...
I CAN'T REALLY USE IT FOR MA—
Come here.
I'll save you, no matter what...!!
I am...
...beautiful ...!!
WHERE DO I SIGN UP!?
NO, NO.
WE DON'T USUALLY DO IT LIKE THIS!!
EVERYONE JUST KINDA STARTED GIVING HIM COOL POSES...
BUT THIS POSE ISN'T VERY COOL.
I—
IS TOO!!!

IN NOZAKI-KUN'S CASE

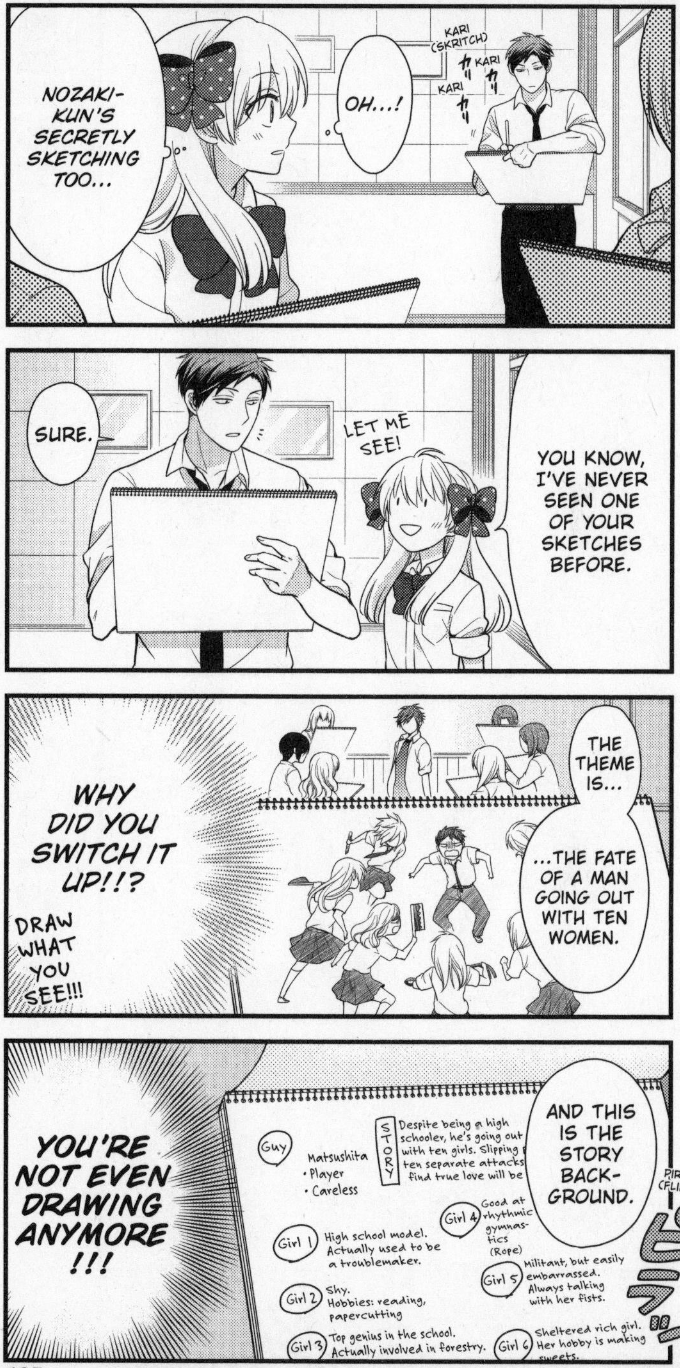
KARI (SKRITCH)
カリ KARI カリ KARI カリ
OH...!
NOZAKI-KUN'S SECRETLY SKETCHING TOO...
YOU KNOW, I'VE NEVER SEEN ONE OF YOUR SKETCHES BEFORE.
LET ME SEE!
SURE.
THE THEME IS...
...THE FATE OF A MAN GOING OUT WITH TEN WOMEN.
WHY DID YOU SWITCH IT UP!!?
DRAW WHAT YOU SEE!!!
PIRA (FLIP)
ピラッ
AND THIS IS THE STORY BACKGROUND.
STORY
Despite being a high schooler, he's going out with ten girls. Slipping
ten separate attacks
find true love will be
Guy
Matsushita
• Player
• Careless
Girl 1 High school model. Actually used to be a troublemaker.
Girl 2 Shy. Hobbies: reading, papercutting
Girl 3 Top genius in the school. Actually involved in forestry.
Girl 4 Good at rhythmic gymnastics (Rope)
Girl 5 Militant, but easily embarrassed. Always talking with her fists.
Girl 6 Sheltered rich girl. Her hobby is making sweets.
YOU'RE NOT EVEN DRAWING ANYMORE!!!

THE ART CLUB AND THE OUTSIDER

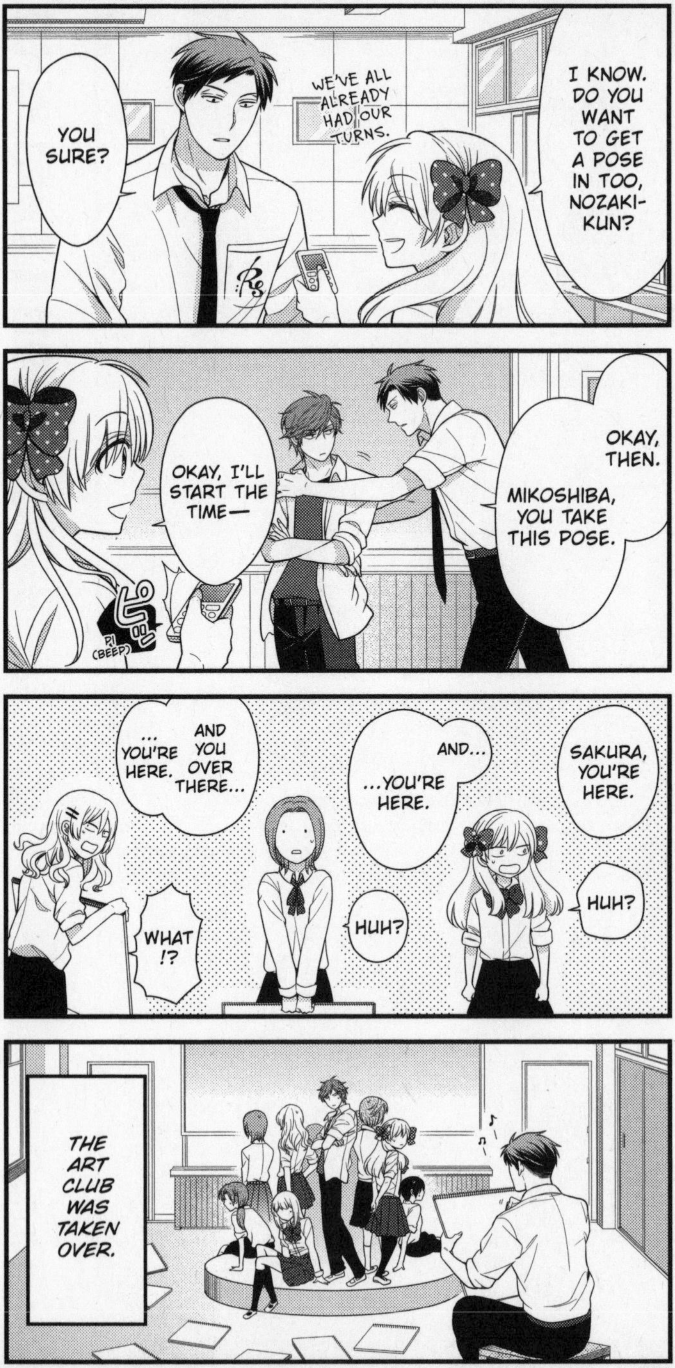
I KNOW. DO YOU WANT TO GET A POSE IN TOO, NOZAKI-KUN?
WE'VE ALL ALREADY HAD OUR TURNS.
YOU SURE?
OKAY, THEN.
MIKOSHIBA, YOU TAKE THIS POSE.
OKAY, I'LL START THE TIME—
ピッ
PI (BEEP)
SAKURA, YOU'RE HERE.
HUH?
AND...
...YOU'RE HERE.
HUH?
AND YOU OVER THERE...
...YOU'RE HERE.
WHAT!?
THE ART CLUB WAS TAKEN OVER.

AND HE'S TREMBLING AGAIN TODAY

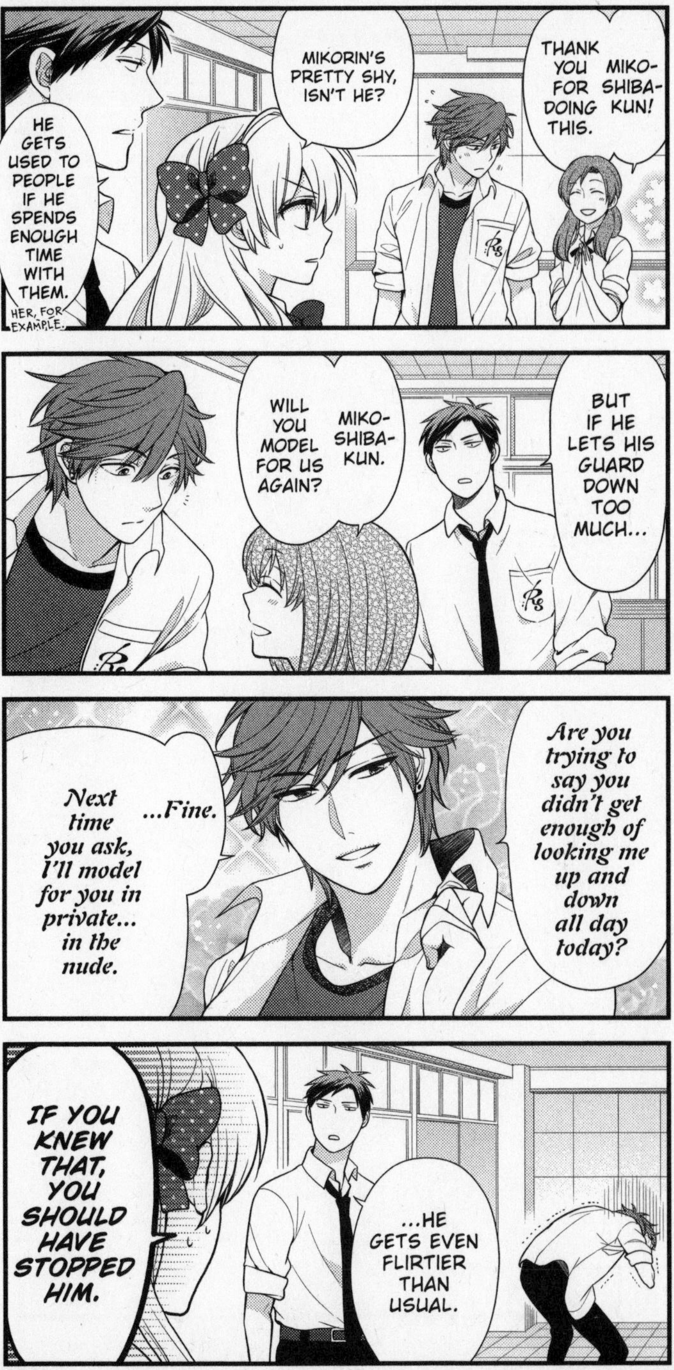
THANK YOU FOR DOING THIS. MIKO-SHIBA-KUN!
MIKORIN'S PRETTY SHY, ISN'T HE?
HE GETS USED TO PEOPLE IF HE SPENDS ENOUGH TIME WITH THEM.
HER, FOR EXAMPLE.
BUT IF HE LETS HIS GUARD DOWN TOO MUCH...
MIKO-SHIBA-KUN. WILL YOU MODEL FOR US AGAIN?
Are you trying to say you didn't get enough of looking me up and down all day today?
...Fine.
Next time you ask, I'll model for you in private... in the nude.
...HE GETS EVEN FLIRTIER THAN USUAL.
IF YOU KNEW THAT, YOU SHOULD HAVE STOPPED HIM.

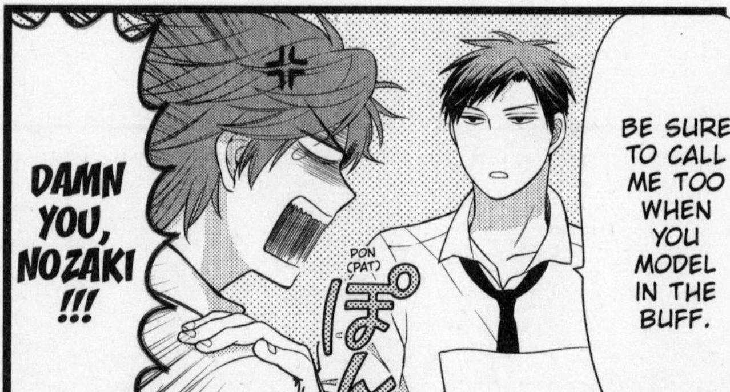
BE SURE TO CALL ME TOO WHEN YOU MODEL IN THE BUFF.
ぽんっ
PON (PAT)
DAMN YOU, NOZAKI !!!

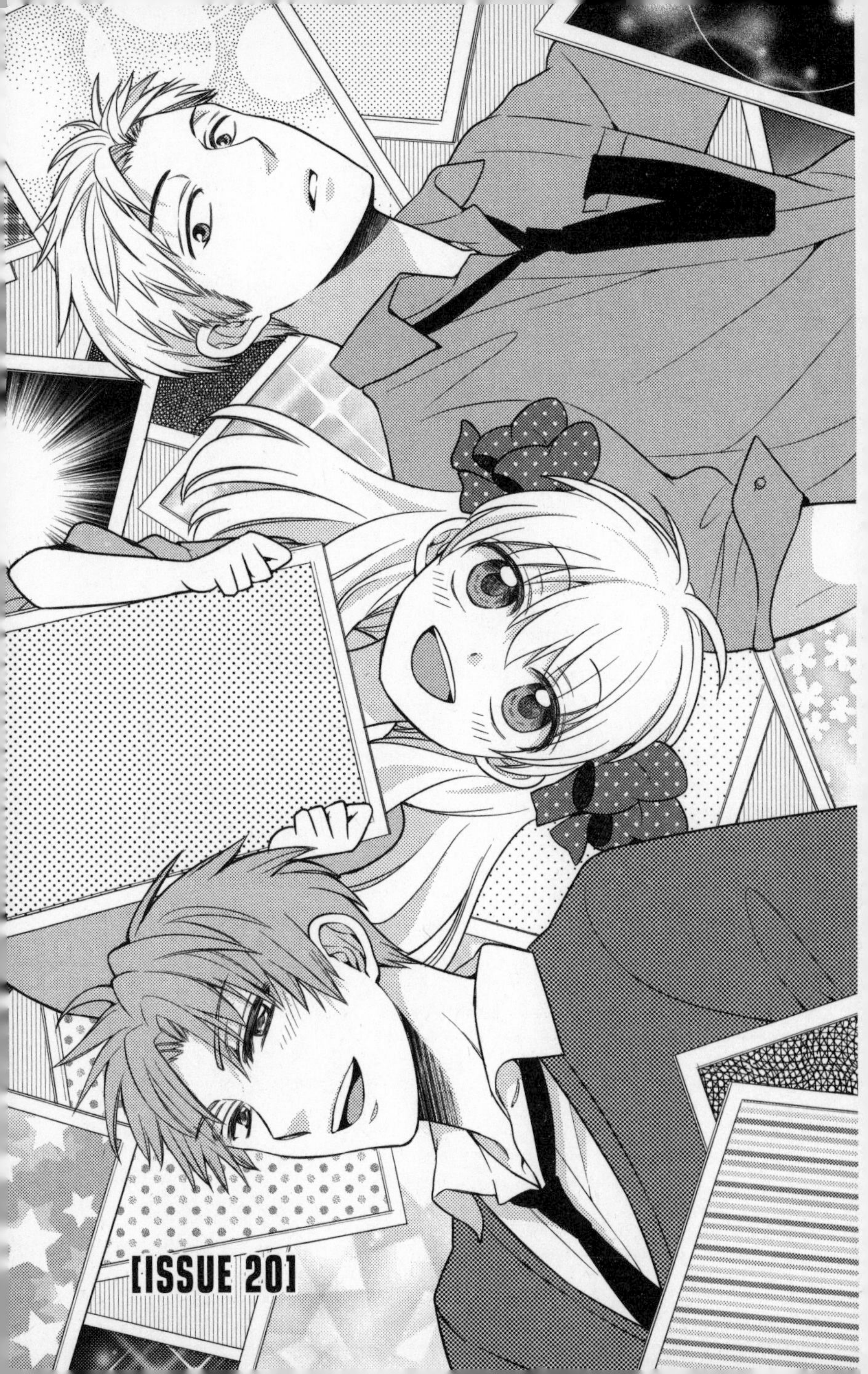
[ISSUE 20]

SICKNESS EVENT

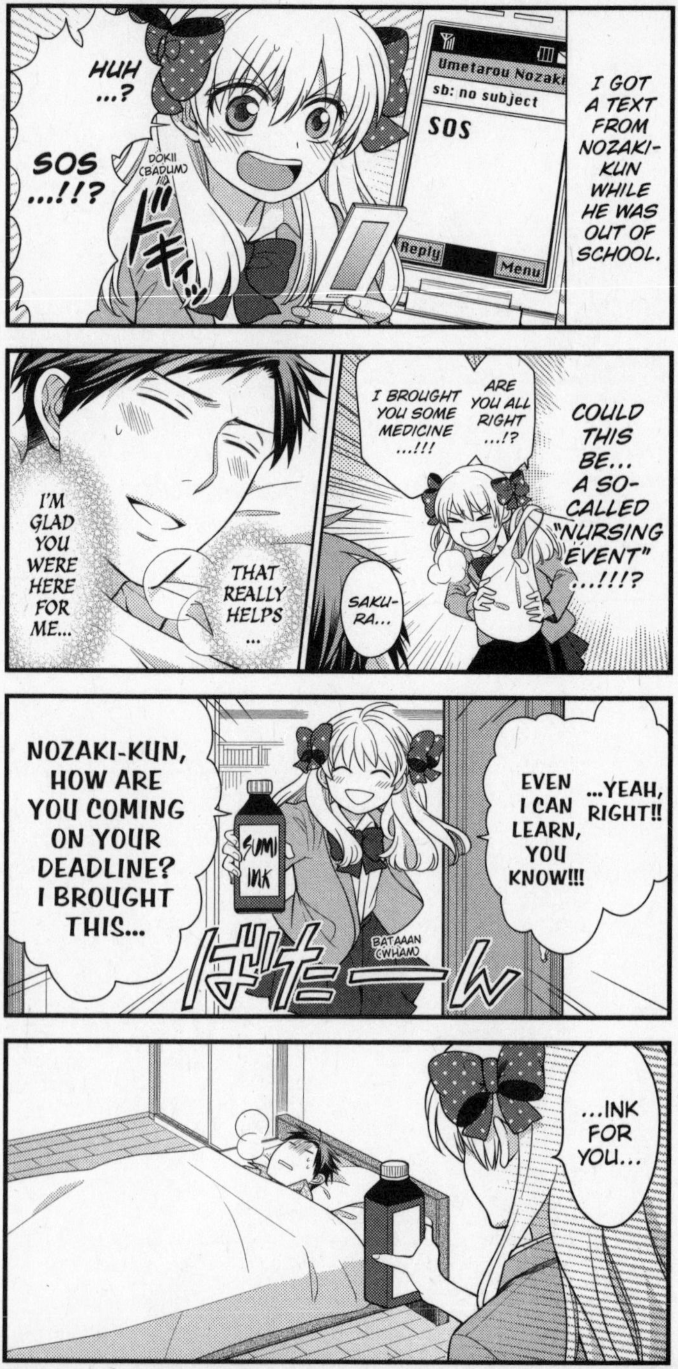
I GOT A TEXT FROM NOZAKI-KUN WHILE HE WAS OUT OF SCHOOL.
Umetarou Nozaki
sb: no subject
SOS
Reply
Menu
HUH ...?
DOKII (BADUM)
SOS ...!!?
COULD THIS BE... A SO-CALLED "NURSING EVENT" ...!!!?
ARE YOU ALL RIGHT ...!?
I BROUGHT YOU SOME MEDICINE ...!!!
SAKU-RA...
THAT REALLY HELPS ...
I'M GLAD YOU WERE HERE FOR ME...
...YEAH, RIGHT!!
EVEN I CAN LEARN, YOU KNOW!!!
NOZAKI-KUN, HOW ARE YOU COMING ON YOUR DEADLINE? I BROUGHT THIS...
SUMI INK
BATAAAN (WHAM)
...INK FOR YOU...

NOZAKI'S SOS

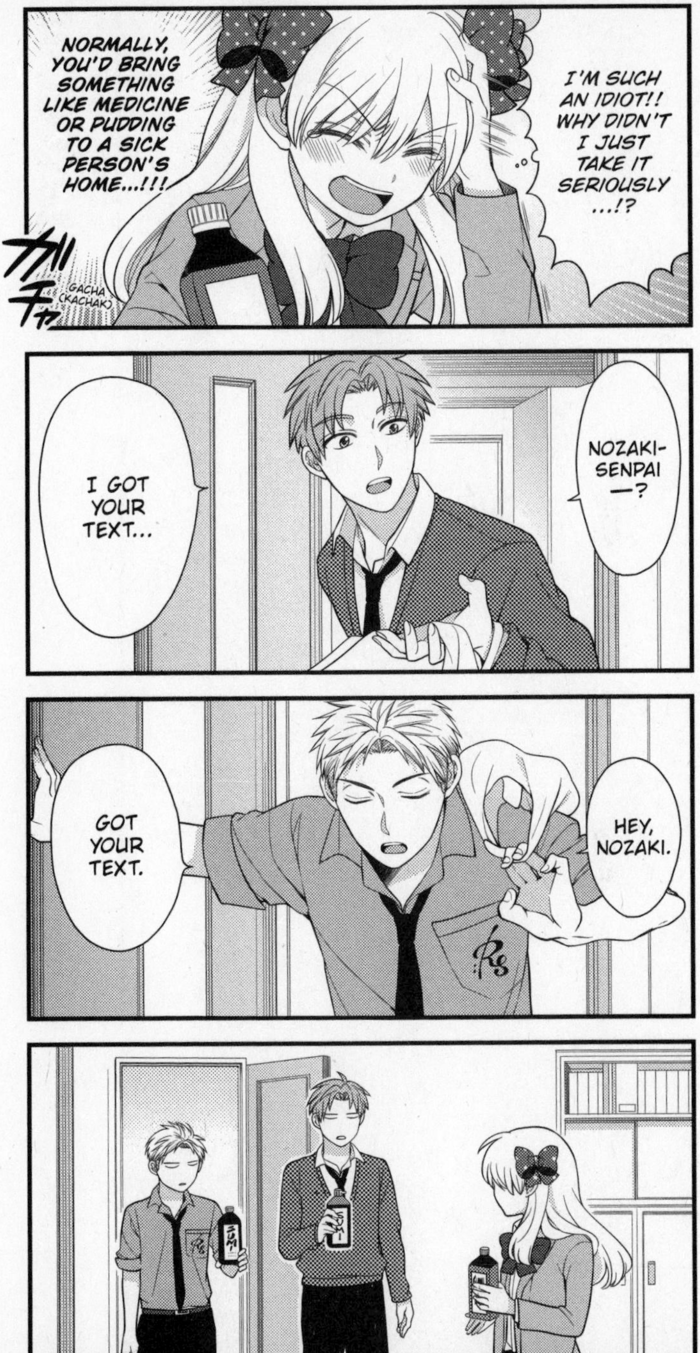
I'M SUCH AN IDIOT!! WHY DIDN'T I JUST TAKE IT SERIOUSLY ...!?
NORMALLY, YOU'D BRING SOMETHING LIKE MEDICINE OR PUDDING TO A SICK PERSON'S HOME...!!!
GACHA (KACHAK)
NOZAKI-SENPAI—?
I GOT YOUR TEXT...
HEY, NOZAKI.
GOT YOUR TEXT.

IN MY PLACE

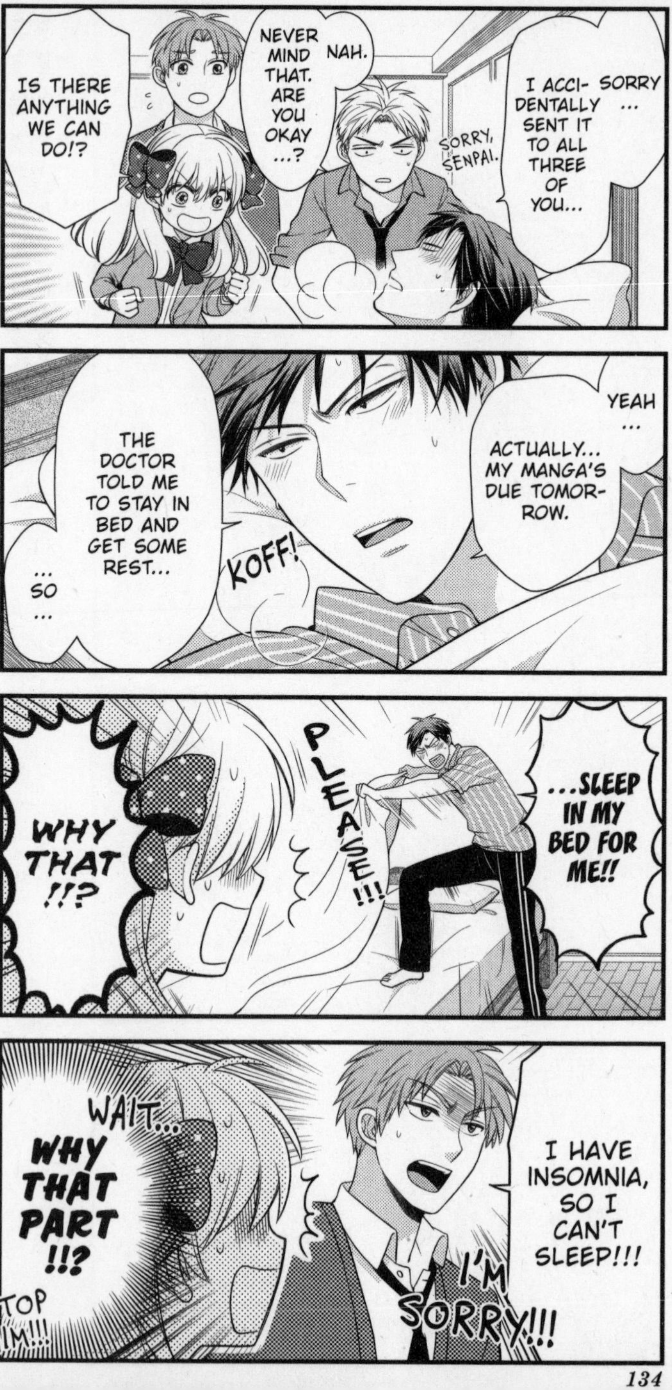
SORRY ...
I ACCIDENTALLY SENT IT TO ALL THREE OF YOU...
SORRY, SENPAI.
NAH.
NEVER MIND THAT. ARE YOU OKAY ...?
IS THERE ANYTHING WE CAN DO!?
YEAH ...
ACTUALLY... MY MANGA'S DUE TOMORROW.
KOFF!
THE DOCTOR TOLD ME TO STAY IN BED AND GET SOME REST...
... SO ...
...SLEEP IN MY BED FOR ME!!
PLEASE!!!
WHY THAT!!?
I HAVE INSOMNIA, SO I CAN'T SLEEP!!!
I'M SORRY!!!
WAIT...
WHY THAT PART!!?
STOP HIM!!!

THE HIDDEN STRENGTH OF A PRO

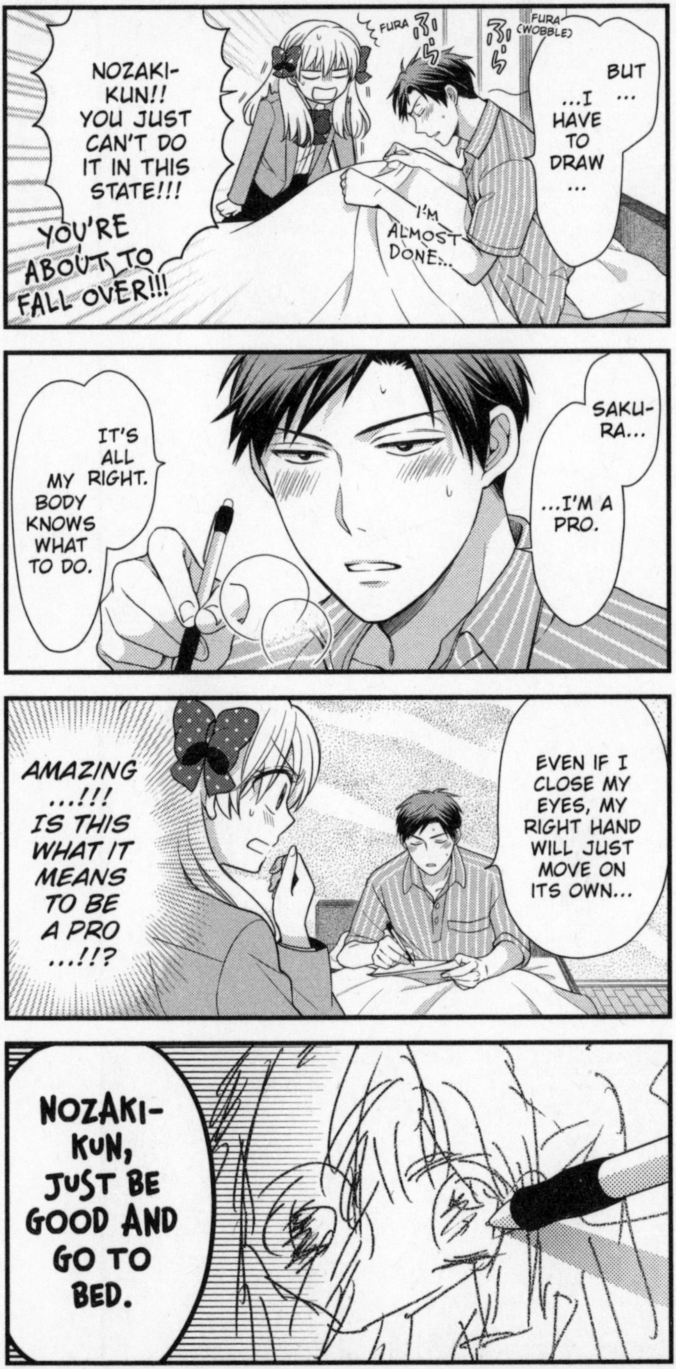
ふら
FURA (WOBBLE)
ふら
FURA
BUT... ...I HAVE TO DRAW...
I'M ALMOST DONE...
NOZAKI-KUN!! YOU JUST CAN'T DO IT IN THIS STATE!!!
YOU'RE ABOUT TO FALL OVER!!!
SAKURA... ...I'M A PRO.
IT'S ALL RIGHT. MY BODY KNOWS WHAT TO DO.
EVEN IF I CLOSE MY EYES, MY RIGHT HAND WILL JUST MOVE ON ITS OWN...
AMAZING...!!! IS THIS WHAT IT MEANS TO BE A PRO...!!?
NOZAKI-KUN, JUST BE GOOD AND GO TO BED.

BEGINNERS

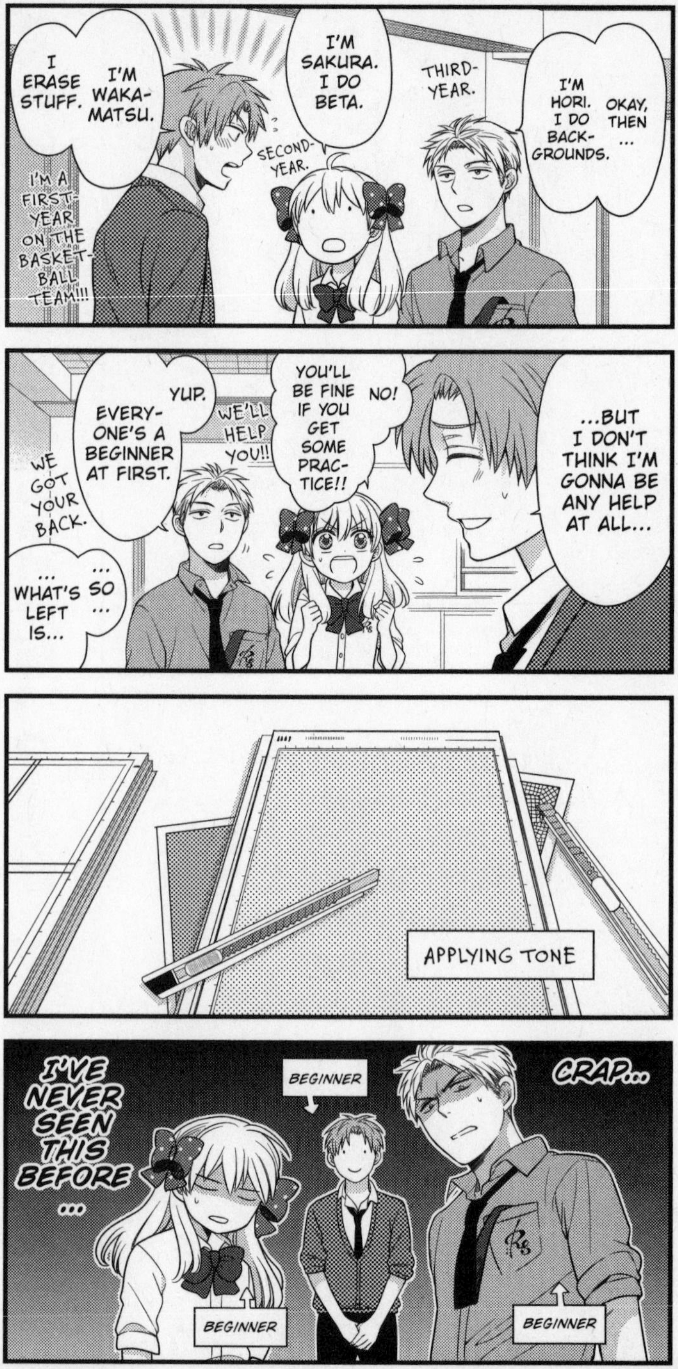

OKAY, THEN ...
I'M HORI. I DO BACKGROUNDS.
THIRD-YEAR.
I'M SAKURA. I DO BETA.
SECOND-YEAR.
I'M WAKAMATSU.
I ERASE STUFF.
I'M A FIRST-YEAR ON THE BASKETBALL TEAM!!!
...BUT I DON'T THINK I'M GONNA BE ANY HELP AT ALL...
NO!
YOU'LL BE FINE IF YOU GET SOME PRACTICE!!
WE'LL HELP YOU!!
YUP.
EVERYONE'S A BEGINNER AT FIRST.
WE GOT YOUR BACK.
... SO ...
... WHAT'S LEFT IS...
APPLYING TONE
CRAP...
BEGINNER
I'VE NEVER SEEN THIS BEFORE ...
BEGINNER
BEGINNER

GO, TEAM ARTS!

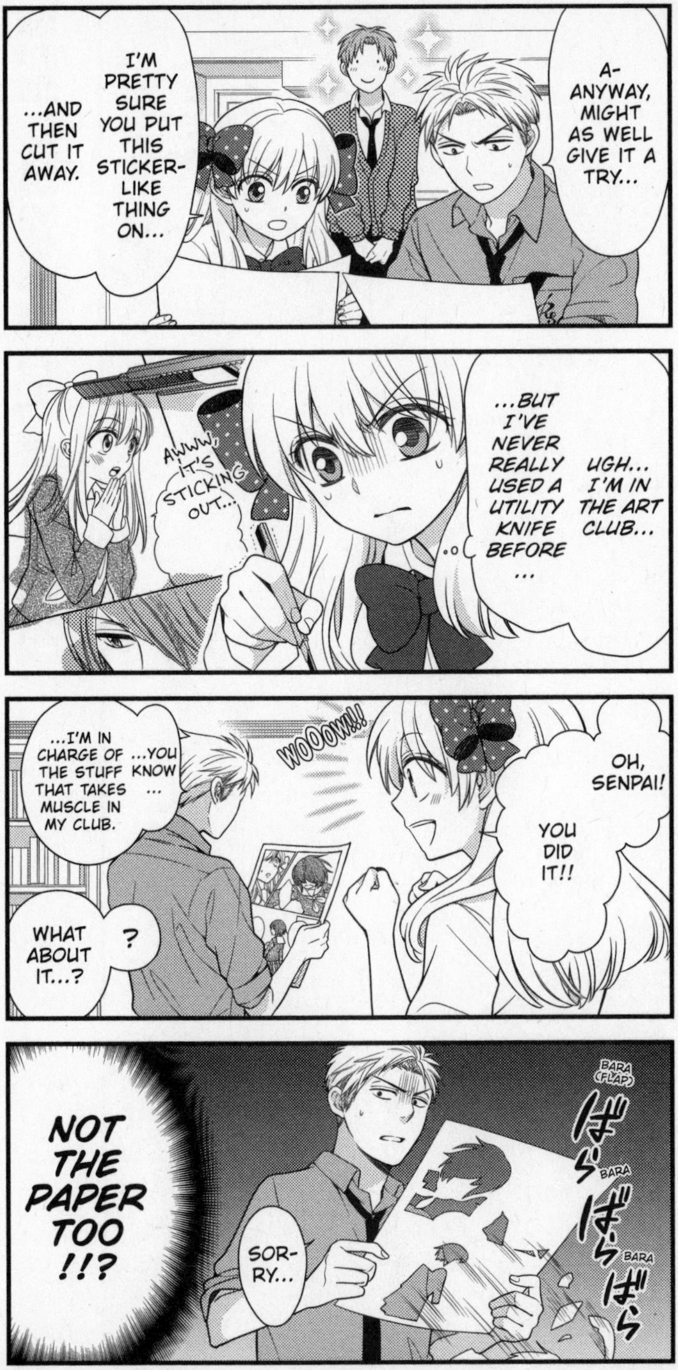
A-ANYWAY, MIGHT AS WELL GIVE IT A TRY...
I'M PRETTY SURE YOU PUT THIS STICKER-LIKE THING ON...
...AND THEN CUT IT AWAY.
UGH... I'M IN THE ART CLUB...
...BUT I'VE NEVER REALLY USED A UTILITY KNIFE BEFORE ...
AWWW, IT'S STICKING OUT...
OH, SENPAI!
YOU DID IT!!
WOOOW!!!
...YOU KNOW ...
...I'M IN CHARGE OF THE STUFF THAT TAKES MUSCLE IN MY CLUB.
?
WHAT ABOUT IT...?
BARA (FLAP)
ばら
BARA
ばら
BARA
ばら
SOR-RY...
NOT THE PAPER TOO!!?

THE NATURE OF A SENPAI

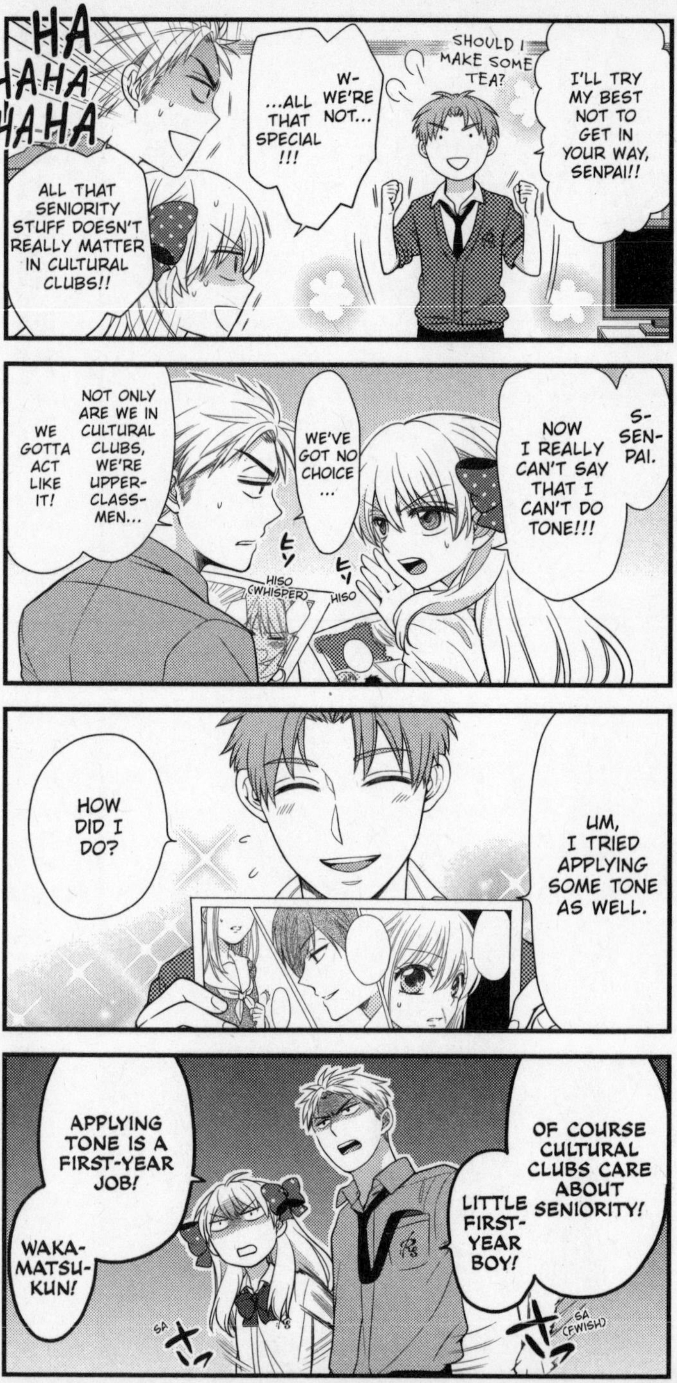
I'LL TRY MY BEST NOT TO GET IN YOUR WAY, SENPAI!!
SHOULD I MAKE SOME TEA?
W-WE'RE NOT...
...ALL THAT SPECIAL!!!
HA HAHAHA HAHA
ALL THAT SENIORITY STUFF DOESN'T REALLY MATTER IN CULTURAL CLUBS!!
S-SEN-PAI.
NOW I REALLY CAN'T SAY THAT I CAN'T DO TONE!!!
WE'VE GOT NO CHOICE...
HISO
HISO (WHISPER)
NOT ONLY ARE WE IN CULTURAL CLUBS, WE'RE UPPER-CLASS-MEN...
WE GOTTA ACT LIKE IT!
UM, I TRIED APPLYING SOME TONE AS WELL.
HOW DID I DO?
OF COURSE CULTURAL CLUBS CARE ABOUT SENIORITY!
LITTLE FIRST-YEAR BOY!
SA (FWISH)
APPLYING TONE IS A FIRST-YEAR JOB!
WAKA-MATSU-KUN!
SA

THE COMPLICATED HEART OF A GIRL

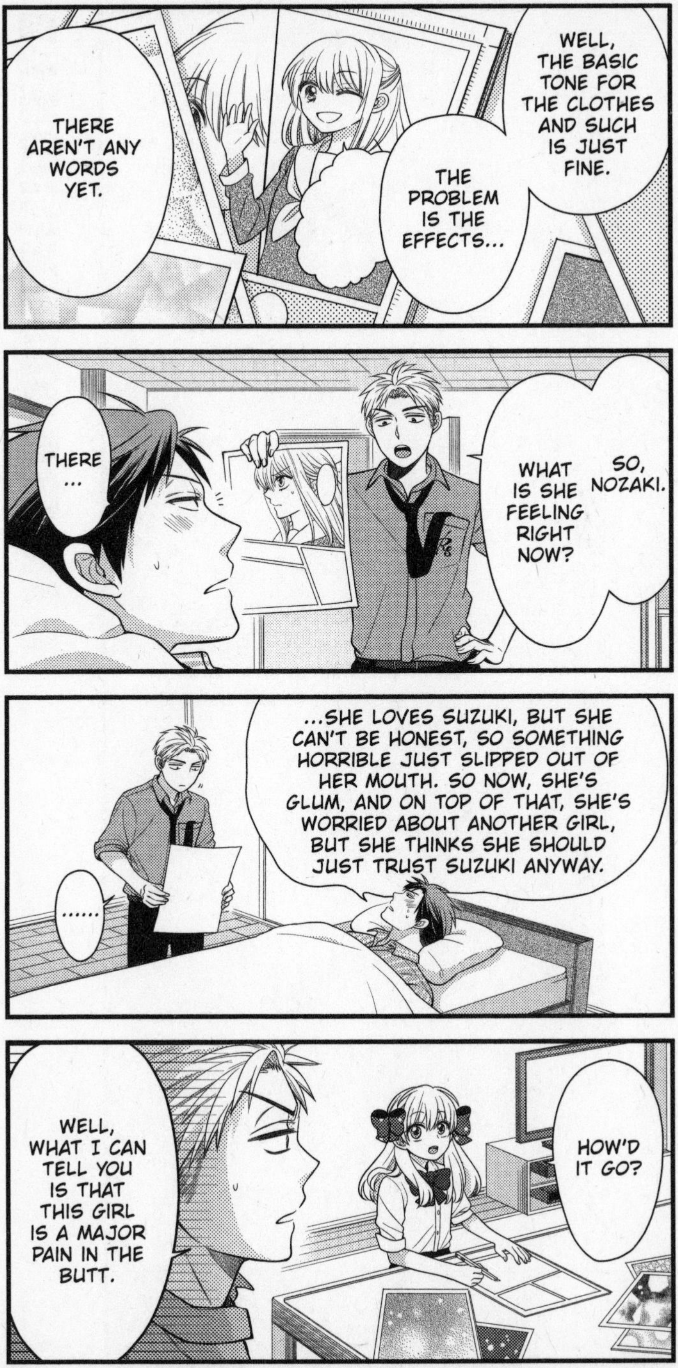
WELL, THE BASIC TONE FOR THE CLOTHES AND SUCH IS JUST FINE.
THE PROBLEM IS THE EFFECTS...
THERE AREN'T ANY WORDS YET.
SO, NOZAKI.
WHAT IS SHE FEELING RIGHT NOW?
THERE ...
...SHE LOVES SUZUKI, BUT SHE CAN'T BE HONEST, SO SOMETHING HORRIBLE JUST SLIPPED OUT OF HER MOUTH. SO NOW, SHE'S GLUM, AND ON TOP OF THAT, SHE'S WORRIED ABOUT ANOTHER GIRL, BUT SHE THINKS SHE SHOULD JUST TRUST SUZUKI ANYWAY.
......
HOW'D IT GO?
WELL, WHAT I CAN TELL YOU IS THAT THIS GIRL IS A MAJOR PAIN IN THE BUTT.

A FAMILIAR MODEL

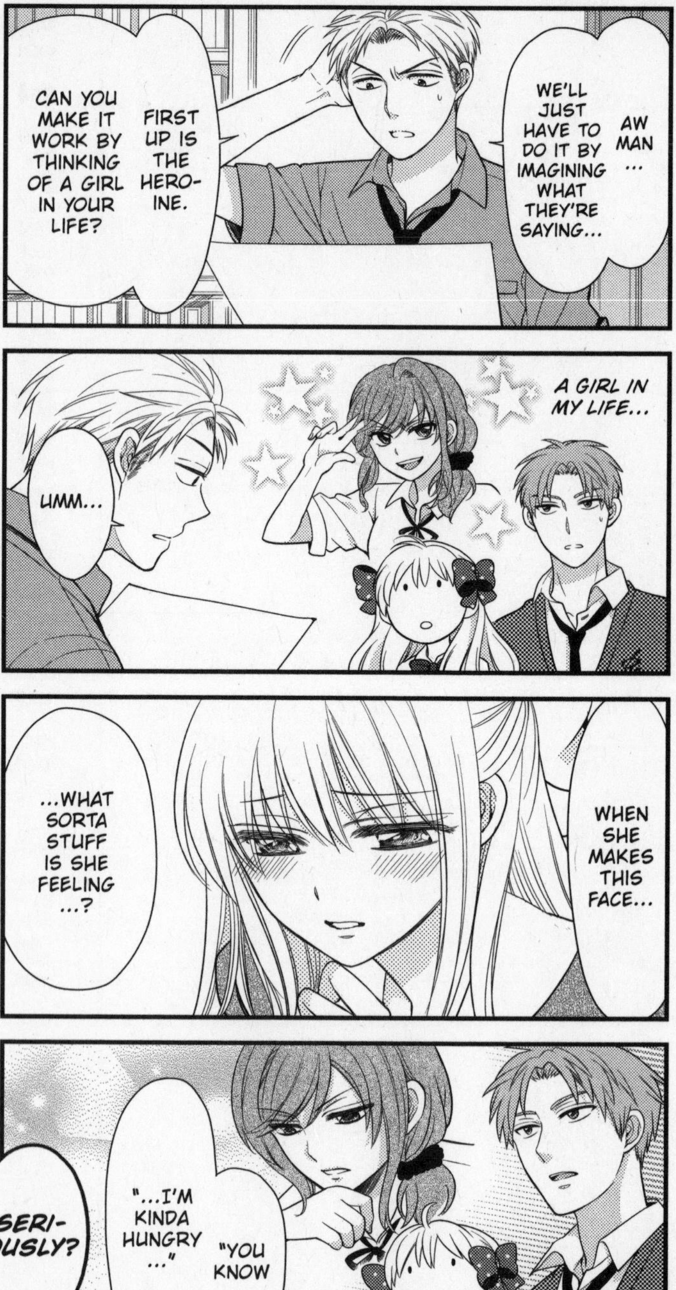
AW MAN ...
WE'LL JUST HAVE TO DO IT BY IMAGINING WHAT THEY'RE SAYING...
FIRST UP IS THE HERO-INE.
CAN YOU MAKE IT WORK BY THINKING OF A GIRL IN YOUR LIFE?
A GIRL IN MY LIFE...
UMM...
WHEN SHE MAKES THIS FACE...
...WHAT SORTA STUFF IS SHE FEELING ...?
"YOU KNOW ...
...I'M KINDA HUNGRY ..."
SERI-OUSLY?

YUZUKI IN MAMIKO

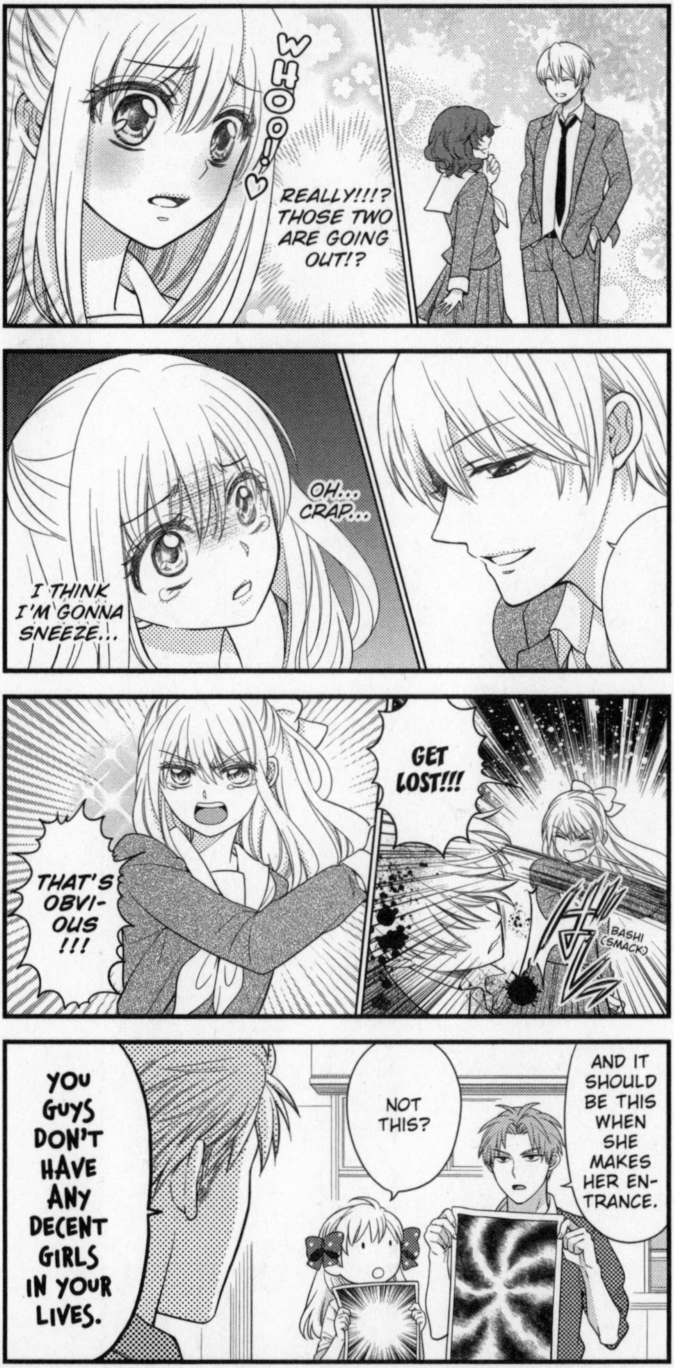

REALLY!!!? THOSE TWO ARE GOING OUT!?
WHOOO!♥
OH... CRAP...
I THINK I'M GONNA SNEEZE...
GET LOST!!!
BASHI (SMACK)
THAT'S OBVI-OUS!!!
AND IT SHOULD BE THIS WHEN SHE MAKES HER EN-TRANCE.
NOT THIS?
YOU GUYS DON'T HAVE ANY DECENT GIRLS IN YOUR LIVES.

HANDSOME GUY TONE

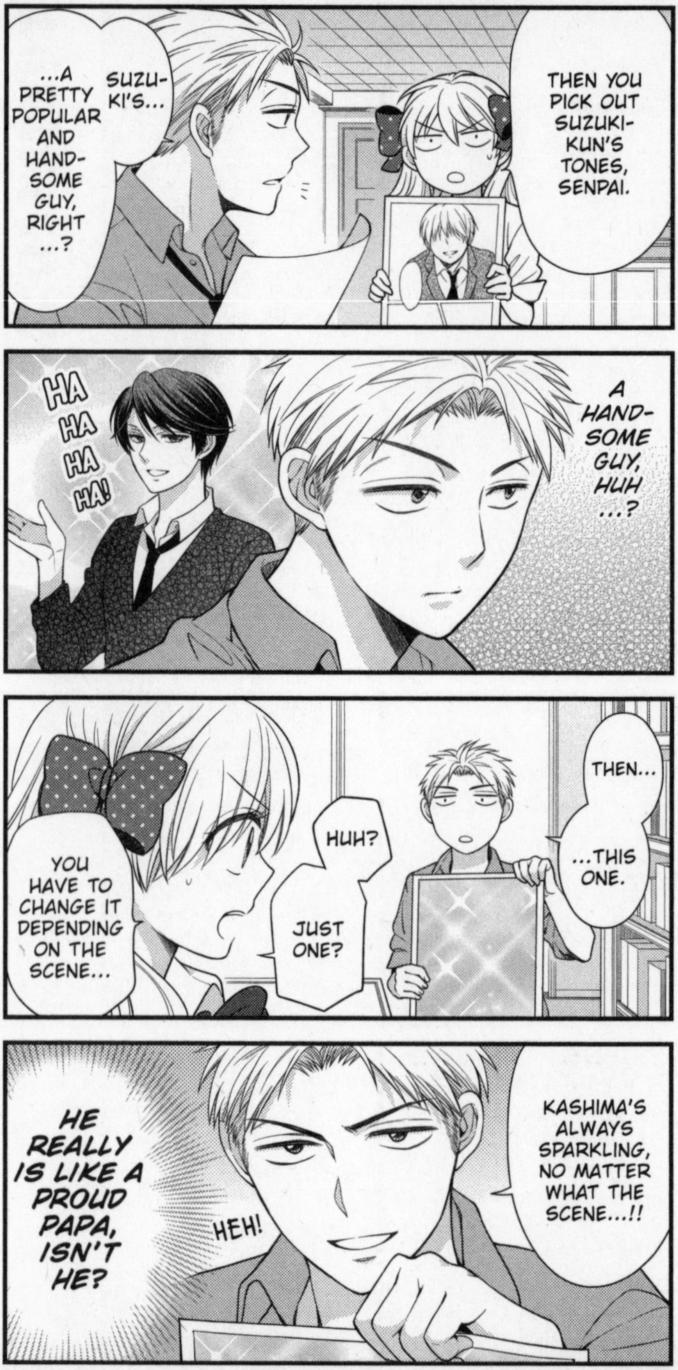
THEN YOU PICK OUT SUZUKI-KUN'S TONES, SENPAI.
SUZUKI'S...
...A PRETTY POPULAR AND HANDSOME GUY, RIGHT...?
A HANDSOME GUY, HUH...?
HA HA HA HA!
THEN...
...THIS ONE.
HUH?
JUST ONE?
YOU HAVE TO CHANGE IT DEPENDING ON THE SCENE...
KASHIMA'S ALWAYS SPARKLING, NO MATTER WHAT THE SCENE...!!
HEH!
HE REALLY IS LIKE A PROUD PAPA, ISN'T HE?

THE ELVES' WORK

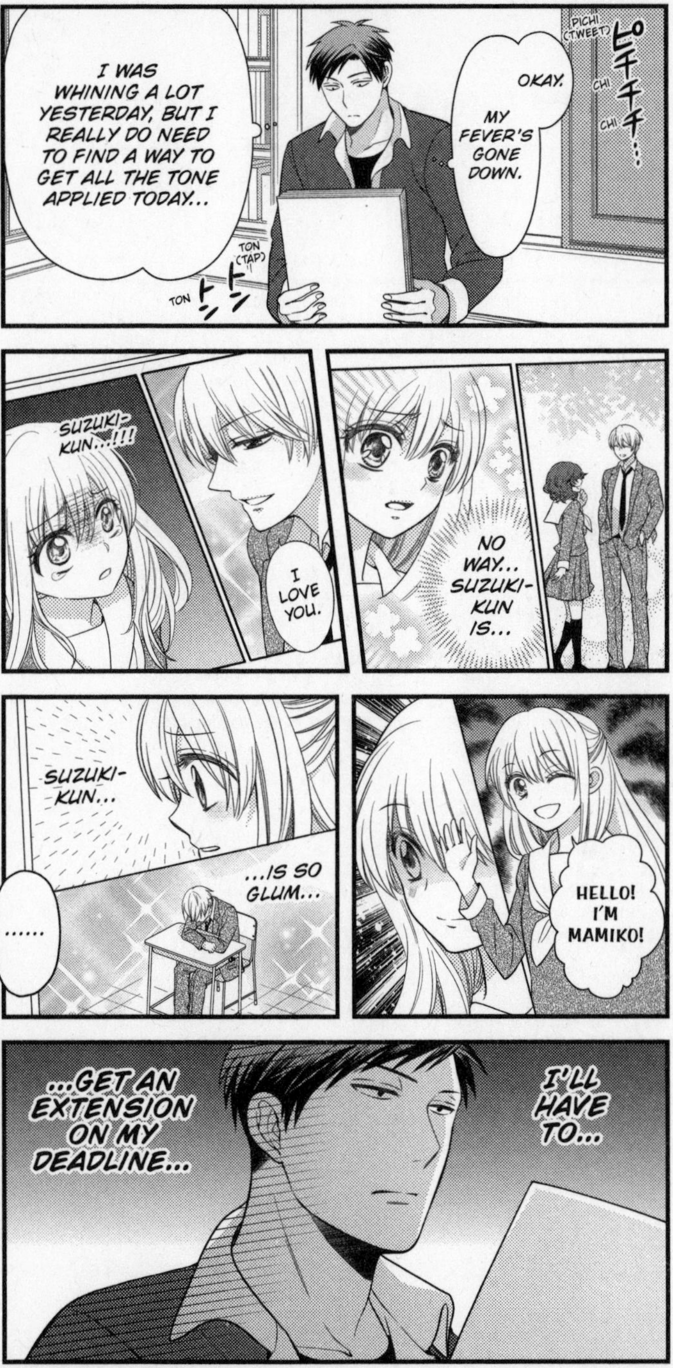
PICHI (TWEET)
CHI
CHI
OKAY.
MY FEVER'S GONE DOWN.
I WAS WHINING A LOT YESTERDAY, BUT I REALLY DO NEED TO FIND A WAY TO GET ALL THE TONE APPLIED TODAY...
TON (TAP)
TON
NO WAY... SUZUKI-KUN IS...
I LOVE YOU.
SUZUKI-KUN...!!!
HELLO! I'M MAMIKO!
SUZUKI-KUN...
...IS SO GLUM...
......
I'LL HAVE TO...
...GET AN EXTENSION ON MY DEADLINE...

MONTHLY GIRLS' NOZAKI-KUN 2 END

MONTHLY GIRLS' NOZAKI-KUN 2

IZUMI TSUBAKI

Translation: Leighann Harvey
Lettering: Lys Blakeslee

GEKKAN SHOJO NOZAKI KUN Volume 2 © 2012 Izumi Tsubaki / SQUARE ENIX CO., LTD. First published in Japan in 2012 by SQUARE ENIX CO., LTD. English translation rights arranged with SQUARE ENIX CO., LTD. and Yen Press, LLC through Tuttle-Mori Agency, Inc.

English translation © 2016 SQUARE ENIX CO., LTD.

Yen Press
1290 Avenue of the Americas
New York, NY 10104

Visit us at yenpress.com
facebook.com/yenpress
twitter.com/yenpress
yenpress.tumblr.com
instagram.com/yenpress

First Yen Press Print Edition: May 2016

Yen Press is an imprint of Yen Press, LLC.
The Yen Press name and logo are trademarks of Yen Press, LLC.

The publisher is not responsible for websites (or their content) that are not owned by the publisher.

Library of Congress Control Number: 2015952610

ISBN: 978-0-316-39157-3 (paperback)

10 9 8 7 6 5 4

WOR

Printed in the United States of America

[Extra] SCHEDULE

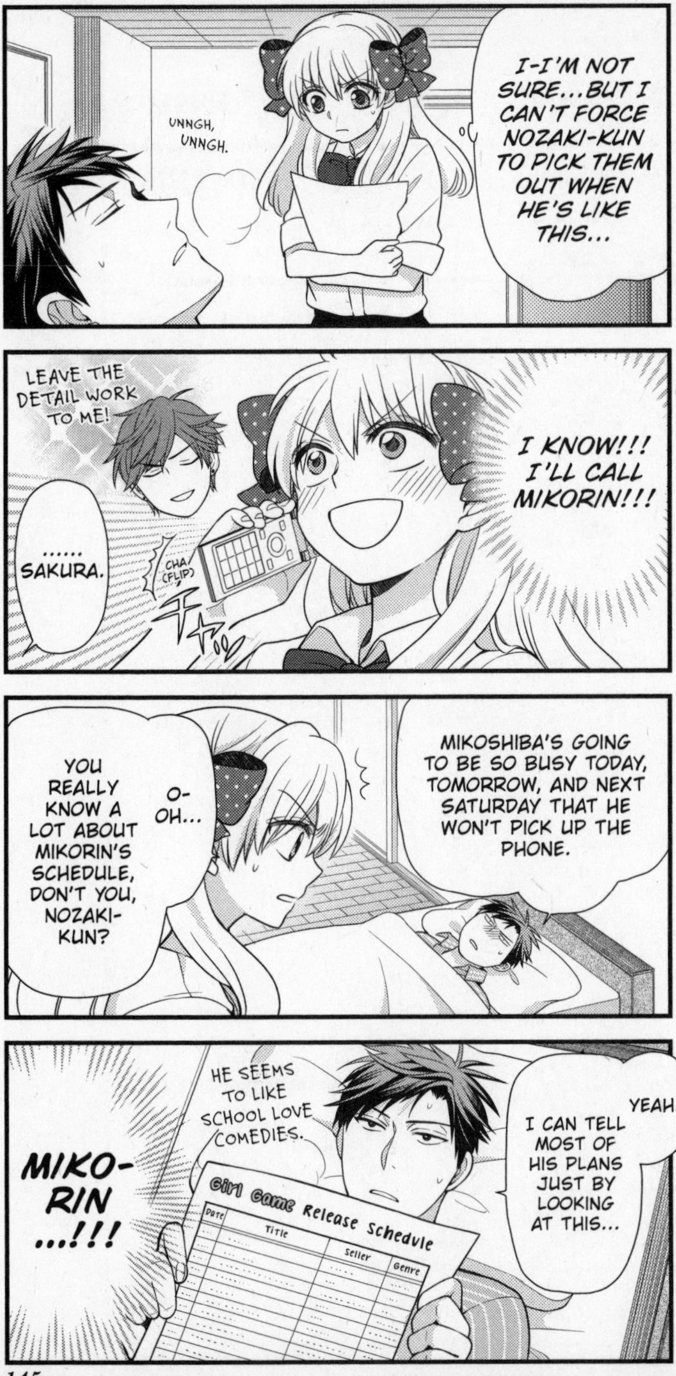

I-I'M NOT SURE...BUT I CAN'T FORCE NOZAKI-KUN TO PICK THEM OUT WHEN HE'S LIKE THIS...
UNNGH, UNNGH.
I KNOW!!! I'LL CALL MIKORIN!!!
CHA (FLIP)
LEAVE THE DETAIL WORK TO ME!
...... SAKURA.
MIKOSHIBA'S GOING TO BE SO BUSY TODAY, TOMORROW, AND NEXT SATURDAY THAT HE WON'T PICK UP THE PHONE.
O-OH...
YOU REALLY KNOW A LOT ABOUT MIKORIN'S SCHEDULE, DON'T YOU, NOZAKI-KUN?
YEAH.
I CAN TELL MOST OF HIS PLANS JUST BY LOOKING AT THIS...
HE SEEMS TO LIKE SCHOOL LOVE COMEDIES.
Girl Game Release Schedule
Date
Title
Seller
Genre
MIKO-RIN ...!!!

[Extra]

TALKING IN HIS SLEEP

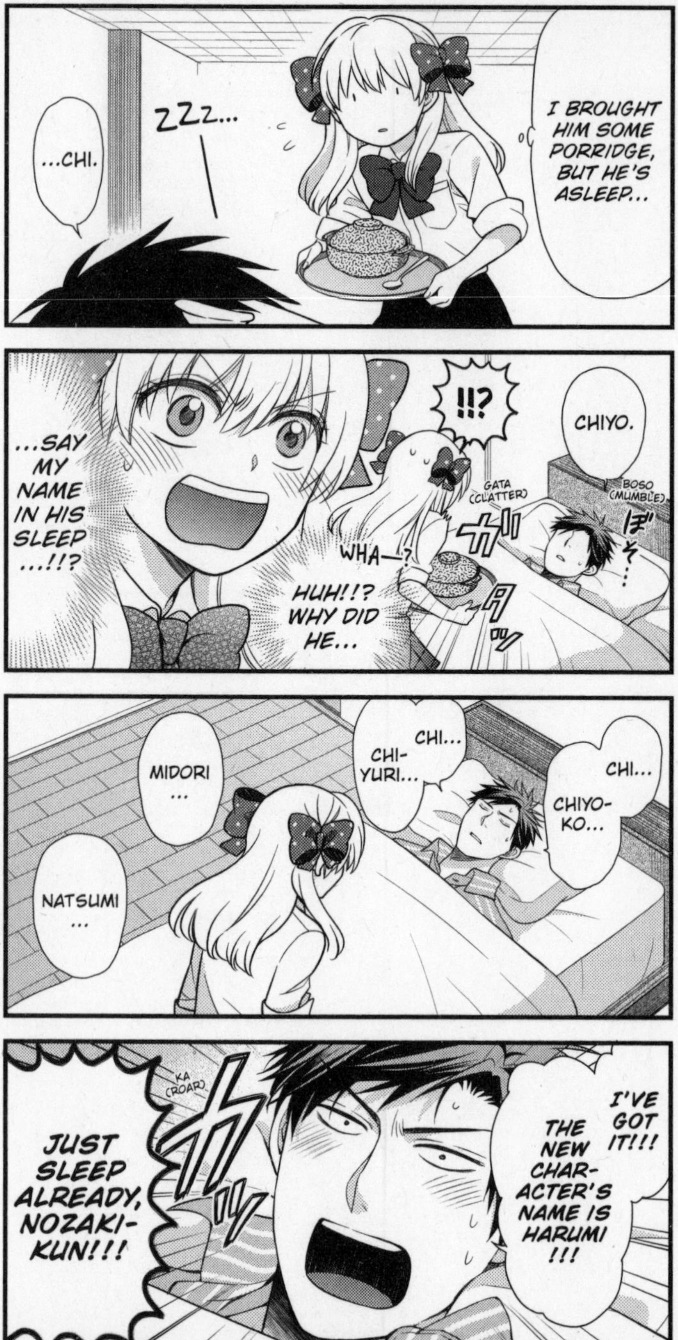
I BROUGHT HIM SOME PORRIDGE, BUT HE'S ASLEEP...
ZZZ...
...CHI.
BOSO (MUMBLE)
ぼそ…
CHIYO.
!!?
GATA (CLATTER)
WHA—?
HUH!!? WHY DID HE...
...SAY MY NAME IN HIS SLEEP...!!?
CHI... CHIYO-KO...
CHI... CHI-YURI...
MIDORI ...
NATSUMI ...
I'VE GOT IT!!!
THE NEW CHARACTER'S NAME IS HARUMI !!!
KA (ROAR)
JUST SLEEP ALREADY, NOZAKI-KUN!!!